# Research Methods in Criminal Justice
## An Introduction

Jack D. Fitzgerald
Steven M. Cox

**Nelson-Hall Series in Law, Crime, and Justice**
Consulting Editor: **Jon R. Waltz**
Northwestern University
School of Law

Nelson-Hall Chicago

LIBRARY OF CONGRESS CATALOGING-IN-PUBLICATION DATA

Fitzgerald, Jack D.
    Research methods in criminal justice.

    Bibliography: p.
    Includes index.
    1. Crime and criminals—Research.     2. Criminal
justice, Administration of—Research.     3. Corrections—
Research.     4. Criminal statistics.     I. Cox, Steven M.
II. Title.
HV6024.5.F58     1987          364          86-16383
ISBN 0-8304-1099-6

Copyright© 1987 by Nelson-Hall Inc.
Reprinted 1992

Manufactured in the United States of America

10     9     8     7     6

# Contents

# *Preface*

This book is addressed to two audiences. First, we hope the book will help fill a gap we perceive in the materials available for use in introductory-level college courses in research methods in criminal justice. Our experiences as teachers suggest that many students do not recognize the crucial role of perspectives in understanding human activity, including science, and are unaccustomed to working with or being critical about the analyses and presentation of data in statistical, graph, or table form. Very few criminal justice research methods textbooks, in our view, do an adequate job of discussing research methodology, and almost none give due consideration to its weaknesses and limitations as well as its strengths. We hope that this book will be useful to students in introductory research methods courses, and to teachers who have been as frustrated as we have been in attempting to educate their students in a methodology so central to criminal justice research.

Second, we hope that the book will be of use to anyone who is a practitioner in criminal justice. Because training in many disciplines and occupations is so highly specialized, many practitioners in criminal justice have limited knowledge of research methods. As researchers continue to make substantial contributions to our understanding of criminal justice issues, each of us, whether as practitioners in criminal justice or as concerned citizens, will be asked to participate in choosing among alternatives in criminal justice policy, some or all of which may be supported by social science research. To participate as intelligently and effectively as possible in these decision-making processes, an acquaintance with some of the basics of research methods is needed.

Furthermore, more students or practitioners of criminal justice will be doing research themselves or assisting others in the research process. For these people, too, knowledge of some basic techniques of data collection, analysis, and presentation is essential.

Our purpose, however, goes beyond simply describing some basic ideas and techniques employed by researchers; for while we are firmly committed to the notion that theories and data, properly used, can be of great benefit, we are also aware that they have been, and undoubtedly will continue to be, misused, both with and without malice aforethought. Consequently, we have attempted to provide information that will permit practitioners and students to ask intelligent questions about and make informed criticisms of their own or others' research. We believe that there is less chance of deceiving or of being deceived if one is familiar with basic research methods.

## *Acknowledgments*

We are especially grateful to Professors Norman Denzin and William Erbe, who initially stimulated our interest in and taught us a great deal about both the potentials and problems of science and scientific methods in the study of human behavior. Our students, too, have taught us a great deal about teaching the scientific perspective and methods.

Thanks to Professor Robert Bonde for his substantive contributions and to Professors Giri Raj Gupta, Robert J. Fischer, and Dean Rodney Fink, who have assisted us in many ways.

We would also like to express our gratitude to Allene Jones, who once again was able to decipher our initial scratchings and turn them into a typed manuscript.

To the Nelson-Hall staff, especially Ron Warncke, who gave us the opportunity to publish this book, and Kristen Westman, our editor, we owe a special thanks for their encouragement, support, and expert guidance.

Finally, our thanks to Sheila, Matthew, and Melissa for their support.

# 1

# *Research and Criminal Justice*

Students and practitioners of criminal justice, like those involved in virtually every occupation or profession in our society, increasingly find themselves using the research of others and/or conducting research themselves. In order to understand the nature and current state of affairs in criminal justice, practitioners and students alike must be able to read and comprehend research reports and must know when and how to apply the results of such research. Many will also find it necessary or advantageous to conduct research themselves to do their jobs as effectively and efficiently as possible. Consider, for example, a director of a Department of Corrections who wants to know the extent to which personnel turnover is a result of job-related stress among correctional officers, or a judge who wants to know which of the various dispositions she uses in juvenile cases are most effective in preventing recidivism, or the police chief who has to know whether the citizens in his community would support a bond issue to build a new headquarters. These practitioners could (and often do) gather information based on hearsay, word-of-mouth, or other accidental contacts to arrive at their answers. However, their chances of obtaining accurate information would be enhanced considerably through the use of scientific research techniques.

To those who believe that research methods and statistics are extremely complex and technical matters that should best be left to the experts, we would offer the following observations. It is quite true that any in-depth study of research methods and statistical analysis would take years, but it is equally true that a student can achieve a basic understanding in a relatively short period of time. Complicated research designs and sophisticated statistical procedures do not necessarily result in better or more useful research, and often, useful information can be gained through relatively simple research designs and elementary statistical analyses. Moreover, with a basic knowledge of research methods and statistics, students can ask important questions about simple and complex research undertaken by others and evaluate the quality of the researcher's results and conclusions.

Finally, knowing what questions to ask about research projects helps protect one from misinterpreting and misapplying research results. Just as your work can be helped by effective research, your work can be harmed by poor research techniques. Therefore, simply as a matter of self-defense, one should know something about research methods and data analysis. As a first step, we will look at two types of research, basic and applied.

## *Basic and Applied Research*

**Basic research** addresses general and fundamental questions that are not easily answered. What is the relative importance of heredity and environment in explaining human behavior? How do people learn? How can human behavior be changed? Why do some people become mentally ill? Under what circumstances do people conform to rules, and under what circumstances are they likely to violate such rules? Because these questions are so fundamental and far-reaching in their implications and applications, even partial answers are exciting. Social scientists often research these issues purely for the satisfaction derived from struggling with important questions and helping to put another piece into an important, basic theoretical puzzle, with little or no concern for how the research results might be used in a practical way. Basic research is often described as the pursuit of knowledge for its own sake.

**Applied research,** on the other hand, has a more practical aim. It addresses specific questions about how to accomplish a task better or more efficiently. Because applied research establishes connections among formulated goals, actions taken, and results obtained, individuals can use it to solve a particular, pragmatic problem. Is psychological counseling more or less effective than incarceration in reforming offenders? Is arresting one or more of the participants in a family dispute a more or less effective strategy for preventing further family violence than insisting on a temporary separation without invoking the law? Does the frequency of personal contacts between parole officer and parolee make any difference in the frequency of parole violations? How effective are seat belts and infant seats in preventing injuries to children? These questions arise from practical concerns and problems, and their answers have immediate implications in terms of policy decisions and behavior of criminal justice personnel.

Basic research may, of course, lead to applied research, and applied research often has implications for basic research. Furthermore, the distinction between applied and basic research is sometimes hazy. Still, it is probably safe to say that most research with which criminal justice practitioners are concerned falls more toward the applied than the basic end of the research continuum. Insofar as criminal justice practitioners make day-to-day decisions about how to deal with their clients, and insofar as applied research assists them in making the best possible decisions, doing good research or critically evaluating the research of others is an important, relevant skill. In short, competent research can enhance the quality of day-to-day decisions and help administrators manage both human and financial resources in the most efficient and effective way possible. Good research can significantly improve the formulation and implementation of policies and programs as well as increase the likelihood that intended results will, in fact, be achieved.

## *In-House, Hired-Hand, and Third-Party Research*

Research projects can also be divided into three categories according to the different relationships that exist between the researchers and those being researched. **In-house research** is conducted by a staff member of the organization or agency under study. Sometimes an organization will have a separate research division or department that operates at the request of other departments, or individuals within the organization who ordinarily perform other duties can be requested to conduct an investigation from time to time. In any event, it is called "in-house" research because someone *within* the organization conducts research *about* the organization *for* the organization. Any criminal justice practitioner who does research about his own activities or any other aspect of the organization, office, or agency for which he works is doing in-house research.

**Hired-hand research** is carried on by an outside organization (typically one which specializes in research) which is independent of but paid by the organization under study. For example, independent consultants may be retained by a criminal justice agency to advise and help agency administrators make changes in organizational structure or policy. In formulating their recommendations, these consultants often engage in information gathering and analysis.

**Third-party research** is conducted by an independent outsider, rather than someone who is part of the organization being studied or someone paid by the organization to conduct the research. Third-party research is paid for by the researching group itself or by a grant from some independent source (e.g., a private or public foundation or a government agency such as the National Science Foundation). A

sociologist, for example, might be given a grant by the Ford Foundation to study the process and effects of plea bargaining; although he
might deal with a number of law firms, judges, or defendants, he has
no direct organizational or financial affiliations with them. As a general rule, the third-party researcher has greater independence and
freedom in the conduct of the research project than either of the other
types of researchers.

## Advantages and Disadvantages

Each of these types of research has its advantages and disadvantages.
For example, in-house researchers have the advantage of being closer
to the problem at hand. Hence, they are in a better position than an
outside research group, whether hired hand or third party, to design a
project that will produce information of benefit to the organization. In
addition, for some types of research—especially that which is concerned directly with the activities of criminal justice agency
personnel—in-house researchers may have an easier time gaining the
cooperation of the staff involved. Being studied by someone who is
considered to be a member of one's own team or part of one's own
group usually reduces the suspicion and mistrust that accompany being scrutinized.

However, the factors in the research situation that encourage this
very sense of security may pose difficulties for in-house researchers.
For example, there may be built-in biases because the researchers are
part of the organization being studied and so share the perspectives
and prejudices of that particular organization. Further, consumers of
the research results may be suspicious of the research and its conclusions because they were derived by someone with a potentially vested
interest in the results. It is not easy for an organization to admit that its
present policies and practices may be ineffective, that some of its
members have made significant errors, or that its financial resources
have been used inappropriately. For example, the public is often suspicious of investigations conducted by internal investigation units in
local police departments or of studies by lawyers on the ethical practices of attorneys—and with good reason. Some members of the organization may look bad as a result of the research. The reputation of
both individual staff members and the organization as a whole may be
harmed. In-house researchers may therefore be reluctant to ask controversial or potentially damaging questions. Even if they do, they
may not report some of their findings in order to protect their own, the
organization's, or the profession's interests.

Hired-hand research has the advantage of putting the control of the research process and the reporting of results into the hands of an outside organization with less of a direct stake in the results of the research. Because they are not part of the organizational structure they are studying, hired-hand researchers escape many of the potentially biasing pressures that can be brought to bear on in-house researchers. Also, in cases where there are no in-house research specialists, greater research expertise can be obtained and no in-house personnel have to be taken from their assigned duties in order to conduct the research. In short, by placing the research project in the hands of outsiders, an organization loses some degree of control over the research process. This helps eliminate biases that can affect in-house researchers and contributes to the credibility of the research findings.

However, less control over the research may, in some circumstances, be disadvantageous. Outsiders may not fully understand what they are expected to do and, as a result, fail to generate information which would be most useful to the organization. Furthermore, the outside research organization may have its own biases on entering the situation. These biases may influence the research design and the reporting of results so as to diminish their usefulness. Of course, the fact that the researchers are hired usually means that the "employer" maintains some degree of control. Therefore, it is extremely important that a representative of the organization hiring the researchers communicate clearly to the hired researchers the goals of the research, participate in its design as much as possible, and have some knowledge of the research process and data analysis techniques. Only then will the organization itself get the information it needs and be able to evaluate the research and its results.

Third-party research maximizes the "distance" between researchers and subjects because there are no organizational or financial connections between the researchers and the organization under study. Hence, the third-party researcher is typically less susceptible to pressures, preferences, and biases that are likely to impinge on in-house or hired-hand researchers.

Third-party research has its own problems, however. Because there are no built-in ties, there is a lesser tendency on the part of organization personnel to cooperate with the researcher. This may diminish the completeness and accuracy, as well as the potential usefulness, of the data obtained. Furthermore, in hired-hand research, the organization at least has the power to choose which researchers will conduct the study. To that degree, the organization exercises some control over the research. In third-party research, even this control is relinquished. This lack of control by the organization (perhaps especially in criminal justice) becomes very important when the third-party researcher has negative prejudices or biases concerning the organization, especially since the researcher has a freer hand in expressing those biases. Because third-party researchers usually choose the topics to be studied and the research methods to be employed according to their own theoretical interests, research results may be of limited value to the organization.

It should be remembered that the organization being studied is not entirely without leverage in third-party research. The organization may, and in some cases should, choose to deny or limit cooperation with third-party researchers. The professional reputation of the researcher is crucial for inspiring confidence and cooperation. In any case, it is usually possible for the organization to bargain with reputable third-party researchers, trading access to information, endorsement of the study, and cooperation of personnel for some influence over the research process and the inclusion of research topics that are of special interest to the organization.

Credibility of research results also deserves brief mention, and the reputation of the third-party researcher is crucial here as well. For example, the results of research conducted by a third party known to be biased either positively or negatively toward the organization or policies being studied are likely to (and should) be regarded with skepticism by the public. In general, however, the greater degree of independence of the third-party researcher contributes to the public's confidence in the research and analysis.

Figure 1.1 summarizes some of the more important aspects of in-house, hired-hand, and third-party research.

## *Common Sense and the Scientific Perspective*

Humans are creatures with a well-developed sense of curiosity. We enjoy acquiring knowledge, figuring out how some piece of machinery operates, or assessing people's behavior. As we attempt to understand the objects, people, and events around us, we gather information, or **data,** by *observing* them in an informal but often careful way. Above all, we watch for *patterns,* that is, sequences or relationships among events. Suppose you have just purchased a car. You might ask, What's the best way to get this car started on a cold morning? If I pump the accelerator three times before I turn on the ignition switch, does it usually start? If it doesn't, you might try not pumping at all, or if that doesn't work, you might try pumping the accelerator six times and then turning on the ignition switch. If one patterns works with reasonable regularity, you will use that pattern. In a sense, this is research by "trial and error." You try one thing, and if that doesn't work, you try something else—until eventually, you hit upon a combination that works at least most of the time. You also become especially aware of those instances where the pattern of actions and responses does not work. If it is colder, does it help to pump the accelerator a few more times? Does the humidity in the air make a difference? In short, you search for other characteristics or properties that may affect the outcome you desire—getting the engine started. We call these characteristics or properties **variables**—factors in the situation that change from time to time and alter the chances of getting the engine started. In this very simple and crude way, you may be said to be performing an **experiment**—changing something and observing the effects of having done what you did.

In the process of trying to figure out what works best, you develop hunches or guesses about what might work and then try them out in practice. This process is quite similar to developing a **hypothesis**—a statement about what effects or results certain causes or actions might produce. You then proceed to *test* the hypothesis by trying the things you think will get the car started and observing the results of each attempt. If the car does not start, you formulate another hypothesis and proceed to test it and to observe the results.

**Figure 1.1  Relationship Between Researcher and Organization in Three Types of Research**

| Relationship | Type of Research | | |
|---|---|---|---|
| | In-house | Hired-hand | Third-party |
| Dependence of researcher on researched: | | | |
| organizational | high | moderate | low |
| financial | high | high | low |
| Degree of organization's control over research process | high | moderate | low |
| Likelihood of cooperation from organization's personnel in research project | high | moderate | low |
| Public's confidence in research results | low | moderate | high/low* |

*Depends on reputation of researcher.

In the previous paragraphs, we have not strayed very far from everyday experiences. Yet, by applying some new terms to an everyday situation, you are well on your way to understanding some of the fundamental concepts in the study of research methods.

We do not want you to conclude, however, that everything you will encounter in this book will be that simple. To grasp some of the intricacies of the research process will take some careful study and clear thinking—in short, some hard work. We do want to suggest, though, that (if you will forgive the pun) "getting started" may not be as difficult as it first appears, and keeping going may not be so difficult, either.

## *Criminal Investigation and Scientific Research*

Even if you have not studied the criminal justice field in detail, you are probably familiar with some of the basic aspects of criminal investigation. The process of investigating a criminal offense bears close resemblance to the research process, since, like all researchers, a criminal investigator gathers, documents, and evaluates facts about an event, in this case a crime. The investigator's first concern is gathering *facts,* for each investigation is initiated by assembling as many specific pieces of accurate information about the crime and the events surrounding it as possible. This information is assembled by carefully and systematically observing the particular details of the crime scene, especially the physical evidence (e.g., objects and individuals present, wounds to the body, the position of objects and persons relative to each other and to the scene). For the most part, these initial steps are *descriptive* in nature, since the investigator attempts simply to describe those things and persons present without making inferences about their relationship to each other or to the crime itself.

Furthermore, the facts that are assembled must be recorded in some way; for example, the scene itself must remain untouched until appropriate photographic records can be made. Accurate written records, which are used for reference and analysis later, are also essential to a successful investigation.

However, any good investigator knows that the simple observation and recording of facts is not enough. Some attempt must be made to link the information to the crime. To complete the investigation successfully, the investigator must eventually create hypotheses which link one fact to another and then, by linking the hypotheses, construct a *theory* that explains the crime as a whole. In part, this is a process of determining which "apparent" facts are "real" facts, which facts are or are not relevant to the crime, and how the facts are interrelated.

For example, a knife with apparent blood stains is present at the scene of a crime. This may lead the investigator to infer, or hypothesize, that the knife was used as a weapon in the commission of the crime. The mere presence of a blood-stained knife, however, does not necessarily mean that the knife caused the wound or killed the victim. The confirmation or rejection of this hypothesis depends upon establishing the validity of other "facts." Laboratory work to match the blood type of the stains on the knife to the blood type of the victim is required. An examination of the wounds to determine if the knife could have produced the kinds of wounds that appear on the victim is also necessary. If the blood types do not match or if the observations of the body wounds do not confirm the hypothesis, the investigator will probably abandon that particular hypothesis and formulate another.

If the additional evidence does support or corroborate the hypothesis, it must be remembered that the hypothesis has not been completely confirmed. There are probably other possible explanations for the observed "facts"; however, the investigator has narrowed the possibilities and produced evidence that is consistent with one of his hypotheses. The investigator is likely to regard this linkage between the knife and the crime as factual or true unless further evidence assembled later in the investigation fails to conform with the hypothesis.

A good investigator also often pays as much attention to what is missing at the scene of a crime as to what is present. The observation that something is absent may be important as evidence that can either support or undermine the validity of the hypothesis.

The investigator, then, has to put all the pieces together into a comprehensive pattern that links all of the facts and hypotheses to each other and contains no internal contradictions. These linkages constitute a **theory of the crime.** The more facts that can be shown to be consistent with this theory, and the tighter its elements are linked together (i.e., the fewer the gaps in the evidence), the more confidence the investigator has in the theory of the crime that he has formulated.

Making the linkages typically requires the application of reasoning and inductive or deductive logic. **Inductive logic** moves from a number of particular and separate observations to a generalization. For example, from the blood stains and the wounds, together with the laboratory reports, the investigator induces that the knife was the weapon used in the crime.

**Deductive logic,** on the other hand, moves from the general to the particular. For example, from the general observation that violent assaults on persons are typically committed by a person with whom the victim has at least some social acquaintance, and that the last person the victim had been seen with was one of the victim's relatives, the investigator might *deduce* that the victim was assaulted by this particular relative. Of course, the deduced conclusion is only as good as the elements of the investigator's argument that led to it. Mistakes in reasoning or incorrect assertations of fact that make up the basic general observation invalidate the conclusion just as certainly as does inconsistent evidence.

Above all, it should be remembered that both criminal investigations and research are *human* endeavors, and as such are subject to human weaknesses and strengths. It is vital that an investigator remain as objective as possible throughout the investigation process. Preconceptions and prejudices must be held at bay, especially during the hypothesis-testing phases, so that they do not interfere with an accurate reading of the assembled information or produce conclusions that are not consistent with the data. At the same time, the appropriate use of expertise, learning from mistakes, intuition, patience, ingenuity, curiosity, and opportunism (in the form of taking advantage of fortuitous occurrences), all play a vital role in successful research.

## *Research in Criminal Justice: An Illustration*

Reprinted below are excerpts from an article in the *American Journal of Sociology* describing some research conducted by Irving Piliavin and Scott Briar on police encounters with juveniles. The article has been widely cited in the professional literature, textbooks, and publications dealing with police training, police discretion, juvenile delinquency, and police community relations. It has also stimulated a great deal of additional research. As you read it, see if you can identify some of the similarities between the research described in the excerpt and the investigation processes discussed above.

### *Police Encounters with Juveniles\**

As the first of a series of decisions made in the channeling of youthful offenders through the agencies concerned with juvenile justice and corrections, the

*From "Police Encounters with Juveniles" by Irving Piliavin and Scott Briar, Sept. 1964, *American Journal of Sociology*, 70, no. 2, pp. 206–14. Copyright by The University of Chicago Press. Reprinted by permission.

disposition decisions made by police officers have potentially profound consequences for apprehended juveniles. Thus arrest, the most severe of the dispositions available to police, may not only lead to confinement of the suspected offender but also bring him loss of social status, restriction of educational and employment opportunities, and future harassment by law-enforcement personnel. According to some criminologists, the stigmatization resulting from police apprehension, arrest, and detention actually reinforces deviant behavior. . . . Despite their presumed significance, however, little empirical analysis has been reported regarding the factors influencing, or consequences resulting from, police actions with juvenile offenders. . . .

The above considerations have led the writers to undertake a longitudinal study of the conditions influencing, and consequences flowing from, police actions with juveniles. In the present paper findings will be presented indicating the influence of certain factors on police actions. Research data consist primarily of notes and records based on nine months' observation of all juvenile officers in one police department. The officers were observed in the course of their regular tours of duty. . . . [T]he candor shown by the officers in their interviews with the investigators and their use of officially frowned-upon practices while under observation provide some assurance that the materials presented below accurately reflect the typical operations and attitudes of the law-enforcement personnel studied.

The setting for the research, a metropolitan police department serving an industrial city with approximately 450,000 inhabitants, was noted within the community it served and among law-enforcement officials elsewhere for the honesty and superior quality of its personnel. . . .

In the field, juvenile officers operated essentially as patrol officers. They cruised assigned beats and, although concerned primarily with juvenile offenders, frequently had occasion to apprehend and arrest adults. Confrontations between the officers and juveniles occurred in one of the following three ways, in order of increasing frequency: (1) encounters resulting from officers' spotting officially "wanted" youths; (2) encounters taking place at or near the scene of offenses reported to police headquarters; and (3) encounters occurring as the result of officers' directly observing youths either committing offenses or in "suspicious circumstances." However, the probability that a confrontation would take place between officer and juvenile, or that a particular disposition of an identified offender would be made, was only in part determined by the knowledge that an offense had occurred or that a particular juvenile had committed an offense. The bases for and utilization of non-offense related criteria by police in accosting and disposing of juveniles are the focuses of the following discussion.

### Sanctions for Discretion

In each encounter with juveniles, with the minor exception of officially "wanted" youths, a central task confronting the officer was to decide what official action to take against the boys involved. In making these disposition decisions, officers could select any one of five discrete alternatives:

1. outright release
2. release and submission of a "field interrogation report" briefly describing the circumstances initiating the police-juvenile confrontation
3. "official reprimand" and release to parents or guardian
4. citation to juvenile court
5. arrest and confinement in juvenile hall. . . .

In practice, the official policy justifying use of discretion served as a demand that discretion be exercised. As such, it posed . . . problems for juvenile officers. . . . [I]t represented a departure from the traditional police practice . . . in the sense that they were expected to justify their juvenile dispositions decisions not simply by evidence proving a youth had committed a crime—grounds on which police were officially expected to base their dispositions of non-juvenile offenders—but in the *character* of the youth. . . . [Also,] the shift from the offense to the offender as the basis for determining the appropriate disposition substantially increased the uncertainty and ambiguity for officers in the situation of apprehension because no explicit rules existed for determining which disposition different types of youths should receive. Despite these problems, officers were constrained to base disposition decisions on the character of the apprehended youth, not only because they wanted to be fair, but because persistent failure to do so could result in judicial criticism, departmental censure, and, they believed, loss of authority with juveniles.

### Disposition Criteria

Assessing the character of apprehended offenders posed relatively few difficulties for officers in the case of youths who had committed serious crimes such as robbery, homicide, aggravated assault, grand theft, auto theft, rape, and arson. Officials generally regarded these juveniles as confirmed delinquents simply by virtue of their involvement in offenses of this magnitude. However, the infraction committed did not always suffice to determine the appropriate disposition for some serious offenders; and, in the case of minor offenders, who comprised over 90 percent of the youths against whom police took action, the violation per se generally played an insignificant role in the choice of disposition. While a number of minor offenders were seen as serious delinquents deserving arrest, many others were perceived either as "good" boys whose offenses were atypical of their customary behavior, as pawns of undesirable associates or, in any case, as boys for whom arrest was regarded as an unwarranted and possibly harmful punishment. Thus, for nearly all minor violators and for some serious delinquents, the assessment of character—the distinction between serious delinquents, "good" boys, misguided youths, and so on—and the dispositions which followed from these assessments were based on youths' personal characteristics and not their offenses.

Despite this dependence of disposition decisions on the personal characteristics of these youths, however, police officers actually had access only to very limited information about boys at the time they had to decide what to do with them. In the field, officers typically had no data concerning the past offense records, school performance, family situation, or personal adjustment of apprehended youths. Furthermore, files at police headquarters provided data only about each boy's prior offense record. Thus both the decision made in the field—whether or not to bring the boy in—and the decision made at the station—which disposition to invoke—were based largely on cues which emerged from the interaction between the officer and the youth, cues from which the officer inferred the youth's character. These cues included the youth's group affiliations, age, race, grooming, dress, and demeanor. Older juveniles, members of known delinquent gangs, Negroes, youths with well-oiled hair, black jackets, and soiled denims or jeans (the presumed uniform of "tough" boys), and boys who in their interactions with officers did not manifest what were considered to be appropriate signs of respect tended to receive the more severe dispositions.

### Table A  Severity of police disposition by youth's demeanor

| Severity of Police Disposition | Youth's Demeanor | | |
| --- | --- | --- | --- |
| | Cooperative | Uncooperative | Total |
| Arrest (most severe) | 2 | 14 | 16 |
| Citation or official reprimand | 4 | 5 | 9 |
| Informal reprimand | 15 | 1 | 16 |
| Admonish and release (least severe) | 24 | 1 | 25 |
| Total | 45 | 21 | 66 |

Other than prior record, the most important of the above cues was a youth's demeanor. In the opinion of juvenile patrolmen themselves the demeanor of apprehended juveniles was a major determinant of their decisions for 50–60 percent of the juvenile cases they processed. A less subjective indication of the association between a youth's demeanor and police disposition is provided by Table [A,] which presents the police dispositions for sixty-six youths whose encounters with police were observed in the course of this study. For purposes of this analysis, each youth's demeanor in the encounter was classified as either cooperative or uncooperative. The results clearly reveal a marked association between youth demeanor and the severity of police dispositions.

The cues used by police to assess demeanor were fairly simple. Juveniles who were contrite about their infractions, respectful to officers, and fearful of the sanctions that might be employed against them tended to be viewed by patrolmen as basically law-abiding or at least "salvageable." For these youths it was usually assumed that informal or formal reprimand would suffice to guarantee their future conformity. In contrast, youthful offenders who were fractious, obdurate, or who appeared nonchalant in their encounters with patrolmen were likely to be viewed as "would-be tough guys" or "punks" who fully deserved the most severe sanctions: arrest. . . .

### Implications

It is apparent from the findings presented above that the police officers studied in this research were permitted and even encouraged to exercise immense latitude in disposing of the juveniles they encountered. That is, it was within the officers' discretionary authority, except in extreme limiting cases, to decide which juveniles were to come to the attention of the courts and correctional agencies and thereby be identified officially as delinquents. In exercising this discretion policemen were strongly guided by the demeanor of those who were apprehended, a practice which ultimately led, as seen above, to certain youths being treated more severely than other juveniles for comparable offenses. . . .

The observations made in this study serve to underscore the fact that the official delinquent, as distinguished from the juvenile who simply commits a delinquent act, is the product of a social judgment, in this case a judgment made by the police. He is a delinquent because someone in authority has defined him as one, often on the basis of the public face he has presented to officials rather than on the kind of offense he has committed.

---

The research report you have just read has been recognized as providing theoretically significant and practically relevant information by academic experts as well as practitioners in the field of criminal justice. Yet, the chances are you had relatively little difficulty understanding the "theoretical" issues discussed, the general nature of the research conducted, the data that were presented and the conclusions that were reached. The chances are, too, that you could, without a great deal of difficulty, imagine yourself doing a research project like the one described and writing a report like the one you read.

The researchers begin their discussion by suggesting that people interested in the criminal justice field have numerous ideas about what factors influence or cause police officers to take certain actions with the juveniles they encounter and what consequences, or effects, these police actions have on the juveniles' future behavior. These ideas can be regarded as *hypotheses* about cause-and-effect relationships among the factors identified as significant in police and juvenile behavior.

The authors also indicate that not many of these hypotheses have been *tested* by actually *observing* police–juvenile encounters. Therefore, they decided to watch some of these encounters and gather some relevant *data* about the behavior of police officers and juveniles when they interact with each other. On the basis of their past experience and from what they had read about these encounters, they selected "demeanor" as a potentially relevant fact about the juveniles. The authors' definition of demeanor included both the youth's manner of dress and the extent to which the youth was respectful of and cooperated with the officer. With respect to the behavior of the officers, they chose to observe the variety of dispositional decisions that were made. The youths' demeanor and officers' dispositional decisions were the *variables*. What the researchers hoped to discover was whether there was some connection—some cause-and-effect relationship—between the two behavioral variables.

To gather the facts that would help determine if there was such a relationship, they accompanied the juvenile officers as they carried out their day-to-day activities. For each officer—juvenile encounter the researchers observed, the various aspects of the juvenile's demeanor and the actions taken by the officer were written down for future reference.

When their observations were over, the recorded facts were assembled in a way that permitted the researchers to determine if a *pattern* existed. To do this, they created a table which contained a simple count of the number of times an uncooperative youth was arrested, a cooperative youth was arrested, an uncooperative youth was admonished and released, a cooperative youth was released, and so on. Upon examining the data, they concluded that a rough pattern was present in the data. Because uncooperative youths received more severe dispositions than cooperative youths, they concluded that there is some relationship between a juvenile's demeanor and the actions taken by the officers: uncooperative behavior causes more severe dispositional decisions.

There were probably parts of the research report that you did not understand. Concepts like *longitudinal study*, which appeared in the excerpt, will be covered later in the text. Also, you will learn that the research described here is only one of several kinds, and that this particular type of research, like all of the others, has its advantages and disadvantages. You will discover, too, that the data analysis might have been done in several different ways. Our purpose here is simply to convince you that significant research projects and reports are not beyond your understanding. In the following chapters, some of the complexities of research concepts and activities will be introduced, so that your knowledge of the research process can be expanded and refined. You will be able to better understand the research process, to analyze data, to raise significant questions about research projects, to evaluate the contributions of research projects to the criminal justice field, and to prepare research reports.

## *Review Questions*

1. What are the similarities and differences between basic and applied research?
2. What are the advantages and disadvantages of in-house, hired-hand and third-party research?
3. Why should someone know about research methods as a matter of self-defense?
4. What distinguishes scientific research from common sense?
5. What were the variables studied by Piliavin and Briar?
6. What hypothesis were Piliavin and Briar investigating?

## *Exercises*

1. Write three basic and three applied research questions, and discuss the similarities and differences between the two types of research questions.
2. Write an essay discussing the parallels between everyday problem solving and Piliavin and Briar's study of encounters between police officers and juveniles.
3. Write an essay on what type of research (in-house, hired-hand, or third-party) the Piliavin and Briar excerpt represents. If you can't decide on the basis of the information given, what else would you need to know to decide? Would your opinion or evaluation of the results of the study be different if it were in-house, hired-hand, or third-party research?

# 2

## Perspectives and Research

To appreciate both the power and the limitations of scientific research methods, the dependence of human knowledge on perspectives must be understood. In this chapter, the nature and functions of perspectives in general, and of social-science perspectives in particular, will be discussed.

### What Is a Perspective?

In responding to their environments, humans typically act on the assumption that the world *is* as they *perceive* it. In a general sense, our actions must be guided by our sensory perceptions because, presumably, we have no other way of knowing about the environment in which we live. Yet, we all have had experiences that make us wary of trusting completely in our perceptions. Becoming acquainted with people of a different culture or difficulties in communicating with people in our own culture sometimes indicate the limitations of our perceptions. Have you ever extended a greeting to one of your friends as you passed on the street, only to discover that you had mistaken a stranger for that friend? Experiences of this kind clearly demonstrate that, while we depend on our senses to guide our interpretations of reality, we should also be aware that the information they convey and the interpretations we make are sometimes inaccurate. Furthermore, even when they are accurate they reflect only some aspects of the world around us. A **perspective** selects and organizes our sensory experiences. The selection is rooted in both our physiology and our language.

Suppose we could magically transform ourselves into newborn infants whose only knowledge consisted of a jumble of fleeting sensations of varying duration and intensity. It would be difficult for us to tell where we stopped and the rest of the world began. None of our experiences would have "meaning." The philosopher-psychologist William James described the world experienced in this way as a "blooming, buzzing confusion."[1]

As we mature, we learn to make sense of the world. Patterns in sensations that tend to occur together are recognized, distinguished from each other, and responded to in different ways. As the process of selecting and organizing sensory information becomes more sophisticated, we learn that some sensations seem to come from within us while others come from our environment. We learn, in effect, that we are a part of, but distinguishable from, our environment.

Our senses connect us with the outside world, but the connections are not perfect. Because our senses are physiologically limited, they transmit only some of the stimuli that impinge on us. As a result, the knowledge acquired through our senses is at best incomplete. For example, we cannot directly observe the ultraviolent zone of the light spectrum, hear some high-pitched whistles that dogs can hear, or detect odors that many animals can smell. Still, whatever their physiological limitations, our senses are the only means initially available to us for relating to the world. For each of us, the world becomes the patterns of sensations we learn to recognize.

Among the environmental events that make an impression on our senses is the spoken language of our fellow humans. As infants, we learn to recognize and repeat sounds and eventually to associate these sounds with other patterns of sensation. We are taught that "things" have "names," that certain sounds stand for particular objects and events in our experience. As we learn to organize these sounds into larger and larger units, we rely more and more on language as our primary means of communicating. Eventually, we take language for granted. Precisely because we do take it for granted, we are apt to miss the significant role language plays in our perceptions. We are inclined to believe that the language we use completely and accurately reflects the world as it really is. However, as we shall see, this impression is dangerously misleading, especially for the researcher.

Why is it misleading? A language system comes to each of us prepackaged. We do not invent it ourselves; we learn it from others. Since words learned from others stand for objects and events in *their* experience, the world, in a sense, also comes to us prepackaged. When we acquire a language, we acquire as well a framework for interpreting reality. Language directs our attention, sensitizes us to particular aspects of our experience, and shapes our thoughts.[2] Language mediates our perceptions of the world.

Although we are not accustomed to thinking about it in this way, the English language is a perspective. English grammar makes a basic distinction between nouns (words for persons, places, and things) and verbs (action words). Sentences are constructed by linking a noun with a verb. To write or speak English, we are forced to make this distinction. As difficult as it is to understand for those of us who only speak English, linguists tell us that some languages do not have this noun-verb structure. Furthermore, even among languages with the same basic grammatical structure, there are many differences in vocabulary. Swahili, Chinese, Hopi, and all other languages are perspectives that reflect the cultures and histories within which they developed. Through its basic grammatical structure and its vocabulary, a language represents one particular way of conceiving the world. As users of a particular language, we *perceive* the world largely in accordance with how, through that language, we *conceive* it.

The general characteristics of a perspective—selectivity and organization—are familiar to us in everyday life. We say, for example, that two photographs, one taken from a point above an object and the other from below it provide two different perspectives on the same object. Likewise, a conservative and a liberal columnist have different points of view about the same social issue.

Consider how a variety of individuals, each having a particular perspective, might analyze events occurring as a group of people frolic in and around a swimming pool. A physicist might focus on the mechanics of the waves in the pool, the pressure the water exerts on the side of the pool, the relative density of objects in the water (including the bodies of the swimmers), the elastic properties of the diving board, the force with which it propels the swimmer into the air, the diver's mass, center of gravity and momentum, the height reached in the dive, the acceleration achieved on descent, and the friction of the air and water on the swimmer's body.

A minister might concentrate on the morality of the behavior of the people at the pool, the vocabulary used, the swimming apparel worn (or not worn, as the case may be), the extent to which sin, love, and charity are manifested, and the importance of these behaviors for the person's soul, salvation, and redemption.

The perspective of the sociologist could lead to inquiries about the social class of the persons at the pool, the status and roles assumed and enacted, the social selves projected, the strategies employed to protect self-images, the social pressures exerted on particular members of cliques, and the norms guiding behavior.

A lifeguard on duty at the pool will focus on activities that might cause injury to those using the pool: pushing or jostling, especially near the edge of the pool. Only one person at a time will be allowed on a diving board. Special attention will be paid to any signs of a swimmer in distress. In short, the lifeguard's perspective will be shaped by his or her responsibilities as rule enforcer and life saver.

A police officer might also choose to observe the "goings on" at a swimming pool. The officer might be watching who "hangs around" with whom in order to identify networks of juveniles whom the officer suspects may be involved in delinquent activities. The pool and its surroundings might also be a place where criminal activities, such as the selling of drugs, take place. The officer will be alert for evidence that such activities are occurring. The officer's perspective, like that of the lifeguard, is shaped by his or her role as a rule enforcer, but the officer's perspective focuses on different activities and different rules.

Similarly, in a courtroom, the accused, the victim, the prosecuting attorney, counsel for the defense, the judge, and each jury member may have very different perspectives on the same set of events. The chief administrator, the supervisor, the secretary, and the janitor of a criminal justice agency may perceive the agency in very different ways. Researchers may see the same courtroom or criminal justice agency in still other ways.

The point here is that each of these observers, making use of a different perspective, selects different aspects of the events and subjects them to observation, interpretation, and prediction. To restate the idea, a perspective is a selective device that focuses the observer's attention and organizes his perceptions, making certain aspects of an event salient.

This inherent selectivity, which emphasizes certain aspects of an event, also implies that other aspects must be de-emphasized. Thus, a social scientist attempting to explain a given set of events from a social-science perspective would likely ignore the observations and explanations that a physicist, lifeguard, minister, or police officer might regard as crucial. Certainly, it is not possible for any of us as observers to pay attention to everything at once, but we may easily become so captivated by our own perspective that we forget that it selects out as well as in. It is important that we recognize that any perspective represents only one of many possible worldviews.

Perhaps you feel that the existence of several different worldviews is not in itself problematic—and you are probably right, for different perspectives can be compatible. The swimmer's social class presumably has nothing to do with the rate of acceleration achieved in a dive. The fact that the sociological perspective includes social class and excludes the rate of acceleration as relevant variables does not mean that the sociologist's observations are inaccurate. It simply means that the sociologist's perspective may lead him to select different aspects of events for observation and analysis than would a physicist. The observations and explanations of the physicist can, in most instances, exist side by side with those of the sociologist without obliging us to choose one or the other as the best or most accurate.

Furthermore, each of these perspectives can be used at different times for different purposes. Which perspective is best or most accurate depends in large part upon the interests or purposes of a particular observer at a particular time.

But suppose two perspectives are fundamentally incompatible, and that significantly different conclusions are arrived at, depending upon which of those incompatible perspectives we use. Under these circumstances, it becomes very important to ask which perspective is more accurate or more useful. Whether it is the perspective of the defense or the prosecuting attorney that prevails in a courtroom will surely make a great deal of difference to those involved, especially the defendant. The biologist who believes that criminal behavior is genetically determined and the sociologist who believes that criminal behavior is a product of the social structure and environment would ask different research questions, investigate different aspects of the problem, and probably find different answers to the question of what causes criminal behavior. Research undertaken from one perspective may suggest that severe punishment has a greater deterrent effect on crime, while research done from another perspective might suggest that the severity of punishment is unrelated to deterrence. Whether we are laypersons, criminal justice practitioners, or researchers, both the questions we ask and the answers we get are, to a very great extent, shaped by the particular perspective we employ.

## *Principles of a Scientific Perspective*

Robert Bierstedt has observed that "as a method of approach to the investigation of any phenomenon whatever, science implies primarily an attitude of mind, an attitude distinguished by adherence to several principles."[3] These principles, which we shall discuss here, are empiricism, objectivity, relativism, skepticism, ethical neutrality, parsimony, and determinism. While science can be seen as either a method of approach (process) or a body of content (product), in this book we are primarily concerned with it as a process. With this definition of science in mind, let us examine some of the principles characteristic of a scientific perspective.

### Empiricism

The first principle, **empiricism,** requires that the scientist seek answers to questions through direct observation of the events being studied. Although the selective aspects of a particular perspective cannot be eliminated (the scientist still selects what he will study and how he will study it), scientists must constantly validate their conclusions through careful, first-hand observations. Insisting upon empirical observation as the basis for investigation provides a powerful, though not infallible, check on the scientist's prejudices.

## Objectivity

When scientists consciously attempt to ensure that their conclusions are based on careful observation rather than personal prejudices, they are adhering to the principle of **objectivity.** While scientists are human and cannot ever become entirely free of personal biases, they are especially concerned with becoming aware of and controlling these sources of distortion. Objectivity is perhaps a more difficult goal to attain in the social sciences than in the physical sciences because social scientists interact with their subject matter—human beings—in a way that physicists or chemists do not.[4]

## Relativism

The principle of **relativism** encourages scientists not to consider their conclusions as permanent, universal, absolute truths. Instead, they assume that their conclusions are tentative and limited. Careful scientists not only attempt to specify the precise set of conditions under which their findings may be expected to hold, they also look for cases that do not support their conclusions. If they discover such cases, they either reject their previous conclusions or modify their statements to account for these discrepancies.

## Skepticism

The search for disconfirming evidence and the scientist's unwillingness to believe he knows the final, absolute truth are closely related to the fourth principle characteristic of the scientific perspective, **skepticism.** As skeptics, scientists are willing to question almost everything, especially common sense and common knowledge, accepting little at face value and looking beneath the surface in an attempt to determine for themselves the validity of an argument or conclusion. They maintain a healthy sense of curiosity and a desire to look behind closed doors to learn more about their subject.[5]

## Ethical Neutrality

By applying the principle of **ethical neutrality,** scientists try not to permit their moral or ethical beliefs to influence their data gathering or their conclusions. As researchers, scientists are concerned only with what is true or false, not what is right or wrong, good or bad. It should be noted that ethical neutrality during the research process does not prevent the scientist from making ethical judgments after his research is completed, when the scientist can view the findings from another perspective. (Furthermore, as we note later in this chapter, the researcher must be concerned with the ethics of the research process itself.) However, when the researcher makes moral judgments about phenomena during the investigation, other principles of the scientific perspective, such as objectivity, relativism, and skepticism, are threatened.[6]

## Parsimony

**Parsimony,** another principle of the scientific perspective, holds that the numerous alternative explanations of a particular phenomenon should be reduced to the smallest number possible. As scientific knowledge grows, competing explanations of the same phenomenon are incorporated into a more general theory or rejected as incorrect. Whatever the scope of the phenomenon being studied, the simplest explanation with the most empirical support is preferred.

## Determinism

One additional principle sometimes said to be characteristic of science deserves brief mention. **Determinism,** which is closely related to the concepts of cause and effect, is based on the idea that every event is preceded by one or more other events which cause it to occur. Actually, we have some reservations about including determinism as a principle of science. To be sure, science assumes that connections of some kind exist among events. Whether those connections are best described as deterministic, however, is a matter of considerable controversy in the contemporary philosophy of science. We agree with some philosophers of science who suspect that a probabilistic rather than a deterministic principle is more appropriate. The probabilistic principle holds that the best we can hope for in the physical or social sciences is a statement that there is some probability that event x is connected to event y. Perhaps the necessity of relying on probabilistic statements is attributable to the inadequacies of our research methods or our current state of knowledge. But it is also possible that this uncertainty is due to the very nature of the empirical world itself. At least for the moment, there seems no way of resolving the dilemma, although perhaps we do not need to settle it for our purposes here. We can treat reality as if it were deterministic, bearing in mind that if we take that principle too seriously, we may ultimately be frustrated.

**Science** as a process, then, may be defined as a systematic search for the most accurate and complete description and explanation of events, relying on the principles of empiricism, objectivity, relativism, skepticism, ethical neutrality, parsimony and at least a modified determinism as guides.

## *Social Science as Science*

Most criminal justice research involves social science research, which is based upon adherence to the principles of the scientific perspective we have just outlined and the methods discussed in the following chapters. While the nature of the subject matter and the research techniques social scientists use usually differ from those used by natural scientists, both are based on scientific principles.

A sociologist, for example, can imagine herself in the place of the persons she is studying in order to better understand their behavior and formulate research questions. She recognizes that both she and her subjects are unique and can influence and be influenced by each other. On the other hand, a chemist cannot imagine herself to be an atom, nor can the atom imagine being her; she does not have to be concerned about the atom's influence on her, or hers on it, as a problem of human interaction. (She clearly does, of course, have to be concerned about the possible influences of the machinery and techniques she uses to study it, but that is not an interactive process in which mutual influence can determine the nature of the relationship.) When a sociologist asks respondents questions, she must be concerned about whether they understand the questions and whether their responses are honest. The chemist knows that the atom cannot deliberately deceive her. Nonetheless, if both the sociologist and the chemist are attempting to be objective, ethically neutral, skeptical, and parsimonious, and if both regard their conclusions as tentative and search for disconfirming empirical evidence, both are employing the scientific perspective.

Any given perspective is composed of a set of words (concepts) that guide observation and thought. In the case of the sciences, some of these words are common to all of the perspectives, while others are unique to certain categories of science. For example, the word *theory* is common to all scientific enterprise (and to other types of enterprise as well). Most scientists would agree that a theory is a set of logically interrelated propositions (hypotheses) that describes or explains some phenomenon, and that these propositions consist of stated relationships between concepts or variables. Most scientists would also agree that *concepts* represent selected characteristics of specific objects or ideas, and that the term *scientific method* refers to the application of scientific principles to a set of procedures for gathering information.

While many of the terms used by natural scientists are recognized by laypersons as technical and specialized, social scientists often use words that are part of almost everyone's vocabulary. Words such as *role, culture, society, norm, bureaucracy, gang,* and *delinquent* are often found in social science research reports; because they are familiar, laypersons often think that social scientists are simply repeating common knowledge. We all "know" that an actor plays a role while on stage, that a person who attends symphony concerts is cultured, that we live in a society, and that norms are rules that normal people follow. Misunderstandings arise, however, because social scientists attach different, specialized meanings to these same words. When sociologists use the term *role*, they may be referring to a set of expectations attached to a particular position in a particular social system; when they speak of culture, they may well be identifying the totality of knowledge, objects, and behavior patterns acquired by a group of people and passed on from generation to generation by means other than genetic inheritance. When they speak of society, they may be examining two or more people and the physical and symbolic interactions among them; and when they speak of norms, they are probably alluding to at least three types of regulations governing human behavior—folkways, mores, and laws. In comparison, *symbiosis, oxide, ionization,* or *photosynthesis*, which are used in the physical sciences, are immediately recognizable as technical terms with special, scientific meanings.

The claim that information provided by the social scientist is little more than common sense is also deceiving in another way. It is true that most of us have learned a great deal about human behavior. But, the fact that social science often tells us things we already know is not as important as the fact that the information was obtained by the scientific method. How much confidence we have in knowledge depends a great deal on the method by which we obtained it. Scientific observation has often demonstrated that "common knowledge" is not always true. Until the days of Columbus, almost everyone believed that the world was flat. Not long ago, most people believed that mental illness was caused by demons.

Consider the following assertion: "During World War II, southern black enlisted men preferred northern white officers to southern white officers." This assertion seems to make sense. We may reason that northern whites were more likely to be sympathetic to the idea of equality of treatment than southern whites and, therefore, black enlisted men could expect less discrimination from northern than from southern white officers. Obvious! However, consider this assertion: "During World War II, southern black enlisted men preferred southern white officers to northern white officers." This assertion, too, makes sense, since southern blacks were more accustomed to interacting with southern whites than with northern whites, knew how to conduct such interaction, and were more comfortable interacting since they could predict the officers' expectations. Obvious! While a study by Stouffer found the former to be the case,[7] either conclusion would be easy to explain in terms of common sense.

Similarly, many laypersons believe that police officers are attracted to police work because they like to order people around. They also believe that officers spend most of their time solving crimes and pursuing criminals. However, research studies indicate that most candidates for law enforcement jobs choose police work as an opportunity to help others, and that most patrol officers spend well over three-fourths of their time simply riding or walking their "beats" and responding to requests for assistance that have nothing at all to do with criminal activities.[8]

The point is, information provided by the social scientist often seems obvious to us *after* it is made available. If the information agrees with our predispositions, we think it obvious; if it runs counter to them, it seems unscientific. For this reason, many are inclined to be less impressed by the conclusions reached in social science research (or more inclined to disregard them if we disagree with them) than by the conclusions reached by research in the physical or natural sciences. To understand social science as a *science*, then, we must understand the special nature of its subjects, the technical meanings it assigns to ordinary words, and the credibility of findings obtained through scientific research.

## *An Example of a Social-Science Perspective: Symbolic Interactionism*

Symbolic interactionism, one of several schools of thought in the social sciences, is a set of related concepts purporting to describe and explain certain aspects of human behavior. The basic assumptions of the symbolic interactionist perspective can be stated as follows. Humans are unique animals; they display enormous behavioral variability and they depend on learning rather than biological instincts as the primary mechanism for adjusting to their environment. The most significant difference between humans and other animals is the means by which they communicate—language. Language is a symbolic system. Linguistic symbols are arbitrary sounds or physical gestures to which people, by mutual agreement, attach significance or meaning. When a person uses a symbol to communicate with another person, the symbol means approximately the same thing to the speaker as it does to the hearer. People constantly invent new symbols to refer to new or different aspects of their environment. In that sense, human language is an open system. The communication systems of most other animals that have been studied are closed in the sense that, whether or not learning is an important factor in their development, the systems are composed of a small, fixed number of gestures, noises, etc., that show practically no change over time.

Almost all human experience is mediated by symbols. Put somewhat differently, we live in a world composed not of real but of symbolic objects. When we use language, we create symbolic objects for ourselves and then respond to the symbolic objects we have created as if they are real. That is, we categorize and attach names to objects and respond to the name we assign to the object instead of to the object itself.

A symbolic interactionist's analysis of the conversation of two people might proceed as follows. When two people (symbolic interactionists call them *actors*) are in the same place at the same time, they usually *interact*. That is, each recognizes the presence of the *other* and adjusts his or her behavior accordingly. This mutual adjustment of behaviors involves each of the actors formulating a *self-concept*, presenting the self to the other, *taking the role of the other*, and attributing a self to the other. An actor's self-concept and the self he attributes to the other actor are symbolic. That is, an actor defines himself and the other by placing each in particular categories according to sex, occupation, personality characteristics (e.g., friendly, suspicious) or moods (e.g., happy, sad). Having attributed a self to himself and the other, the actor imagines himself to be that other in order to anticipate the other's behavior, and hence plan his own *line of action* during the interaction. Through his line of action, the actor presents his self to the other. The other is, of course, also an actor and is engaging in the same processes with respect to *his* other (our original actor). Each continually revises the symbolic self he claims through his line of action and the symbolic self he attributes to the other. Hence, by a process of negotiation, the interactants arrive at a consensual *definition of the situation* that includes the roles and selves appropriate in this situation.

According to symbolic interactionists, it is possible to analyze any human interaction in these terms. The meeting between an officer and a juvenile on a street corner, the interrogation of a suspect, a conference between a parole officer and a parolee, and the questioning of a witness by an attorney in a court of law might each be observed, described, and analyzed using this perspective.

An example of the symbolic interactionist approach to research is Erving Goffman's book *Asylums.*[9] Goffman was interested in studying life in what he refers to as *total institutions*, places of "residence and work where a large number of like-situated individuals, cut off from the larger society for an appreciable period of time, together lead an enclosed, formally administered round of life."[10] Total institutions include mental hospitals, prisons, monasteries, and juvenile homes. In his research carried out at St. Elizabeth's, a mental hospital in Washington, D.C., his objective was to learn about the social world of the institution as subjectively experienced by its inmates. He began with the assumptions that any group of inmates in a total institution "develop a life of their own that becomes meaningful, reasonable, and normal once you get close to it; and that a good way to learn about any of these worlds is to submit oneself in the company of members to the daily round of petty contingencies to which they are subject."[11] Thus, Goffman took the role of an assistant at the hospital and passed the day with patients while trying to avoid being identified with staff. Combining his observations with those made by researchers studying other total institutions, Goffman was able to say a great deal about the characteristics of total institutions and what he calls the "underlife" that exists among inmates. For example, he found that inmates have what he refers to as a "moral career" in the institution, during which a number of changes routinely occur. Their self-concepts change dramatically when they realize that decisions about personal hygiene, sleeping, eating, and working are now being made by others. Inmates are stripped of their previous identities (their hair is cut, they wear uniforms) and are treated in much the same way we treat a child. Inmates learn an institutional "lingo" (the vocabulary by which their selves are defined) and a line of action that allows them to maintain some sense of personal dignity while still apparently adhering to institutional rules and enacting the roles the institution prescribes.

As a result of Goffman's research, we learned a great deal about inmate life not only in mental hospitals but in other total institutions as well. Many of his conclusions confirmed the results of prior research, while his somewhat unique approach gave us greater insight into both the symbolic and physical processing and life of inmates.

Like all perspectives, the concepts and assumptions of the symbolic interactionist perspective are selective, emphasizing certain aspects of the situation being studied and organizing the observations for the investigator. A given perspective generates answers to some of the questions one might ask about a phenomenon, but is, by definition, limited in scope, though some are more limited than others. Science, for example, is a fairly comprehensive perspective composed of several more limited perspectives (*social* sciences, *natural* sciences, and so on). Each of these contains yet more limited perspectives. Thus, symbolic interactionism is one perspective within the sociological perspective within the social-science perspective within the scientific perspective. In principle, at least, more limited perspectives must meet the same general requirements as the broader perspectives of which they are a part. Thus, social science must meet all the requirements of the scientific perspective.

## *Theory*

One way of viewing a perspective such as symbolic interactionism is to see it as a kind of theory. A **theory** may be defined as a set of two or more related, empirically testable assertions (statements of alleged facts or relationships among facts) about a particular phenomenon. A theory serves as a symbolic guide to the observation, interpretation, and explanation of phenomena in the empirical world.

Note that our definition of theory leaves considerable room for variation. Theories may vary in scope, degree of integration, and amount of empirical verification.

### Scope

One theory may refer to a narrow range of phenomena while another is broader in scope. For example, a theory on the nature and consequences of plea bargaining has a smaller scope than a theory on the connection between the criminal justice system and the political system in American society.

### Integration

Some theories consist of a relatively "loose" collection of concepts and assertions. The propositions of another theory may be tightly linked with each other, so that each proposition follows logically from the others. To construct a tightly knit theory is the goal toward which all scientists strive. Some theories in the natural sciences have achieved such coherence and integration that they can be expressed in a series of closely related mathematical formulas. While great progress has been made in the last 50 years, there are few theories in the social sciences which approach this level of development.

## Verification

A theory consists of assertions or statements which are *symbolic* in nature. That is, they are humanly generated verbal or mathematical expressions of fact, and not fact themselves. It should be remembered that anyone can say anything, and that a mere verbalization does not make something true. A theoretical assertion is only a *claim* that something is true. Whether scientists accept a theoretical statement as true depends on how much empirical *evidence* there is to support the statement. Remember that scientists must always regard their research findings as tentative rather than absolute truths. But, research conducted according to scientific principles produces the most persuasive evidence concerning the truth of an assertion.

## Relationships Among Theory, Research, and Methodology

While some theories have not been tested through research, others have had some empirical verification, and still others have been subjected to extensive empirical testing.

Both theory and research are essential elements in the scientific pursuit of knowledge. Meaningful research cannot be conducted unless it is guided by a theory. A theory without empirical support is simply one person's claim or speculation, no better and no worse than any other person's claim or speculation.

Viewed in the context of science as process, the relationship between theory and research is dynamic. When research evidence fails to support a proposition in a theory, the theory must change to incorporate the evidence. The revised theory then must be tested and, in turn, either be confirmed or disconfirmed. If disconfirmed, the theory must be revised again. Research improves a theory, which leads to new research, which ideally tends to confirm the improvement in the theory. As a result, our confidence in the theory grows and scientific knowledge progresses.

The support or nonsupport of a particular proposition in a theory has implications for the other propositions in that theory. If research evidence does not support a proposition, confidence in the other proposition(s) of the theory is weakened. This is more true for a tightly integrated theory than for a loosely connected one. This is a principal reason why scientists regard tightly integrated and parsimonious theories as better than theories that are loosely integrated. A more cohesive theory is easier to confirm or reject, and permits a more dynamic relationship between theory and research.

Finally, note that our definition of theory specifies that propositions be *empirically testable*. This implies that a particular methodology for testing the propositions is required. The methodology specifies the general principles and guidelines by which the researcher is to proceed in gathering information or evidence that may help determine the truth of a proposition. Although different methodologies exist, empirically testable propositions can be supported only by using scientific methodology, which follows the principles of empiricism, objectivity, relativism, skepticism, ethical neutrality, parsimony, and determinism.

Hence, we may say that there is an integral relationship among theory, research, and methodology. Only if research is performed according to the guidelines and principles of science can it be called scientific research. Only if research is scientific can it confirm or disconfirm an empirically testable proposition. Moreover, the application of scientific methodology gives the researcher confidence in the results of the research and in its implications for the theory that guided the research.

## *Research Ethics*

As noted earlier, the scientist should maintain ethical neutrality toward the phenomena being investigated during research. In research about drug use, prostitution, organized crime, plea bargaining, sentencing practices, or the use of force by police, for instance, a researcher's personal moral judgments may cloud his observations, bias his conclusions, and otherwise interfere with achieving objectivity. Therefore, the researcher should attempt to identify whatever moral preconceptions he holds and endeavor to set them aside during the research process.

There are, however, some ethical principles that should be very much involved in the design and execution of a research project. These pertain not to the subject matter but to the research process itself, including the human relationships between researchers and the persons they study.

In selecting the scientific perspective as a way of viewing the world, and scientific methodology as a way of studying it, we make ethical commitments. We have obligations to our subjects and to sci-

ence. We must be concerned about the right of our subjects to anonymity, informed consent, and freedom from risk.

## Anonymity

If we promise subjects that their names will not be used or that they
will not be identifiable in our report of findings, we are ethically obli-
gated to keep these promises.

Failing to protect subjects' identities can harm the subjects themselves. Suppose we ask a group of patrol officers to evaluate their immediate supervisors. To encourage honest responses, we guarantee
our respondents anonymity. Suppose further that, in reporting our
results, we fail to disguise the identities of patrol officers sufficiently,
and the supervisors, reading the research report, are able to identify
them. The supervisors may subject those respondents who gave us
honest but negative opinions to punitive treatment or refuse to recommend them for a promotion or a salary increase.

In addition to being injurious to respondents, failure to protect
anonymity can have damaging consequences for the research enterprise as a whole. For example, other potential subjects may refuse to
participate in future research projects if their anonymity cannot be
assured.

## Risk and Informed Consent

We must also be concerned about risks to our subjects and their right
to informed consent. For example, we often have to decide whether to
observe people's behavior surreptitiously (i.e., without telling them
that we are observing them) or openly (i.e., making it known to them
that we are observing them). It is generally regarded as ethically preferable to inform subjects that they are being observed. There are occasions, however, when it is scientifically advantageous to gather information without the knowledge or permission of the subjects. The
researcher must be certain in those cases that the interests of the subjects are not compromised. Secret observation should not be prac-
ticed if its use poses any significant physical, mental, or social risks to
those observed. If there is the slightest risk to the psychological or
physical health or safety of subjects in an investigation, the researcher
has a moral obligation to inform subjects about all risks and to obtain
subjects' voluntary agreement to participate in the study. Only if subjects are aware of the risks involved can they make an informed decision concerning participation in the study.

To further complicate the issue of informed consent, suppose we
ask: Are all potential subjects equally capable of giving voluntary in-

formed consent? The answer would seem to be "no." Recently enacted regulations, for example, prohibit the use of prisoners in most research projects. The rationale for these regulations is that, because of their status as prisoners, inmates cannot be regarded as voluntary participants in a study. They may believe that their participation will increase the likelihood of early parole, or they may fear personal repercussions from prison authorities if they refuse to participate, for example. Furthermore, some prisoners as well as other potential subjects may be insufficiently educated or experienced to understand either the nature of research, the vocabulary used by the researcher to describe the research project, or any risks that may be associated with participation in it. It is difficult to argue, in such circumstances, that a person can give voluntary, informed consent.

There is also the issue of the seriousness of risks posed by the research process. In a medical study not too long ago, black prisoners serving life sentences were deliberately denied treatment for venereal diseases, so doctors could study the progression and long-term effects of the diseases and the effectiveness of available treatments. The prisoners were clearly subjected to significant risk in this study.[12] They were not informed that they were subjects in an experiment, nor were they apprised of the risks associated with the withholding of treatment. Their informed, voluntary consent to participate was not sought. While this research strategy may have seemed appropriate and even ethically acceptable to the researchers at the time, these procedures would be considered morally reprehensible by contemporary ethical standards.

## Deception in Research

Stanley Milgram, a research psychologist, wished to understand the effects of various circumstances on the tendency of humans to obey authority figures.[13] To study these phenomena, he created an experimental situation in which subjects who volunteered to participate were asked to teach another person, located in an adjacent room, a simple "word association" task. To encourage learning, the experimenter instructed the subject-teacher to deliver electrical shocks to the learner when the learner made mistakes. The shocks progressed in intensity with each mistake the learner made, to the point where they were potentially lethal and the learners no longer responded at all to the teacher's efforts.

There were many forms of deception involved in this experiment. For example, the subjects were told that they were participating in an experiment on learning, not obedience to authority. Also, the learners were part of the research team and did not actually receive any electrical shocks. But the subjects (the "teachers") did not know this and were led to believe that the shocks were real. The behavior of the teachers, as they "delivered" more and more intense shocks to the learners, confirmed that they did, in fact, believe that the shocks were real. Many of the teachers manifested extremely emotional reactions to the situation, some laughing hysterically, some apparently going into a trancelike state and others shaking and sobbing uncontrollably as they delivered what they believed to be severe shocks to the learner.

Milgram "debriefed" his subjects after their participation, telling them the true nature of the experiment and informing them that the "learner" had not received any shocks. He also contacted the participants several months after their participation in the experiment and reported that there were no long-term negative psychological effects on his subjects. Nevertheless, Milgram agreed to suspend his experiments when ethical issues were raised about them by a committee of the American Psychological Association.

Most contemporary standards of ethical research conduct allow some "benign" deception of subjects in research. The general rationale for permitting benign deception is that subjects who know what the researcher is really studying may deliberately alter their responses or behavior in a way that distorts the research findings. We agree that benign deception of subjects is ethically permissible, but we cannot leave the topic without asking you to think about this: How valid is the researcher's assumption that data gathered when subjects are deceived is "better" than data gathered when subjects have been informed of the true purpose of the study?

## Responsibility to Scientific Community

Finally, science itself imposes ethical demands on the researchers. As scientists, we must present the research process and the findings in an honest fashion, even when they do not support our hypotheses. It would be irresponsible deliberately to omit, alter, or misrepresent data in a research report so that they appear to support a favored proposition or belief.

While most researchers do not deliberately violate this principle, some ask us to ignore or discount the fact that some or all of their findings do not support their contentions by attempting to explain away their results. The researcher has an ethical obligation to note weaknesses in the design or execution of the research. These weaknesses may have a direct bearing on the confidence one has in the results obtained, but merely providing excuses does not serve science. Omitted or altered data may mislead us into believing that something has been demonstrated when it has not. We may then fail to propose alternative hypotheses that might better explain what has been observed, and the development of scientific knowledge is impeded. To guide their members during the research process and in other professional activities, most associations of research scientists and governmental funding organizations have developed and published standards of ethical conduct. One example, from the Illinois Department of Mental Health, is included in appendix D. We urge you to peruse this statement now in order to understand more fully some of the ethical dimensions of research.

The application of ethics in research, as in other realms of human behavior, often poses dilemmas for which there are no clear and absolute resolutions. Nevertheless, for ethical reasons, as well as for practical and professional ones, protection of subjects and honest presentation of data should be overriding concerns in all research activities.

## *Notes*

1. Of course, this discussion is speculative, since we cannot get testimony from an infant. For James's analysis, see his *Psychology: Briefer Course* (New York: Collier, 1962).
2. For a more thorough discussion of the influence of language on thought and perception, see Benjamin Lee Whorf, *Language, Thought and Reality: Selected Writings,* ed. John G. Carroll (New York: Technology Press and Wiley, 1959).
3. Robert Bierstedt, *The Social Order* (New York: McGraw-Hill, 1970), p. 16.
4. This is not to say, of course, that physical scientists ever achieve complete objectivity. They, too, have personal prejudices and biases which find their way into their research projects.
5. For a more thorough discussion of the social scientist as voyeur, see Peter L. Berger, *Invitation to Sociology: A Humanistic Perspective* (Garden City, N.Y.: Doubleday Anchor, 1963).
6. Bierstedt, p. 19. Actually, this is a matter of considerable controversy in both the social and natural sciences at present. Many laymen as well as scientists contend that scientists must recognize the ethical and moral implications of their work, both while they are engaged in research and in deciding whether, when, and in what way the results are to be published or employed. We agree with this position inasmuch as we recognize that questions of ethics and morality are relevant to all human behavior, including the behavior of the human being who happens to be a scientist. For a more detailed discussion of the issues involved, see Howard S. Becker, ''Whose Side Are We On?'' *Social Problems* 14

(1967): 239–48; George A. Lundberg, *Can Science Save Us?* (New York: David McKay, 1961); or Jacob Bronowski, *Science and Human Values* (New York: Harper Torchbooks, 1956).

7. See Samuel A. Stouffer, Edward A. Suchman, Leland C. DeVinney, Shirly A. Star, and Robin M. Williams, Jr., *The American Soldier: Adjustment During Army Life* (New York: John Wiley, 1949), especially pp. 580–82.
8. See, for example, Steven M. Cox and Jack D. Fitzgerald, *Police in Community Relations: Critical Issues* (Dubuque, Iowa: Wm. C. Brown, 1983), pp. 20–21.
9. Erving Goffman, *Asylums* (Garden City, N.Y.: Doubleday, 1961).
10. Goffman, p. xiii.
11. Goffman, p. x.
12. For example, see H. M. Pappworth, *Human Guinea Pigs* (Boston: Beacon Press, 1967).
13. Stanley Milgram, *Obedience to Authority: An Experimental View* (New York: Harper & Row, 1974).

## *Review Questions*

1. What are some of the physiological limitations of our senses of hearing, sight, touch, taste and smell? Can we overcome these limitations?
2. How does the language we learn influence what our senses tell us? Why is it potentially misleading for a researcher to think that language merely reflects the world? Do people who speak different languages perceive the "same" object or events in different ways?
3. What does it mean when we say that language mediates our perceptions?
4. What is a perspective? What is the relationship between language and perspective?
5. What are the seven principles of the scientific perspective?
6. What is a theory? How do theories differ?
7. Can we have a theory without a language?
8. What is the relationship that exists among theory, research, and methodology?
9. Why are research ethics important?
10. What ethical principals should guide all research?

## *Exercises*

1. How does an aerial photograph of a city building differ from one

taken at ground level? How would an article about a police department written from a liberal perspective differ from one about the same department written from a conservative perspective?

2. Pick some local social scene (e.g., a bar, a fraternity or sorority house, a church service, a pool hall, a courtroom, a street corner "hangout," a university cafeteria), and describe the scene from the perspective of people playing different roles on the scene (e.g., a police officer, a minister, an attorney, a criminal justice researcher, a janitor, a hustler, a biologist, a bouncer). To what extent are the different perspectives compatible with each other? Is it possible or necessary to resolve all the differences in perspective?

3. Discuss the application of the principles of the scientific perspective to the Piliavin and Briar research described in chapter 1.

4. Formulate at least two different theories about one or more of the following: police juvenile encounters, the causes of crime, the effects of imprisonment, the training of police officers, the courtroom behavior of prosecuting attorneys, a researcher's relationship with police officers.

5. For two of the theories you developed in question 4, identify at least two research projects that would produce evidence concerning the theory.

6. What ethical problems might have confronted Piliavin and Briar as they did the research described in chapter 1?

# 3

## *An Introduction to Research Methodology and Design*

In the previous two chapters, we have discussed some key aspects of the larger context within which research takes place. In this chapter, we begin our discussion of the research process itself.

As a point of departure, it is important to distinguish between two related aspects of the research process: methodology and methods. This distinction is analogous to the difference between strategy and tactics. Research **methodology,** like strategy, is concerned with the researcher's ultimate goals and the general plan the researcher formulates for achieving those goals. Research **methods,** like tactics, are the specific techniques the researcher uses to implement the plan and collect data. Methodology includes such things as the study of the role of concepts, variables and their definitions in research, the purposes and structures as well as the advantages and disadvantages of different types of research design, the logic of causal inferences, and sampling theory. Methods include specific data-gathering and analyzing techniques to be used (e.g., direct observation, interviews or questionnaires, and making graphs and tables). An appropriate general methodology must be selected before specific methods are chosen. In fact, as we shall see, the credibility of research depends as much on the quality of the researcher's methodology as it does on the quality of his methods. In this chapter and most of the next one on sampling, methodological issues will be considered. The remainder of the book will be concerned primarily with methods.

The research process is typically divided into a number of related phases:

1. choosing a research topic;
2. defining concepts and variables;
3. selecting a research design;
4. gathering the data;
5. summarizing and analyzing data;
6. interpreting the data;
7. writing the research report.

In this chapter, the first three stages of the research process will be discussed.

## *Choosing a Research Topic*

A number of factors may influence the selection of a research topic. Of course, the particular social-scientific perspective (e.g., symbolic interactionism, behaviorism) the researcher uses determines in part the kinds of topic areas that come to his attention. The topic a researcher chooses always reflects to some extent his judgments or feelings about what is important to study. The personal values of the researcher also clearly influence his choice of topic. Selection of a topic may also be based on theoretical or intellectual concerns or the practical desire to alleviate a specific problem. Finally, it is not uncommon for a researcher to choose a topic because funding is available for its study.

A symbolic interactionist, for example, may choose a research topic that involves the self-concepts and face-to-face interactions of judges and defendants, or correctional officials and prison inmates. A behaviorist would be more likely to focus on a topic that emphasized the role of punishment and reward in shaping human behavior. A researcher whose primary interest was the legal profession would likely choose a different topic than one whose interests were in probation, parole, or cross-cultural analysis of crime. A researcher who is personally convinced that the plea bargaining system is in serious need of reform may select a research topic related to this personal belief.

While research questions may originate from a variety of sources and assume a variety of forms, they must all be questions for which scientific answers are possible. Not all questions, not even all important or interesting questions, can be approached scientifically. Questions like Does God exist? or Is premarital sex immoral? cannot be answered scientifically because supreme beings and ultimate moral standards are not subject to direct observation or measurement. To be sure, people's beliefs concerning such matters can be subjected to empirical investigation, but the matters themselves are beyond the scope of the scientific perspective and cannot be approached through scientific methodology. Issues such as the relationship between police response time and the number of crimes cleared by arrest, or between court disposition of convicted offenders and recidivism, however, can be approached scientifically because relevant data can be obtained through systematic, controlled observation of empirical and at least potentially measurable phenomena.

# *Defining Concepts and Variables*

The language of science is primarily a language of concepts and variables. **Concepts** are symbolic, shorthand ways of representing some aspect of perceived reality. That is, they are words or other symbols the scientist uses to describe one or more dimensions of an object or event. Remember that concepts, like perspectives, are selective devices; they emphasize certain aspects of an object or event and ignore others. For example, the concept of color refers to only one dimension of our experience, only one property of an object. Similarly, the concept crime refers to one dimension of a person's behavior, the concepts judge and correctional officer to one property of the person. Many different objects or events can have certain characteristics or properties in common; hence, we can *categorize* them according to the properties that they share. Remember, though, that although two objects or events have properties that are alike, they may have many others that are different. A group of acts categorized as *crimes* are similar in some respects (they all violate criminal law), but may be quite different in others. To say that murder, arson, and theft are all crimes is to emphasize what they have in common and to ignore their differences.

Using language precisely is crucial to good scientific research. Because different researchers use the same words (e.g., crime, delinquency, poverty, justice, and stress) but attach different meanings to them, researchers *define* key concepts in their research reports so that they and others who read their reports will know as clearly as possible what they mean.

## Types of Definitions

There are several different kinds of definitions used by researchers. Some concepts are defined in terms of other concepts. When we define crime as any act which violates the criminal law, we are using a collection of other concepts to define the concept crime. Concepts which are defined in terms of other concepts are called *constructs.*[1]

A concept may also be defined by physically pointing to an example of it in the empirical world—definition by indication. We might define a courtroom, for example, by showing one to the person for whom we are defining it. Concepts that we can define by pointing to something in the empirical world are said to have direct empirical referents.

Closely related to definitions by indication are **operational definitions.** To operationally define a concept, such as ''delinquent,'' the researcher specifies exactly how she will identify the objects or events that fall under that category. They are called operational definitions because they specify the operations the scientist will perform in order to recognize an instance of a category. Consider the category "delinquent." If the research is primarily a study of police records and documentation, *delinquent* may be operationally defined by specifying that "any juvenile whose name appears two or more times in the police records" will be placed in the category "delinquent." If the research includes interviews of young people, *delinquent* may be operationally defined as "any juvenile who indicates involvement in two or more acts of illegal or antisocial behavior" during the interview. If both records and interviews are used, the operational definition of delinquent may include information from both sources. Because different "operations" applied to the same group of juveniles may well produce different lists of delinquents, and because a particular operational definition may have important consequences for what is discovered about delinquents, specifying the definitions used is crucial.

## Variables

A category may be divided into two or more subcategories to create a variable. Each subcategory is then called a value of the variable. The concept or category *sex*, for example, has two subcategories (two values)—male and female. Categories may be subdivided in different ways, depending on the requirements of the research. One researcher may assign the concept *crime* the values misdemeanor and felony, while another might assign the values murder, robbery, breaking and entering, and theft. Stress may be assigned the values low stress, moderate stress, and high stress. Size of police department may be assigned any number of values from one to 30,000, for example.

By converting concepts into variables and specifying operational definitions for each value, the researcher is in a position to observe stability or change (i.e., variability) in the values of the variable. The researcher can also look for relationships (related changes) between two variables.

## Validity, Reliability, and Precision in Categorization

For scientists, as for all humans, there is always the possibility that the conceptual categories or subcategories themselves don't represent reality very well or that the process of applying the categories to the empirical world is to some degree faulty. In scientific methodology, the examination of these issues is concerned with the degree of validity, reliability, and precision of categorizations.

A categorization is *valid* if it reflects a characteristic or property of the real, empirical world. We are raising the issue of validity when we ask questions such as, Is what we are categorizing a crime actually a crime? Is what we are calling stress really stress, or is it something else? Is the person we are calling a criminal really a criminal, or perhaps the victim of social prejudice in the criminal justice network?

*Reliability* refers to the extent to which the procedures we use to make our categorizations (including, perhaps, measurements) of the empirical world produce the same results upon repeated application of those same procedures to the same objects or events. A yardstick, for example, is a fairly reliable devise for observing the length of an object. Counting the number of recorded arrests in a given period of time is a fairly reliable way of observing arrest activity of a police officer or department. Asking a judge one or more questions about the factors which enter into her sentencing decisions may or may not be a very reliable way of categorizing the factors in her decision-making process, since asking her the same questions a day or a week later may not produce the same results. To the extent that repeated categorizations of the same phenomenon produce different results, the procedures employed to make those observations are unreliable.

*Precision* refers to the number of subcategorizations of a concept (values of a variable) that are available. Some subcategorizations divide a phenomenon into relatively few parts, while others produce many subdivisions. One procedure might result in categorizing objects simply as longer or shorter than some standard we have chosen, while another permits us to say how many inches longer or shorter one object is compared to another, and still another may permit us to determine such differences in 1/100s of an inch. Many, though not all, categorizations in criminal justice research are relatively imprecise, at least compared to those in the physical sciences. The time an officer takes to respond to a call can be quite precisely determined by using a stopwatch, for example, but the levels of stress experienced by the officer in different types of law enforcement situations may not be subject to very precise determination.

Validity, reliability, and precision are separate dimensions of categories and categorizations. That is, a category we are using may be valid, but our process of categorization is unreliable, or the process can be reliable but imprecise, or it may be precise but neither valid nor reliable. Furthermore, we are always dealing with *degrees* of validity, reliability, and precision. We shall have more to say about these concepts when we discuss quantitative research in a later chapter.

# *Choosing a Research Design*

A research design is the general plan for carrying out the research project and must be established well in advance of the actual data collection. It specifies who or what will be observed, sets how many times and in what time sequence observations of the variables will take place, and lays the logical foundation for drawing conclusions on the basis of the data gathered. The choice among the wide range of designs available depends first and foremost on the basic goal of the researcher, which may be either the description or the explanation of some phenomenon in terms of the variables which have been defined. Exploratory research, which may have either description or explanation as its goal, and prediction of future trends on the basis of previous descriptive and explanatory research, are also discussed.

## Descriptive Research

Many social science studies are descriptive. The researcher's goal is to identify and communicate important properties or characteristics of a particular category of objects or events. The census of the population of the United States and the Uniform Crime Reports are good examples of very large-scale descriptive studies. A survey on the nature and types of unreported delinquent behavior or a study on the extent of drug use in a community are also examples of descriptive research. The aim in all these cases is to describe some phenomenon as it exists. No attempt is made to determine why the phenomenon is as it is.

While the structure of descriptive research is generally less complicated than explanatory research, it is not easy to conduct. The researcher must formulate and define useful concepts, contend with the issues of reliability, validity, and precision of the observations, and select an appropriate research design.

Suppose we were interested in the incidence of crime in a particular population. We must decide if we are interested in crime as a single category or as a variable with several subcategories. If we choose the latter, how many subcategories shall we include? How shall we operationally define crime or its subcategories? We might decide to look at police records of crime, but would this provide us with a valid measure of the actual incidence of crime? A survey of the population could be conducted, but how could the validity and reliability of self-reports about criminal activities be determined? Should we compare the information obtained from a survey with crime statistics maintained by the police? The answers to these depend at least to some extent upon what we want to do with the data we collect. Each of the possible answers to these questions has merit, depending upon the goals of the researcher.

In the case of a delinquency survey, how should we define *delinquency*? What behaviors should count as delinquent? Whom shall we survey about this behavior—teenagers or adults? How reliable are self-reports of delinquent behavior? If we ask the same juveniles to report their delinquent behaviors on two different occasions, will the same delinquent behaviors be reported by each juvenile? Again, these are only some of the questions that the investigator must consciously and deliberately attempt to resolve if he is to have any confidence in the description provided by the data. The investigator who conducts descriptive research, then, must be methodologically aware, skillful, and attentive to detail if he hopes to obtain credible results.

Then, too, there are issues related to the overall design of the research which must be resolved. Many descriptive studies are like the ones described above—single "snapshots" of a particular phenomenon at a given point in time. Others, however, are designed to describe changes in some phenomenon over time. Research designs of this nature are **longitudinal,** including panel designs and multiple group trend designs, or cross-sectional.

## Panel Designs

Suppose that we wanted to study changes in drug use among teenagers over time. In a **panel design,** one group of teenagers might be selected for study. (We shall have more to say about selection procedures—called sampling—in the following chapter.) The same group of individuals would be asked about their current drug usage at as many different points in time as we felt appropriate or necessary. We might diagram a panel design like this:

Time →

panel    T1    T2    T3    T4

This diagram indicates that the panel would be observed (i.e., the variable "current drug use" would be measured) at four different points (T1, T2, T3, T4).

Sometimes entire populations rather than small, selected groups are described using the same design. Each census might be considered a single observation of the entire population of the United States; each Uniform Crime Report is a single observation of all the crimes reported to police in a particular year. By comparing several of these descriptive reports, changes over time in various aspects of the phenomenon being described can be observed and analyzed.

The most difficult problem encountered by researchers using the panel design is dealing with the almost inevitable loss of some panel members from one observation time to the next, especially if the time between observations is relatively long. Members of the panel may die, refuse to participate in the study again, change address or otherwise be unavailable for subsequent observations. When panel members are lost, any observed changes in the values of the variables may reflect the change in panel membership rather than actual changes over time in variable values. In addition, being repeatedly asked questions (about drug use, for example) may change the panel members' behavior because participating in the study has made them more aware of and self-conscious about their opinions or activities. This possibility is a general problem with which researchers must contend whenever people are aware of being observed: if we know someone is watching us, sometimes we change our behavior. (We shall have more to say about this phenomenon, called the **Hawthorne effect,** in chapter 6.)

## Multiple Group Trend Analysis

In **multiple group trend designs,** different groups are selected at different points in time from the same larger group. This design can be diagrammed as follows:

Time →

| | | | | |
|---|---|---|---|---|
| Group 1 | T1 | | | |
| Group 2 | | T2 | | |
| Group 3 | | | T3 | |
| Group 4 | | | | T4 |

In our drug use study, for example, we might have selected four different groups at different points in time from students attending a particular high school and asked each group about their current drug use.

In this design, the problem of repeated exposure to observation is solved because each is observed only once. Furthermore, since different groups are chosen each time an observation is made, we don't have to worry about loss of subjects from one observation time to the next, as we did in the panel design. Unfortunately, though, in solving some problems, we have created others. The most serious problem in interpreting data from this design is the possibility that differences among the groups selected for observation, rather than changes in the phenomenon itself, may be responsible for any variations in the values of the variables we have chosen to observe.

## Cross-Sectional Designs

In **cross-sectional designs,** a larger group is divided into subgroups and each of the subgroups is observed at a given point in time. The subgroups are chosen so that differences in their memberships may reflect changes over time. That is, rather than observing a given phenomenon at different points in time, we observe at a single point in time persons whom we believe are at different stages in a process of change. Returning to our study of drug use, we might divide students from a particular high school into four age groups (14 or younger, 15, 16, and 17 or older) and then compare drug usage among the different groups. We might diagram our cross-sectional design like this:

Time $\rightarrow$

| | |
|---|---|
| Subgroup 1 (14 or younger) | T1 |
| Subgroup 2 (15 yrs. old) | T1 |
| Subgroup 3 (16 yrs. old) | T1 |
| Subgroup 4 (17 & older) | T1 |

Differences in drug use among age groups might be interpreted as reflecting changes that have occurred through time as those being observed have grown older. Of course, this interpretation may be questioned because, as with multiple group trend studies, there may be differences other than the passage of time among the subgroups. For example, to interpret any observed differences among the subgroups as real changes in drug use patterns we have to assume that the "17 or older" group had the same patterns of drug use when they were "14 or younger" that the "14 or younger" group we actually observed has. Nevertheless, this design is often used because it requires less time and is less expensive to complete than longitudinal designs.

Descriptive research has a basic structure, in the sense that it is executed according to a carefully devised plan designed to produce valid, reliable information about a particular phenomenon at a given point in time or changes in a phenomenon over time. The quality and usefulness of a description depends on the appropriateness of the concepts, constructs, or variables the researcher chooses, the validity and reliability of the categorizations, and the effectiveness of the research design. Repeated "testing" of the adequacy and usefulness of the descriptions by comparing them with the reality to which they refer improves their quality.

## Explanatory Research

Describing phenomena is an essential part of all scientific activity, but many researchers also attempt to determine *why* some phenomenon has occurred—to go beyond description to explanation. Scientific explanation is accomplished when statements about the causal relationships among variables have both empirical and logical support. Empirical support for an explanatory statement is provided by gathering and analyzing data. Logical support is provided by reasoning guided by the rules of logic. The investigator who does explanatory research must be concerned with the logical structure of the research design as well as the empirical evidence—the data—collected. In order to understand explanatory research, we need to be familiar with some elementary principles of logic.

## Logic and Causality

Logic is a system of rules for making arguments and drawing conclusions. It is primarily concerned with the *form* of those arguments rather than their content. Most causal arguments in the social sciences proceed from statements in the conditional form. A *conditional proposition* takes the general form, if *a*, then *b*. This statement is called conditional because it states the condition(s) (*a*) that must be present if another condition (*b*) is to be present as well. Arguments involving conditional statements proceed as follows:

| | |
|---|---|
| Major premise | If *a*, then *b* |
| Minor premise | *a* is present |
| Conclusion | Therefore, *b* is present |

In this case, *a* is often referred to as an *antecedent* or *independent* condition, and b as the *consequent* or *dependent* condition. The independent condition (or, in methodological language, the **independent variable**) is defined as a *cause*, and the dependent condition (or **dependent variable**) is defined as its *effect*. The presence of b is said to be explained by the major and minor premises through deduction.

Research hypotheses often take the form of conditional statements. Suppose we believe that larger cities have higher rates of crime. We can convert this statement into conditional form as follows: If city T is larger than city R(a), then city T has a higher crime rate than city R(b). This is, as you will note, simply another way of hypothesizing that city size is causally related to crime rate.

Conditional statements may appear in both logically valid and logically invalid forms of argument. (Note that the term *validity* in this context has a different meaning than that assigned to it in the earlier section on categorization. Here it refers to the form of an argument; there it referred to the application of concepts to reality.) The argument given above is an instance of *affirming the antecedent;* that is, given the major premise, if we can affirm that the antecedent a is present, we may then validly conclude that the consequent b is present as well. We may also argue validly by *denying the consequent;* that is, if we can show that b is not present, we can validly conclude that a is not present either. According to the rules of logic, however, given the statement, if a, then b, we cannot make a logically valid argument either by denying the antecedent or affirming the consequent. In the former case, if a is not present, b may nonetheless be present, because a may not be the only antecedent to b. Similarly, in the latter case, the fact that b is present does not permit us to conclude validly that a is present, because b may be present without a.

Causes can be related to resultant conditions in a variety of ways. The independent variable may be a *necessary* cause of the dependent variable. If a is a necessary cause of b, then b never occurs without a. The independent variable may also be a *sufficient* cause of the dependent variable. In this case, the occurrence of just a is sufficient for the occurrence of b, although there may be other sufficient causes of b as well. Or the independent variable may be both a necessary and a sufficient cause (b occurs if, and only if, a occurs).

It is easy to assert that one event or condition causes another; justifying the assertion is another matter. Some philosophers of science have even argued that we would be better off if we did not use the concept of cause at all. While it is beyond the scope of this text to go into the details of this debate, we can make four observations. First, as we noted above, saying that one event (the independent condition) is causally related to another event (the dependent condition) does not necessarily mean that there is a one-to-one correspondence between the two. Several conditions may be causally related to a single other condition, with each condition contributing separately or in combination to the determination of another condition. We refer to this as **multiple causation.** Multiple causation is likely in criminal justice.

Second, both students and scholars often think of cause as a unidirectional concept. We can easily imagine a chain of causes in which $a$ causes $b$, $b$ causes $c$, and $c$ causes $d$. But if we consider a system of conditions where each condition is connected to every other condition in the system, a change in condition $a$ will produce changes in some or all of the others. These changes may, in turn, eventually cause another change in $a$. This kind of relationship among conditions is called a **feedback relationship.** For example, the uncivil behavior of a defendent in court ($a$) may change the judge's behavior ($b$) from civil to threatening, which may change the defendant's behavior ($a$) to civil. A researcher bound in his thinking to a unidirectional concept of causality may be unable to recognize this type of relationship upon encountering it.

One other type of variable is often used in explanatory research: the **intervening variable.** An intervening variable is one that comes between the independent and dependent variables in time, so that a "causal chain" or sequence of variables is created. That is, the occurrence of condition $a$ followed by the occurrence of condition $b$ causes condition $c$.

Finally, we must always remember that in science a cause can never be established with absolute certainty: "We are always in a position of *inferring* from observed data that the hypothesis that $a$ is a condition for the occurrence of $b$ is or is not tenable with some specified degree of confidence."[2] Cause, then, is a complex concept, and its application is always subject to question. In spite of the difficulties associated with its use, however, we continue to talk about cause because no better alternative has been found. So long as we bear in mind when using the concept of cause that we are making *inferences* from data, the risks associated with speaking of causal relationships are minimized.

Logic gives researchers rules for making arguments that are valid in form. But scientists must be concerned with an argument's empirical content—the data—as well. Scientists rely on observation to determine the empirical support for statements about the world. The major and minor premises in a scientific argument are assertions about some empirical phenomenon. If these statements are supported through observation and the form of the argument is logically valid, the conclusion arrived at has both empirical and logical support.

In the methodology of explanatory research, both logic and data are combined in reaching conclusions about causal relationships. It is, in fact, this linkage of logical and empirical support that makes science such a powerful tool for acquiring knowledge. Explanatory research designs must be structured so that they permit the assessment of the degree of empirical support for the statements which comprise the major and minor premises in a logically valid argument.

Before we discuss specific types of explanatory research designs, then, we must examine in greater detail the concept of causality, including the conditions logically and empirically necessary for a causal inference.

*Requirements for Causality.* Generally, there are three requirements that must be satisfied to infer a causal relationship between conditions. The first requirement is that of **concomitant variation**; that is, when a change occurs in *a* a change also occurs in *b*. When this situation occurs, we say that *a* is *correlated* or associated with *b*. The conditions must vary systematically with each other. If we contend that greater alienation causes more frequent participation in radical political activities, then the data must show that those people who are more alienated participate in radical political activities more frequently than those who are not. If the data reveal a systematic variation among the conditions, the concomitant variation requirement for making a causal inference has been met.

The second requirement is one of sequence in time: if *a* causes *b*, then *a* must occur before *b*. An event that takes place *after* another event cannot be the cause of that event. To return to our example, if more frequent participation in radical activities precedes increasing feelings of alienation, the feelings of alienation cannot be a cause of the participation. The investigator demonstrates that he has satisfied this requirement by observing that the appropriate temporal sequence of conditions has occurred.

The third requirement is to eliminate from consideration as possible causes all other conditions *in a particular research situation* that satisfy the first two requirements. (We emphasize ''in a particular research situation'' here because we do not wish to deny the possibility of multiple causation. Rather, this requirement pertains only to other possible causal variables which may be involved in a specific research project.) In practice, this requirement, unlike the two preceding ones, is very difficult to satisfy. At best, we can only satisfy this requirement approximately, by eliminating as many alternative, potentially explanatory conditions as we can when we do our research.

We can summarize our discussion with the statement of a major premise in conditional form: If and only if condition $a$ varies concomitantly with condition $b$, and condition $a$ (the independent condition) has preceded condition $b$ (the dependent condition) in time, and all other possible independent conditions have been eliminated, then condition $a$ is a cause of condition $b$.

As we shall see, with varying degrees of precision, the structure of explanatory research designs permits us to establish the concomitant variation of conditions and the time sequence within which the conditions exist or occur. They also take us some, though never the entire, distance toward eliminating other possible independent conditions.

## Hypotheses and Theories

In scientific methodology, explanation is accomplished by establishing a strong logical and empirical argument that a causal relationship exists between two variables, that is, demonstrating that changes in the values of one variable are caused, and therefore explained, by changes in values of a second variable. Some theorists contend that poverty is causally related to crime. In this formulation, poverty is the independent variable and crime the dependent variable. Such assertions about causal relationships between two variables are called hypotheses. We might represent this hypothesis as follows:

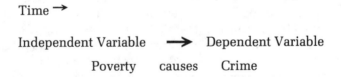

Time $\rightarrow$

Independent Variable    $\longrightarrow$    Dependent Variable

Poverty    causes    Crime

In criminal justice research, we are seldom able to explain a complex phenomenon like crime by referring to a single causal variable. Because several variables taken together are more likely to account for crime, we might hypothesize that poverty, ethnic or racial discrimination, and age cause crime. This is an example of multiple causation, and it can be represented as follows:

Time $\rightarrow$

Income
Ethnicity ——————————→ Crime
Age

Finally, we may hypothesize that persons who are poor and then begin to associate with others who commit crimes are likely to commit a crime. That is, criminal association is an intervening variable between poverty and crime.

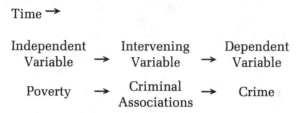

Time →

| Independent Variable | → | Intervening Variable | → | Dependent Variable |
|---|---|---|---|---|
| Poverty | → | Criminal Associations | → | Crime |

All these formulations are hypotheses generated by the researcher. The researcher creates and imposes a tentative, hypothetical structure on the phenomenon he is studying. The same researcher, or another one, seeing the phenomenon from a different perspective, might propose a different hypothetical structure for the same phenomenon. For instance, in a given research project, crime might be considered a hypothetical cause of poverty; in another project, crime might be seen as leading to criminal associations. In any event, it is the researcher who decides how to formulate hypotheses, and he may change his formulation if he desires. In the end, it will be the structure of the research design together with the data collected by the researcher that determines whether or not a particular explanatory hypothesis should be tentatively accepted or rejected.

Sometimes a researcher is working with two or more hypotheses that can be logically connected with each other. A set of logically related, empirically testable hypotheses is called a theory. There are two principal advantages to having a theory. The first is that new hypotheses can often be logically derived from the set of original ones. Consider, for example, the following three hypotheses:

If $a$, then $b$

If $b$, then $c$

If $c$, then $d$

Applying certain rules of logic (the details of which are beyond the scope of this text) to these three hypotheses, we could derive three new ones:

If $a$, then $c$

If $a$, then $d$

If $b$, then $d$

These new hypotheses are then incorporated into the "logical net" that comprises the theory.

The second advantage of theories over single hypotheses is that empirical support for any *one* of the hypotheses in the theory lends empirical support to *all* of the other hypotheses which make up the theory.

With these preliminary considerations of logic and causal analysis in mind, we turn to a discussion of explanatory research designs.

## Preexperimental Designs

Explanatory research, as we have noted, involves the search for causal relationships among two or more conditions or variables through the use of a number of different types of research design. These research designs are differentiated from each other by their forms and by the strength of the arguments they permit the researcher to make concerning the existence of cause-and-effect relationships. The least persuasive of these designs are called **preexperimental designs,** of which there are two kinds, after-only and before-after.

Suppose we let $DV_{T1}$ represent our observation of the value of the dependent variable (DV) at a given point in time (T1). We let $DV_{T2}$ represent a second observation of the same variable at a later point in time (T2). Finally, we let IV represent our observation of the independent variable (IV), the one which we think explains DV. We could then represent a sequence of observations of these two variables in the following way:

$$\text{Time} \rightarrow$$

$$DV_{T1} \quad IV \quad DV_{T2}$$

This indicates that we observed IV at some time between our first and second observations of DV. Now, suppose we compare our two observations of DV—that is, we compare $DV_{T1}$ and $DV_{T2}$. There are two possibilities: either DV changed or did not change in value. If no change in DV is observed, there is, presumably, nothing to explain, since the IV has nothing to do with DV. If DV did change, then there is something to explain and it is at least possible that IV caused the change.

*After-Only Design.*   The after-only design is a strategy for attempting to assess the effect of a particular event after the event has occurred. It is called after-*only* because no observation of the dependent variable

(DV) took place before the presumed cause (IV). The **after-only** design may be represented as follows:

The dotted box around $DV_{T1}$ indicates that the researcher had not observed DV at that time, and therefore has to guess or estimate what he would have observed. In general, this is the only type of design that can be used to study the effects of unexpected events. Studies of the impact of civil disorders or cataclysmic natural events, such as earthquakes or tornadoes, often use an after-only design.

An investigator may use an after-only design when he has no alternative, but its form provides the least persuasive basis for causal inference. Using it for any purpose other than to describe the state of affairs following a significant event and to speculate about its effects is fraught with methodological hazards. Because the investigator has been unable to observe the dependent variable (DV) prior to the hypothesized causal event (IV), he cannot be very confident either that DV actually changed or that the causal factors he hypothesized are really causal. The only requirement of a causal inference that has been met is that of time sequence. Concomitant variation is not established by this design, and nothing has been accomplished in the way of eliminating other possible causal factors.

One strategy a researcher can use to strengthen the inferences drawn from after-only research is to study a similar population that has not been exposed to the *presumed* causal condition (i.e., the earthquake, storm, riot, or revolution). If observations of both of these populations show the same presumed effect, we can be reasonably sure that the presumed cause was not a real cause. If the exposed population shows the effect and the unexposed population does not, we have not proven that the independent variable caused the effect because some other unmeasured or unknown variable may be responsible. However, we have at least increased the likelihood that the presumed independent variable was responsible for the effect, and in doing so, we make the argument for causal inference more persuasive.

*Before-After Design.* If the researcher is able to anticipate the independent variable, or to create it in a research situation, he can use a **before-after** type of explanatory research design. Here, the investigator actually observes DV before IV occurs (a preobservation of the dependent variable). Then, the event (IV) occurs or is introduced by the investigator, and DV is observed again (postobservation of the dependent variable). This design can be diagrammed as follows:

$$Time \rightarrow$$

$$DV_{T1} \quad IV \quad DV_{T2}$$

Finally, the pre- and postobservations of the dependent variable are compared to determine if any change has taken place, and an appropriate inference is drawn about the relationship between the independent and dependent variables. If a change is observed, the independent variable can be viewed as responsible for the change because the before-after design provides reasonably clear evidence of both concomitant variation and appropriate time sequence between the variables.

While the before-after design has significant advantages over the after-only design, it has serious shortcomings. The inference that the dependent and independent variables are causally related is justified only if the event (the independent variable) was the only thing that changed between the pre- and postobservations. If any other changes took place, then any of these changes might have generated the observed effects, or several in combination may have done so. Therefore, the before-after design also fails to provide strong justification for causal inference, since the intervention of unforeseen and/or unobserved events in the research situation is *always* a possibility.

Methodologists have identified several types of changes (besides the occurrence or introduction of the independent variable) that may occur in the time between the pre- and postobservations of the dependent variable. A few of the more common changes will be described here, and others will be covered later. Changes in *maturation* may account for variations in the value of our dependent variable, and generally speaking, the longer the time period between the first and second observations of the dependent variable, the greater are the chances that maturation effects will occur. For example, as time passes, children grow in both the physical and experiential sense.

*History* refers to changes not in the individuals under observation but in the general social environment in which they function. For example, changes in the crime rate may be related in some way to changes in the economic environment, since better economic times mean more employment and, perhaps, less inducement for crime.

Here too, a longer time period usually generates a greater potential impact of historical change.

If we change the method by which we have operationally defined and observed or measured the dependent variable, we are changing how or what we are observing and, in effect, introducing another variable into the investigation. Any differences in our two observations of the dependent variable may be the result of observation or measurement changes and not changes of the independent variable.

Another kind of problem with the before-after design and all other designs incorporating observation is that the process of observation itself may affect the results obtained. Asking people questions (for example, about their attitudes toward the death penalty, the police, or the Supreme Court) or making them aware that they are being observed by researchers (even if they do not know specifically what the researchers are observing) may influence the pre- or postobservation results, quite apart from any effect generated by the independent variable itself. An effect generated by the process of observation itself is known as an experimenter effect or a Hawthorne effect, which will be discussed more thoroughly later.

## Experimental Designs

All of the explanatory research designs considered so far have substantial flaws that seriously weaken the argument that variable *a* causes variable *b*. The basic problem in each case has been satisfying the third condition for a causal inference—the elimination of other possible causes for changes in the dependent variable in the particular research situation. A causal inference is significantly strengthened if the research design includes a control group. This is the advantage of **experimental designs**.

*Before-After-with-Control Design.* When an investigator recognizes that variables other than the independent variable—such as maturation, history, measurement methods, or the Hawthorne effect—are present and potentially influential, and wants to assess or neutralize their effects, he can use a **before-after-with-control** research design:

Time $\rightarrow$

| E | $DV_{T1}$ | IV | $DV_{T2}$ |
|---|-----------|----|-----------|
| C | $DV_{T1}$ |    | $DV_{T2}$ |

Two separate groups of subjects are included in this design: an **experimental group** (E) and a **control group** (C). In the experimental group, the independent variable occurs or is introduced by the investigator, just as in the before-after design. In this design, however, there is also a control group, for which the independent variable does not occur or is not introduced.

The inclusion of the control group in the design permits the researcher to argue quite strongly that the effects of a number of possible alternative causal variables can be measured and then eliminated from consideration. The difference between the values of the dependent variable observed at T1 and T2 in the control group is a measure of the changes that may have occurred because of maturation, history, initial exposure to the measuring device, the Hawthorne effect, or any other changes that occurred between T1 and T2, *without the additional effects, if any, of our independent variable.* Therefore, we can subtract out from the total differences between $DV_{T1}$ and $DV_{T2}$ in the experimental group differences associated with maturation, history, etc., in the control group and we are left with the difference in our dependent variable which can be attributed to the effects of our hypothesized independent variable.[3] We might represent the subtraction as follows:

Experimental Group      Control Group

$(DV_{T1} - DV_{T2})$   –   $(DV_{T1} - DV_{T2})$   =   Effect of IV on DV

If the data indicate that some change in DV remains after this subtraction is performed, this design gives us strong evidence of concomitant variation and appropriate time sequence as well as good reason to believe that the change was caused by the IV, because we have measured and then eliminated many of the possible extraneous causal factors. As a result, we can argue effectively that a causal relationship exists between the independent and dependent variables.

*Solomon Four-Group Design.* **Solomon four-group design** is an extension of the basic experimental design and can be represented as follows:

| E1 | $DV_{T1}$ | IV | $DV_{T2}$ |
|----|-----------|----|-----------|
| C1 | $DV_{T1}$ |    | $DV_{T2}$ |
| E2 |           | IV | $DV_{T2}$ |
| C2 |           |    | $DV_{T2}$ |

In this design, another experimental and another control group are added to the basic experimental design. These additions permit us to assess the effects, if any, of some of the potential causal variables in the experimental situation by comparing observations from the four groups in various combinations. Consider, for example, a comparison of the two experimental groups (E1 and E2). The difference between these two is the absence of the preobservation of the dependent variable in E2. Suppose that we wanted a measure of the effects of the preobservation. Note that while in C (control group) 1 the dependent variable was assessed initially, in C2 it was not. Now, $C1DV_{T1}$ – $C1DV_{T2}$ is a difference which includes the effects of the preobservation *as well as* the effects of any other variables (except the independent variable) which changed between T1 and T2. A measure of the effects of these other variables is provided by $C1DV_{T1}$ – $C2DV_{T2}$. Hence:

$$(C1DV_{T1} - C1DV_{T2}) - (C1DV_{T1} - C2DV_{T2}) = \text{The Effect of the Preobservation}$$

The Solomon four-group design does not provide any stronger support for an inference that there is a causal relationship between the independent and dependent variables than does the before-after-with-control design. However, it does permit the researcher to measure separately the effects of some of the other variables in the research situation, such as the effects of the preobservation.

*Matching and Random Assignment.* While using a control group helped us solve some of the problems associated with justifying a causal inference, unfortunately we have introduced some new ones that demand attention. The most significant new difficulty is the possibility that the experimental and control groups are different from each other in some important way. If they are, the benefits we have derived from this design are negated, because any difference is also a variable that may account for observed changes in our dependent variable. However, two basic strategies can be used to help insure that the experimental and control groups are as similar as possible: matching and random assignment.

   **Matching** is a strategy in which the investigator determines that the two groups are "identical" on certain variables other than the independent variable he believes might be causally related to the dependent variable. To insure that the two groups are as similar as possible with respect to these variables, the investigator assigns people to the two groups on the basis of their similarity on these variables. This strategy requires, of course, that the investigator is able to identify the important variables and to assign individuals to the two groups accordingly. He may select the two groups so that all members of both groups are males, between the ages of 14 and 19, middle-class, white, and so forth. He may also select groups so that the proportions or percentages of certain characteristics are equal in the two groups; that is, both groups are 50 percent male, 25 percent middle-class, 35 percent under age 19, 50 percent felons, and so on. The groups can be matched on as many different variables as the research situation permits, but obviously, the more variables involved, the more difficult the matching process becomes.

Matching does not completely solve the problem of similarity between the experimental and control groups, however. There is always the possibility that the two groups differ on one or more important variables that the researcher did not recognize and therefore did not consider in the matching process. These differences may account for observed changes in the dependent variable.

**Random assignment** involves placing individuals in the two groups according to the laws of probability, a subject about which we shall have more to say in a later chapter. This strategy begins with the total pool or collection of persons or events to be studied, and then assignments are made so that each individual person or event has an equal chance of being placed in either the experimental or control group. This is a way of randomly distributing differences among the people or events between the two groups and minimizing the likelihood of any systematic differences between the two groups. Random assignment does not provide guarantees, for the possibility remains that systematic differences will exist and that these differences, rather than the investigator's hypothesized independent variable, may account for changes in the dependent variable.

Matching and random assignment help ensure that the experimental and control groups are as similar as possible. Nevertheless, as we have seen, there remains some uncertainty concerning this similarity. As a result, causal inference based on an experimental research design remains to some degree uncertain as well.

*Longitudinal Explanatory Designs.* Some kinds of research situations call for modifications of the basic types of research designs we have discussed. Perhaps the most common adaptations involve using the panel and multiple group trend designs discussed in the earlier section on descriptive research. Suppose, for example, that we wanted to assess the effects of a police department's public relations campaign (the independent variable) on attitudes toward the police (the dependent variable) in a particular urban neighborhood. A study might be designed that involved a measurement of the dependent variable before the campaign was launched and three measurements after the campaign was completed. We could choose either a panel or a multiple group trend design. The explanatory panel design might be diagrammed like this:

Where the research situation permits, a control group should be added to this design, consisting, for example, of a neighborhood very similar to the one where the campaign is being conducted, thereby increasing substantially the persuasiveness of an inference that the campaign, rather than some other possible causal variable, is the cause of any observed before-after differences in citizens' attitudes.

A multiple group trend study of the same research question might be diagrammed like this:

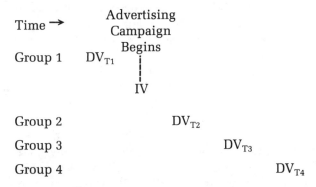

Here, too, control groups should be included in the design whenever possible. Pollsters hired by political candidates often use one of these two designs to gauge the effectiveness of TV, newspapers, or radio advertising campaigns. They are useful, in fact, for assessing the effects of almost any kind of information or persuasion program. Multiple observations following the occurrence of IV provide evidence concerning both the duration and the changes in the intensity of its effects.

Longitudinal explanatory designs have the advantages and disadvantages of their descriptive design counterparts. When used without control groups (as they often are), causal inferences derived from them are no better than those based on preexperimental before-after designs.

## Quasi-experimental Procedures

Research that conforms to all of the aspects of the experimental research design typically takes place in a laboratory setting, since it is imperative that a researcher has control over the assignment of subjects to experimental and control groups and the occurrence of the independent variable. However, exercising these controls is often difficult in criminal justice research. It is virtually impossible, for example, for a researcher to persuade a judge to assign different sentences for the same offense in order to test the effects of sentencing policy on recidivism. It would also be difficult to request public defenders (on a random basis) to act as if they adhered to two different legal strategies in defending their clients to examine the effects of these strategies on conviction rates. Even if subjects could be controlled in such ways, some very difficult ethical issues are raised by these practices.

For ethical, practical, and methodological reasons, then, researchers must often resort to quasi-experimental procedures in some phases of the research process. These procedures diminish some of the persuasive power of experimental design but still provide some logical and empirical support for causal inferences. Perhaps the two aspects of the research process most often compromised through quasi-experimental techniques involve the assignment of subjects to experimental and control groups and separating the time of measurement from the time of occurrence of the variables.

Experimental design requires that membership in the experimental and control groups be determined before the experiment begins so that differences between the two groups can be controlled through matching or random assignment. When the researcher is unable to do this, he may attempt to find two groups in the "real world" who are similar in most ways but who differ in their values on the independent variable. Their values on the dependent variable could then be compared, and any differences observed might be attributed to the differences in the independent variable values. While this procedure has merit, it is often considerably less persuasive than experimental procedure because finding adequately matched groups in the real world is extremely difficult and the researcher is usually forced to use groups that have larger differences than are desirable, which, in turn, undermines support for a causal inference about the relationship between the variables the researcher is studying.

The logic of causal inference also requires that changes in the independent variable occur *before* changes in the dependent variable. The best empirical evidence for this time sequence is provided by the experimental design, where the researcher controls the time at which the independent variable occurs. For many research projects, however, exercising this control is neither possible nor practical. In these cases, it is possible to approximate the strict time sequence requirements of the experimental design by gathering data at one point in time (the *time of measurement*) about variables whose values have changed at some previous time (the *time of occurrence*). Interviews and questionnaires often seek information of this nature.

Suppose we hypothesize that family instability (IV) is related to juvenile delinquency (DV). For obvious reasons, it is not possible to test this hypothesis using an experimental design. However, we could give a large group of older juveniles a questionnaire asking them to tell us (a) if they had ever been convicted of a juvenile offense and, if they had, when the first offense occurred, and (b) if their parents were divorced and, if they were, when the divorce occurred. We could then use the responses to the questions about time of occurrence of IV and DV as evidence concerning their actual time sequence. Of course, when time of occurrence does not coincide with time of measurement, support for the time sequence condition in a causal argument is weakened because serious questions can be raised about the validity of the measurements. Are the reports about times of occurrence accurate? Still, sometimes evidence of this kind is the best we can get.

Whatever the choice of research design, it must be made explicit before the research begins. The quality of the results and the degree of confidence that the researcher can place in the descriptions or causal inferences that result depend upon the structure of the design within the context of which the data were collected. The researcher's knowledge of the characteristics, the strengths, and the limitations of these designs is vital to understanding and doing effective research.

## Exploratory Research

Exploratory research is a loosely structured but valuable methodological strategy. When scientists are interested in some phenomenon, but feel they need to know a great deal more about it before they can put together a well-organized and thorough study of it, they often engage in exploratory research. Suppose you were interested in the significance of adolescent groups to the lives of adolescents in inner city neighborhoods. Unless you had grown up in the inner city or had had contacts with such adolescents and their groups, you would probably not know what to look for or what might be important in understanding the relationship between these individuals and their groups. Under these circumstances, you need to familiarize yourself with the general nature and functioning of such groups. You might contact an inner city neighborhood center and volunteer to work in its youth program. Or you might ask to talk with some of the adolescents who frequent the center. In either case, your purpose would be to observe the lives and activities of the adolescents in a general way, with an eye toward forming some preliminary ideas about important aspects of the relationships between the individuals and the groups to which they belong.

Most researchers undertake exploratory research (a) to familiarize themselves with the selected research "territory," and (b) to determine the desirability and feasibility of conducting a more rigorous investigation in the future. The exploratory researcher typically begins with some general questions but few specific ideas or topics to investigate. When he emerges from this type of research, the researcher has simply become better acquainted with the subject; he has not developed definitive descriptions or explanations. However, the researcher has been able to identify specific aspects of his subject that may be significant, and this information can be useful in preparing a more rigorous study of the phenomenon at a later date. Another potential benefit is the insight that can be gained concerning an appropriate strategy for conducting a subsequent investigation. Often the exploratory researcher is able to identify which research techniques would be feasible and which would not. Occasionally, researchers discover that they are not as interested in the phenomenon as they initially thought, or that there seems to be no feasible means of studying the phenomenon further at the present time. Any of these outcomes of exploratory research would make the effort worthwhile.

## Prediction

Scientific *prediction* is closely related to explanation. The principal difference is that prediction refers to the attempt to say something about the state of affairs which will exist in the future, while explanation attempts to account for something that has already occurred. For example, criminal justice policymakers may be interested in predicting the direction and magnitude of change in crime rates over the next 10 years, or members of a parole board may wish to estimate the likelihood that a given ex-convict will return to prison. As you can imagine, the ability to predict such phenomena accurately can be enhanced by understanding what causes crime rates to change and what causes criminals to recidivate. In other words, if one could explain previous changes in crime rates and instances of recidivism, then at least theoretically one should be able to predict them as well. Actually, being able to explain does not by any means guarantee an accurate prediction. Our theories about and knowledge of social processes and individual behavior are too incomplete and forces which shape the future are too complex to permit accurate prediction in most areas of criminal justice. However, as our ability to explain increases, so should our capacity to predict.

## *Triangulation*

**Triangulation** means collecting different types of data from different sources with respect to a single research question. With *observation*, the researcher records the activities and events he has seen. Our confidence in interpretations based on observation alone, however, is limited by the possibility that the observations may not be accurately recorded or interpreted. If, however, we *interview* the people involved about their behavior, and their remarks concur with the researcher's observations, we can have more confidence in the conclusions. If we are also able to use *document analysis*, that is, read others' accounts of the people and events we have witnessed, and if their observations and conclusions are similar to ours, we can say with still greater assurance that our conclusions are justified. We have, in short, used the technique of triangulation.

Triangulation is valuable not only because it allows us to have more confidence in our findings, but also because it often brings discrepancies in our data to light. People may tell us they behave in one way, but our observations might show they behave in another. We can then focus on the source of this discrepancy and its resolution and, perhaps, design an experiment to investigate the discrepancy we have discovered.

Whenever possible, the researcher should use triangulation to minimize error resulting from the use of any single method for collecting data, to maximize the possibility of discovering discrepancies, and to make full use of the principles characterizing the scientific perspective.

## *Replication and Computer Simulations*

So far, our discussion has focused on factors that affect the confidence we have in the descriptions and explanations produced by a particular researcher on the basis of a particular research project. The fact that there are many difficulties associated with each of the designs and procedures we have discussed cannot be ignored. As we have just seen, triangulation can help us overcome some of these difficulties. However, there are other features of scientific methodology that, in the long run, contribute to the resolution of these difficulties. Science is a thoroughly social enterprise, and the confidence we have in the knowledge generated through the application of scientific methodology is increased through mutual criticism and replication.

Scientists carefully scrutinize and criticize each other's research, pointing out the strengths and weaknesses they see in others' research designs and data-gathering processes, offering alternative interpretations of the data and both criticizing and defending their own work. In these exchanges, hidden biases may be revealed, faulty reasoning exposed, and the quality of subsequent research improved.

Researchers also often **replicate** the work of others by studying the same research question using the same research methodology. If the replication produces results that are the same or similar to those of previous studies, confidence in the descriptions made or causal inferences drawn is increased.

Computer simulations may also be used to examine relationships among variables. The investigator provides real or ''dummy'' data for several variables and mathematical formulas for the relationships among them. The computer is then instructed to change the values of one or more of the variables and work out the corresponding changes in the other variables as determined by the formulas. These simulations are especially useful when complex relationships among many variables are being explored. Of course, unless the data are real and the mathematical formulas used have been empirically verified in actual research, these simulations are little more than computer-aided exercises of the researcher's imagination.

## *A Final Note about the Research Process*

Throughout our discussion, we have emphasized the dangers inherent in accepting the results of scientific research at face value. Our experiences teach us that things are not always as they seem, so the validity and reliability of our categorizations may be questioned. There may be discrepancies between what people say they do and what they actually do. People who say they would welcome minority group members as neighbors are often the first to leave the neighborhood when minorities arrive, and politicians' campaign promises may be regarded with suspicion. Causal inferences, even if based on experimental designs, are subject to debate.

Even the best scientific methodology provides no foolproof mechanism for removing all doubt about the validity and reliability of data collected or causal inferences drawn in its name. The best we can do as researchers is to eliminate as many sources of error as possible in our own work, make it available for the criticism of other scientists, and subject our findings to further tests.

## Notes

1. See F. S. C. Northrop, *The Logic of the Sciences and the Humanities* (New York: World, 1959), especially pp. 102–7, for a thorough discussion of concepts and constructs.
2. Claire Selltiz et al., *Research Methods in Social Relations* (New York: Holt, Rinehart, and Winston, 1965), p. 83.
3. This inference, of course, depends upon the assumption that no other influences have acted on the control group between measurements that have not also acted on the experimental group. If this assumption is correct—and we may have no way to tell whether it is—then we may justifiably infer that the difference between experimental and control groups represents the effect of the independent variable.

## Review Questions

1. What is the difference between research methodology and research methods?
2. From what sources might research topics emerge?
3. How do constructs differ from operational definitions?
4. What is the difference between a category and a variable?
5. What distinguishes validity, reliability and precision in categorizations?
6. What is a research design?
7. How do descriptive and explanatory research designs differ?
8. What are the advantages and disadvantages of panel, multiple group trend, and cross-sectional designs in descriptive research?
9. What are the valid forms of argument from conditional statements?
10. What is the difference between the form and the content of arguments?
11. What is the difference between necessary and sufficient causes?

12. What are the logical conditions necessary for making a causal inference?
13. How do independent, dependent and intervening variables differ?
14. How do preexperimental designs differ from experimental designs? Why are preexperimental designs less persuasive as foundations for causal inference than experimental designs?
15. What is the Hawthorne effect?
16. Compare and contrast experimental and quasi-experimental designs.
17. What is triangulation and why is it an effective research tool?

## *Exercises*

1. Collect at least three physical objects of the same general type (e.g., three writing instruments, or three cups, or three books) and place them in front of you. Identify ways in which the objects are different. Identify the categories (variables) you are using and the subcategories corresponding to each category. (For example, you may say one object is blue and another is red. The concept you are using is color and the subcategories—the values of the color variables—are red and blue.) Construct at least four such variables and their associated values. Then, consider three persons and perform the same comparative activities, identifying variables and corresponding values of each variable. Then, consider three events of the same general type and do the same things.
2. Identify values for each of the following variables and describe at least two different operational definitions for each variable.

   - police officer
   - crimes
   - citizens' evaluation of the performance of the state's attorney
   - laws
   - punishments
   - judges
   - verdicts
   - penal institutions
   - criminals

   Compare your results with another member of the class and discuss any similarities and differences you discover.
3. Identify three different research designs for a research project de-

scribing drug use patterns among students at a particular university over time.

4. Identify at least three possible causal variable chains in criminal justice involving independent, intervening and dependent variables.

5. Suppose you are interested in studying the effects of a human relations or sensitivity training program on white officers working in black neighborhoods. Describe and discuss the logical supports for causal inference provided by each of the following types of design for studying this research question.

- after-only design
- before-after design
- before-after-with-control design
- Solomon four-group design

# 4

# *Sampling*

After stating a research question and developing an appropriate research design, we must select one or more persons, objects, or events on whose properties or characteristics our research will focus.

Sometimes, we can take a **census** of a population by studying every element involved. For example, to determine whether the 400 registered voters in Hitsville would support a tax referendum to provide funds for a new police station, we might interview every voter. This group of persons is called the research **population**, and each individual person is referred to as an *element* of the population. Populations may be *finite* and consist of a specifiable number of elements, or *infinite* and include an unspecifiable number of elements. The population of registered voters in Hitsville is a finite one, while all possible flips of a coin is infinite.

If we were interested in citizens' opinions on a tax referendum not just in Hitsville but statewide or nationally, census-taking would not be feasible for a typical researcher because of the expenses involved. Even the federal government undertakes a national census only once every 10 years because of the tremendous cost. In such cases, we obtain information from some but not all of the elements in our population; that is, from a **sample** of that population. A sample consists of selected elements from a population that will be observed in order to learn something about the entire population.

Because the sample will represent the population for our research purposes, we need to be concerned about the *quality* of that representation. Our goal is to select a "good" sample—one whose characteristics accurately represent the characteristics of the population. To the extent that the sample is representative, inferences can be drawn about the population.

But sampling is inevitably a risky business. Some samples are good representatives of their populations, while others are not. Furthermore, even a good sample may not mirror *exactly* the population from which it is drawn. Any differences between the characteristics of the sample and those of the population are said to be the result of

**sampling error.** We can expect any sampling procedure to produce some sampling error. To make matters worse, the researcher cannot determine the extent of the sampling error because the whole population has not been observed and therefore the characteristics of the sample cannot be directly compared to those of the population.

Given this situation, the procedures that the researcher uses to select the sample become critical. Some sampling techniques are more likely than others to produce "good" samples. Furthermore, some sampling procedures permit us to estimate the amount of the sampling error statistically, and these sampling procedures are clearly preferable to those that do not permit such estimates. Inferential statistics (covered in a subsequent chapter) allow us to say precisely how much risk we are taking when we make an inference about the population on the basis of the sample data. For now, we will discuss the more powerful sampling techniques first and then consider the less powerful ones.

## *Probability Sampling*

Although there are many kinds of sampling techniques, they can be divided broadly into two types: probability and nonprobability sampling. **Probability sampling** allows us to specify the probability that any given element in our population will be included in our sample. **Nonprobability sampling** does not permit us to estimate the likelihood that an element in our population will be selected. Probability sampling has very significant advantages over nonprobability sampling, especially since it allows us to use statistical inference. Statistical inference, in turn, permits us to estimate the extent of sampling error.

Suppose we are interested in theories of crime causation, and we have identified 5 theorists as our population, namely Edwin, Cesare, George, Jeremy, and Robert. This list of all the elements in our population is called a **sampling frame.** Since we cannot afford to visit all 5, we decide to select 2 for our sample. After writing each of the names on a small piece of paper and putting those slips of paper into a hat, we then, without looking, draw one from the hat. Because each theorist is one-fifth or .20 of the total group of 5, each man's probability $(p)$ of being selected is 1 in 5, or $p = .20$, at the outset.

The name on the slip of paper we pick initially is the first element in our sample. After our first draw, we have a decision to make before we make our second draw. We may either put the drawn slip back in the hat or keep it out. If we leave it out, there are only 4 names remaining in the hat, so the probability of drawing 1 of those 4 is 1 in 4 or .25. Hence, the probability of drawing any single name has changed from .20 on the first draw to .25 on the second. To keep the probability of drawing any one name from the hat the same from one draw to the next, we would have to place each name drawn back into the hat before we made the next draw. That creates the possibility that we will draw the same name again, and that possibility will be discussed later. For now, we can simply note that when we put an element back into the population before we select another element for our sample, we are **sampling with replacement.** Not returning the drawn element is called **sampling without replacement.** When we are drawing relatively small samples from relatively large populations, the changes in probability associated with sampling without replacement are very small, and sampling without replacement is quite common.

We can also determine the probability of drawing any 2 particular names from our population of 5 names. The first step would be to list all of the potential combinations of 2 names, and for our purposes we will use the first letters in each of the 5 names. The 10 possible combinations for this population would include the following: EC, EG, EJ, ER, CG, CJ, CR, GJ, GR, JR. The probability of getting any one of the 10 combinations is 1 in 10 or .10. Obviously, if we had a much larger population, the task of determining the probability of getting any one of the combinations would be tedious indeed if we used this rather simple method. Fortunately, statisticians have worked out a formula for determining the number of possible combinations (c) of elements drawn (r; in our example, 2) at a time from a population of size n (in our example, 5). That is:

$$_nC_r = \frac{n!}{r!(n-r)!}.$$

The ! is a mathematical notation for "factorial," and factorial n is given by $n(n-1)(n-2)(n-3)...(1)$. In our example, $(n-4)$ would be the last factor needed since $(5-4) = (1)$. The formula can be computed as follows:

1. $_nC_r = \dfrac{n!}{r!(n-r)!}$

2. $_nC_r = \dfrac{5!}{2!(5-2)!}$

3. $_nC_r = \dfrac{5(n-1)(n-2)(n-3)(n-4)}{2(r-1) \times (3)(3-1)(3-2)}$

4. $_nC_r = \dfrac{5 \times 4 \times 3 \times 2 \times 1}{(2 \times 1)(3 \times 2 \times 1)} = \dfrac{120}{12} = \dfrac{10}{1}$

This tells us that there are 10 possible combinations of 5 things taken two at a time. The probability of getting any one of the combinations, then, is 1 in 10 or .10.

If we take a census, that is, if we contact all persons in our population and ask them appropriate questions, we will have relatively complete information concerning their thoughts on the causes of crime. But if we select only 2 individuals (elements) and learn their views, we will almost certainly not have represented the views of all 5 exactly. Hence, we take a risk when we generalize from the responses of any sample to the population, but that risk decreases as we increase the size of our sample. When we use probability sampling, the larger the number of elements we sample from our population, the more assurance we have that our sample is representative of the population from which it was drawn.[1]

## Simple Random Sampling

The most basic type of probability sample is a **simple random sample,** which gives each individual element an *equal* chance of being selected, and makes all combinations of a specified number of elements equally probable as well. (In our previous example, the probability of drawing any specific name on the first draw was .20, and the probability of any particular combination of two being selected on the first draw was 1 in 10, or $p = .10$.)

Theoretically, in order to select a simple random sample, *all* of the elements in a population must be listed only once; however, a complete list of population elements may be very difficult to obtain, and creating our sampling frame may present a number of problems. Even an accurate and complete list of voting residents of Hitsville collected today might contain inaccuracies tomorrow, because some voting residents may die or move away, and newly qualified residents may register. Often, no list (for example, a list of rape victims in Hitsville) enumerating a population will exist. When lists do exist, they may be biased and inaccurate, for they may systematically exclude or underrepresent some categories of events or people and overrepresent others. Clearly, our initial list of elements must be carefully constructed and evaluated for accuracy, and corrected where possible. Unavoidable inadequacies should be noted and reported. While it is unlikely that any enumeration of elements in a large population will remain accurate for any length of time, checking for these sources of error may improve the quality of the list considerably.

After we have drawn up our list, we can use any of a number of techniques to select a sample of the size we need. Suppose we wish to select a sample of 100 respondents (elements) from a population of 500 by using a table of random numbers. First, our 500 respondents would have to be numbered consecutively, beginning with 001 and ending with 500. Then, we would turn to the table of random numbers (see appendix A), close our eyes, and place a pencil somewhere on the table. Starting from the nearest number, we could move either horizontally or vertically, selecting a respondent for our sample each time we come to a number between 1 and 500, until we have selected 100 subjects. Assuming that we are sampling without replacement, if we encounter the same number a second time or if the number in the table is greater than 500, we simply skip that number and go on to the next number until we find one that does correspond and has not already been chosen.

A simple random sample is less costly both in time and in manpower than taking a census, but it can still be relatively expensive if we have to put a lot of effort into constructing and "purifying" our list of elements. However, when we know little or nothing about our population and can get a reasonably accurate list of its elements, a simple random sample is usually the best choice.

## Stratified Random Sampling and Proportionate Sampling

If we want to be sure that our sample is representative of our population in certain specifiable ways (e.g., proportion of males), or if we believe that a certain variable may affect our subjects' responses (e.g., ethnicity), we can use a **stratified random sample**, assuming that relevant information about each element is available. To draw a sample of this type, we divide our population into categories, or *strata*, ensuring that each population element falls into one and only one of the established categories or strata. Simple random samples could then be selected from each of the subpopulations. Usually, the size of the simple random sample drawn from each strata is adjusted so that the proportion of elements is equal to the proportion of the whole population contained within that stratum. This procedure is referred to as **proportionate sampling**. If we stratified a population of 1,000 subjects by sex and discovered that there were 600 females and 400 males, we could draw a sample of 100 from the whole population consisting of 60 females and 40 males. Our sample would then be exactly representative of the population, at least as far as the sex variable is concerned. Furthermore, each element in the whole population had an equal chance of being selected for the sample. By using a stratified sample, we can often reduce the number of cases we need in order to maximize our chances of representativeness by making certain that members of each of the categories we believe to be important are included. For instance, if we hypothesize that ethnicity is related to the frequency of rape victimization, and we enumerate the population of Hitsville, we could select a simple random sample large enough to ensure that all ethnic groups in the city would be included. If, however, the percentage of ethnic minorities is very small, our sample size would have to be extremely large to include enough minority group members to conduct a meaningful analysis. If we could obtain or construct lists for each of the ethnic minority groups in the population, we could stratify it according to ethnicity and select simple random samples of whites, blacks, Hispanics, and so forth, thus ensuring that all minorities would be represented in our sample in the appropriate proportions.

## Disproportionate Sampling

So far we have discussed only one type of probability sample, a simple random sample, in which each element in the population has an equal chance of being selected. However, the probabilities associated with an element's selection do not have to be equal. We can use a **disproportionate sampling** strategy and draw a sample so that some elements have twice the probability of others of being chosen. The critical characteristic of any probability sample is being able to specify the probability that any given element will be included.

Consider again our example of a population with a small percentage of minority persons, stratified by ethnic group. Suppose we would like to examine our data on blacks in some detail, and to do that, we need a relatively large number of blacks in our sample. We would simply decide that we wanted each black person in our population to have 1 chance in 10 (or 5 or 2, etc.) of being included in the sample, while leaving the probability that a white would be selected at 1 in 100 (or 200 or 1,000, etc.). The result, of course, is that we end up with a greater number and proportion of blacks in our sample, and that our total sample is no longer representative of the ethnic distribution within the population. Therefore, when we analyze our data, we should not place all of the selected people into a single pool and use the data from this pool to generalize to the population as a whole.

Suppose that we are studying whether or not people are in favor of capital punishment in a city whose population is 90 percent white and 10 percent black. We stratify our population by ethnic group and sample disproportionately, selecting 2 percent of the whites and 20 percent of the blacks. In comparison to their respective proportions in the whole population, blacks will be overrepresented and whites will be underrepresented in our sample. If blacks and whites differ in their views on capital punishment, combining these two groups into a single pool to estimate the proportion of people (regardless of ethnic group) in the city who favored capital punishment would be misleading. Our estimate would be distorted by the differences in the proportion of blacks in our sample compared to their proportion in the population as a whole.

We *could* legitimately use the proportion of blacks in our sample to estimate the proportion of blacks in the population who favor capital punishment, and the proportion of whites who favor capital punishment in this sample to estimate the proportion of whites in the population who favor it. We could also legitimately compare the proportion of blacks with the proportion of whites who favor capital punishment because our stratified sampling procedure has produced two separate random samples, one of blacks and one of whites. The differences between the two samples in the proportion that each represents of the population as a whole is, for all practical purposes, irrelevant to a comparison of the proportions in the two separate groups.

There is a relatively simple solution to the problem of making statements about a population as a whole on the basis of sample data when disproportionate sampling is desirable. It consists of drawing a second sample of one or more of the separate strata so that the sample contains proportionate representation of a particular subpopulation (for example, ethnic groups). These proportionate samples from the various strata can then be combined to make estimates of the percent of people in the population as a whole who support capital punishment.

## Systematic Sampling

Sometimes, a reasonable approximation of a random sample can be achieved through a technique called **systematic sampling.** To use systematic sampling, instead of a table of random numbers to select each element in our sample, we randomly select only our first element, and then choose every 10th, 15th, or kth element in the sampling frame. The size of k is determined by the number of elements on our population list and the size of the sample we desire. If there are 500 names on a list and we want a sample of 50, we would select every 10th name (500 ÷ 50 = 10) on the list.

If an adequate list of elements in a particular population is available to the researcher, systematic sampling may save considerable time, but it also entails a potential hazard. This hazard involves lists that are ordered in some way—for example, by rank or cycle. Suppose we have a list of military personnel in which every 5th subject holds a supervisory rank (e.g., sergeant). If we intend to sample every 5th subject, a systematic sample starting with the randomly selected number 2 clearly could provide us with considerably different responses to questions about authority than a sample starting with the number 5. In the first case, we would include only nonsupervisory personnel in our sample; in the second, only supervisory personnel.

## Cluster Sampling

Another type of probability sampling, known as **cluster sampling,** involves dividing our population into a number of groups, called clusters, on the basis of some criteria (e.g., geographic area). Each cluster is assigned a unique number, and, using a random numbers table, we select a random sample of clusters. Data may then be gathered about each element in each of the selected clusters in order to complete the research project.

At first glance, cluster sampling may seem like another version of stratified sampling, but there are four important differences between the two. First, remember that in stratified sampling we used one or more potential independent variables such as age and sex to create the strata. We wanted to be sure that our sample accurately reflected the population on these variables because we thought they were important for our analysis. We create clusters using a criterion which we think is unimportant for our analysis and which merely permits us to divide up the original population into clusters. Cluster sampling is a strategy most often used as a relatively quick, convenient, and inexpensive method of approximating a random sample of individual elements in a population.

Second, the strata created in stratified sampling typically contain unequal numbers of individual elements, while clusters are specified so that they contain approximately equal numbers of individual elements.

Third, a researcher must have information about each element in the population to create the strata from which the samples will be drawn. Cluster sampling requires only that the researcher have a means of dividing the population into a number of subgroups of equal size, so that in sampling clusters, we can argue that each element of the population has about an equal chance of being selected as a part of one of the clusters we draw. No other information about the individual elements in the population is needed to select a cluster sample.

Fourth, in stratified sampling, we first define the strata (groups) and then sample individual elements within each strata. In cluster sampling, we are sampling not individual elements but groups of elements.

Cluster sampling is often used to study public opinion or voter preference in a large and geographically dispersed population. In such studies a small compromise is made with the requirement of equally sized clusters, since an existing territorial basis may be used to define the clusters. Suppose we wish to determine the amount of public support for a bond issue in a city. Rather than attempting to construct a sample frame for a simple random sample of the city's residents, we might define the city as composed of a collection of city blocks as indicated on a city map, and each residential block might be further defined as a cluster of citizens of the city. A researcher might then take a random sample of the city blocks and include the residents on the blocks selected for the cluster sample of the city's population. Congressional districts might also be treated as population clusters; however, not all blocks or congressional districts will have exactly the same number of residents, and, therefore, the rule of equally sized clusters is not strictly met. In many cases, though, the differences in size are relatively small, and the sample that results from such a procedure is regarded as close enough to a random sample of the residents for most research purposes. You might try to identify some circumstances in which such approximations of a cluster sample might lead to distortions in the sample.

## Multistage Sampling

It is possible to draw a sample by applying the cluster sampling technique in successive stages or to combine random cluster sampling with individual-element random sampling in a variety of ways. Suppose we wish to sample the opinion of registered voters on the national level. As a first step, we would randomly select 10 districts from a list of all U.S. congressional districts. In stage two, we would obtain lists of census districts from each of the 10 congressional districts we selected, and randomly select 10 census districts from each of the 10 congressional districts. In the final stage, for each of the census districts we selected we would obtain a list of registered voters, and from that list we would randomly select 100 voters to be interviewed. The three stages can be summarized as follows:

| Sampling Stage | Sampling Technique |
| --- | --- |
| Stage 1 | Random cluster sample of congressional districts |
| Stage 2 | Random cluster sample of census districts |
| Stage 3 | Random sample of individual voters in each census district |

This process generates a sample of 10,000 voters to be interviewed, but unlike a simple random sample of the registered voter population in the United States, our voters are all located in 100 census districts in 10 congressional districts. It would be much less expensive to send interviewers to these people than to all of the congressional districts and to thousands of census districts. In addition, we are not faced with stratifying our population and then interviewing subjects from each stratum, a task of considerable difficulty if we were to hypothesize that ethnicity, religious affiliation, education, and occupation, for example, affect voting behavior.

Though cluster sampling may save us much time, money, and personnel, it also increases the risk of making errors when generalizing from our sample to the population from which it was selected. Congressional and census districts may vary substantially in population, and at each stage in the sampling process after the first one, some clusters and some elements (individual voters) have no chance of being included in the final sample. Generalizations about a population based on that kind of procedure have some obvious shortcomings. In the foregoing example, we have excluded all voters residing outside the 10 congressional districts and the 100 census districts chosen. In using cluster sampling plans, whether single or multiple stage, we must always be concerned with balancing the cost of our operation with the amount of sampling error we are willing to accept.

Figure 4.1 summarizes the various types of probability sampling we have discussed.

## *Nonprobability Sampling*

The major advantages of nonprobability sampling, the second basic type of sampling, are economy and convenience. However, its major disadvantage is that sampling error cannot be accurately estimated, for biases introduced in nonprobability sampling cannot be evaluated. Because we cannot determine the probability that any given element will be included in our sample, we cannot legitimately use inferential statistics in the analysis of our data. Therefore, making statements about the population on the basis of data obtained from such samples is very risky.

Three different types of nonprobability samples—an accidental, quota, and typical-case or purposive sample—will be considered briefly. An **accidental sample** is composed of respondents who "accidently" happen to come into contact with the researcher and become part of his sample. Man-in-the-street interviews, which are typical of accidental samples, are not very likely to represent their populations well. Too many biasing factors, such as the time of day or the place, influence the type of respondents that the researcher accidentally encounters.

A **quota sample** offers some improvements over the accidental sample because the sampling procedure insures that various elements of a population will be included in the sample. Here a researcher selects a sample that replicates the population by establishing an appropriate quota for each subgroup in the sample. Thus, a quota sample for the United States might include 12 percent blacks, 4 percent Jews, 25 percent Catholics, and 25 percent poor, assuming that these are the correct population proportions for these particular groups.

The final type of nonprobability sample is called a **typical-case** or **purposive sample,** and its underlying assumption is that the researcher has enough skill to select subjects who ought to be included in the sample. He hopes to select cases that are "typical" of the population in question, and assumes that errors in his judgment will cancel out one another.[2] The problem with the typical-case method is that one cannot know whether the cases chosen really are typical. Nonetheless, purposive sampling is still used, for example, to predict election outcomes by interviewing voters in counties or states that have "typically" or "always" voted for the winner.

In addition to sampling people, the researcher may also take samples of places, times, and events. Although it is clearly possible to conduct such samples *randomly* and to observe subjects at the places, times, and dates so selected, this usually is a waste of time for the researcher whose investigation is concerned with particular types of events. It is more sensible to observe at those times when and in those areas where specified, relevant events are likely to occur. The researcher may spend long periods of time with his subjects and record information about the events as they happen to occur (a type of accidental sampling), or he may determine in advance where and when such events will occur and then observe during these periods of time (a type of purposive sampling). For example, interaction among police officers, patients, and staff in a hospital emergency room could be observed in one or two emergency rooms, around the clock for several weeks, thus including in our sample *all* time periods and interactions during that specified period. This procedure would clearly be costly, since we would need at least four researchers (one for each eight-hour shift and an alternate in case of an observer's personal emergency or illness), and we would be paying salaries on a continuous basis (24 hours per day). However, a review of emergency room records might show that most cases are seen between the hours of three o'clock in the afternoon and two o'clock in the morning. If we were willing to

# Figure 4.1 Probability Sampling Techniques

## A. Simple Random Sampling

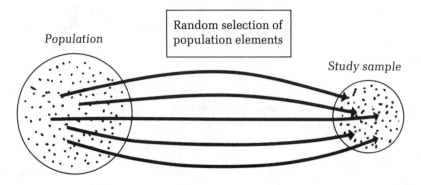

Population

Random selection of population elements

Study sample

## B. Stratified Sampling

Population

Strata samples should not be combined for analysis unless sampling has been proportionate.

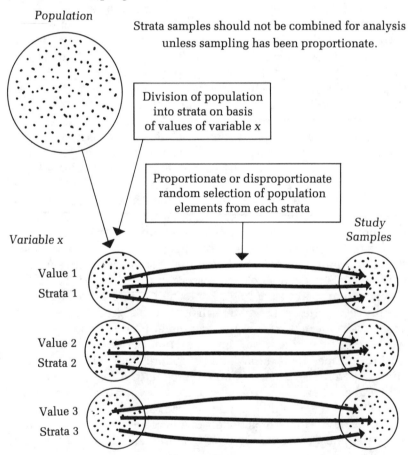

Division of population into strata on basis of values of variable x

Proportionate or disproportionate random selection of population elements from each strata

Study Samples

Variable x

Value 1
Strata 1

Value 2
Strata 2

Value 3
Strata 3

## C. Cluster Sampling

*Population*

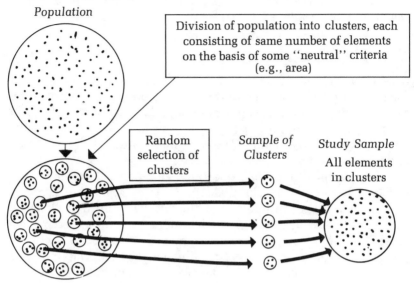

Division of population into clusters, each consisting of same number of elements on the basis of some "neutral" criteria (e.g., area)

Random selection of clusters

*Sample of Clusters*

*Study Sample*

All elements in clusters

## D. Multistage Sampling

*Population*

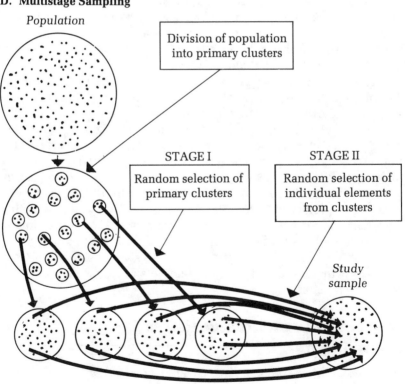

Division of population into primary clusters

STAGE I

Random selection of primary clusters

STAGE II

Random selection of individual elements from clusters

*Study sample*

allow a small percentage of cases (events) to go unobserved, our research staff and salary outlay could be reduced considerably.

## Sample Size

In assessing a research project, we should begin with an evaluation of the sampling techniques employed. The important questions to ask are: (a) Is the sample a probability or nonprobability sample? (b) Is the specific type of sampling procedure used (simple random, multistage, purposive, etc.) appropriate to the hypotheses and the data? and (c) What is the size of the sample?

The relevance of the third question will become clearer in our discussion of statistics, but a brief example here will illustrate its importance. Not long ago, an auto parts manufacturer claimed that taxis using its products in a large American city had not experienced a breakdown for "450,000 taxi-tough miles." Apparently, the company hoped to convince readers of the ad that their parts last mile after mile after mile. Unfortunately, the advertisement failed to mention how many taxis were included in the study. If the number of taxis using these parts was, for example, 4, the manufacturer's claim would appear to have some substance, because, on the average, each taxi could have driven over 100,000 miles on the parts. The reader can estimate for himself the substance of the claim if the number of taxis sampled was not 4, but 4,000!

The objective of any sampling plan is to obtain a representative sample of the population involved that is large enough to permit data analysis and can be studied within the researcher's time and budgetary limits. While small samples can be used, they do not permit very sophisticated analysis because there are too few cases to sort into the various categories of our variables. As a rule of thumb, the sample size should not be less than 30, and most researchers would prefer a sample size nearer 100. For samples drawn from extremely large populations, a sample size of up to 1,500 may be desirable.[3] With probability sampling there are ways to determine the size of sample required to meet specified limits of sampling error, and these techniques are discussed in detail in most statistics texts.[4] We shall consider some elementary principles of determining sample size in the chapter on inferential statistics.

## Determining the Population to Be Sampled

Many research questions can be answered by selecting samples from a number of different populations. The selection of the actual population to be sampled depends largely upon the objectives of the researcher. If, for example, we wanted to determine citizens' attitudes toward the police in a particular community, we might select our sample from the phone book, the city directory, or voter registration lists. However, each of these populations contains some inherent biases since some people, for example, do not own phones and others have unlisted numbers. The city directory is compiled on the basis of volunteered information and not everyone chooses to be included; moreover, not all citizens register to vote. Which of these populations we select, then, depends upon our research goals. If we want to investigate citizen attitudes toward the police to determine if they will support a bond issue to finance a new police building, we might sample the list of registered voters. If our goals were different, one of the other populations might be more appropriate.

Whatever population we identify, it is important for a researcher to remember the basic requisite of any sample: it must represent as well as possible the population from which it was drawn. Furthermore, generalizations made on the basis of the sample data refer at best only to the population sampled. It is tempting to overgeneralize, giving the impression that the results of a study of police officers in Chicago, for example, apply to police officers elsewhere. If Chicago police officers were sampled, then it is to that population that one can generalize. Any implications for police officers in other cities that might be drawn cannot be justified by the Chicago data. To talk about police officers elsewhere, we must sample and study them too.

## Notes

1. For a more complete discussion of probability sampling, see Hubert M. Blalock, Jr., *Social Statistics*, 2nd ed. (New York: McGraw-Hill, 1972), pp. 392–409.
2. Clair Selltiz, Marie Jahoda, Morton Deutsch, and Stuart W. Cook, *Research Methods in Social Relations* (New York: Holt, Rinehart, and Winston, 1965), p. 520.
3. Edwin S. Johnson, *Research Methods in Criminology and Criminal Justice* (Englewood Cliffs, N.J.: Prentice-Hall, 1981), p. 156.
4. Blalock, *Social Statistics*, for example.

## Review Questions

1. Why do researchers sample?
2. What is the essential difference between probability and nonprobability sampling procedures?

3. How can we maximize our chances that a sample represents the population from which it was drawn?
4. What is sampling error?
5. What are some of the principal sources of sampling error?
6. What is the difference between a population and a corresponding sampling frame?
7. How does a simple random sample differ from a stratified random sample?
8. How do random sampling and systematic sampling differ?
9. Why would a researcher use disproportionate sampling?
10. How does cluster sampling differ from simple random sampling and stratified random sampling?
11. Compare and contrast purposive sampling, quota sampling and accidental sampling.
12. Populations of people are often sampled. What are some other types of populations that might be sampled?

## *Exercises*

Use the directory of students for your college or university for exercises 1 through 7:

1. Pick two adjacent pages and consider the persons named on these two pages as a sampling frame. Using the random numbers table, draw a random sample of 20 names, writing down each step you went through in drawing the sample. Then using the same pages, draw a systematic sample of the same size, writing down each step you went through.
2. Discuss the possible differences between the sampling frame you used in exercise 1 and the corresponding population. Then discuss what you might do to improve the sampling frame.
3. Consider each page of the directory as a cluster and draw a two-stage sample, randomly selecting 20 clusters and then a simple 5 percent random sample of each of the clusters, writing down the steps you went through at each step in the sampling process.
4. Using data available in the directory about a variable (e.g., dormitory, or home state or year in school) draw a proportionate stratified random sample of students at the school. Then draw a disproportionate stratified random sample.
5. Is the proportionate stratified random sample you drew in exercise 4 a "better" sample than a simple random sample of the same population?

6. Draw a purposive, an accidental, and a quota sample of size 20 from the two adjacent pages of the directory you used in exercise 1. Then discuss the similarities and differences in sampling techniques used.

7. Why should we consider the sample you drew in exercise 1 "better" than the ones you drew in exercise 6?

8. Consider each 15-minute period in a day an element of the population of 15-minute periods in a two day-period. Draw a simple random sample of 20 elements, writing down each step in the process.

9. Specify some population of events occurring in your immediate environment and draw a simple random sample of them, writing down each step in the process.

# 5

## Research Tools and Techniques: Survey Research through Questionnaires and Interviews

In our daily attempts to understand the world around us, we rely on three basic techniques for gathering information: we observe directly, we communicate with others about what they have observed, and we learn from recorded sources such as books, newspapers, films, and television. The scientific approach to understanding relies on the same techniques for gathering information, but uses them more systematically with respect to specific problem situations. We will consider direct observation and use of recorded sources of information (e.g., document research) in the next chapter. Here we shall be concerned with information gathering through communication with others, that is, through surveys.

**Surveys** can be conducted either by **interview**, with an interviewer asking the questions and recording the subjects' responses, or by **questionnaire**, with the respondents reading the questions and recording their own responses.

## Questionnaires

Researchers often use questionnaires rather than interviews to collect information about a large number of subjects because they require less time and fewer trained staff members to administer. Questionnaires can also provide anonymity to respondents, which is a desirable feature in many criminal justice research projects. They are frequently distributed by mail, because that is an inexpensive, easy way to reach a large number of subjects in many types of groups for which a mailing list can be obtained (such as residents of a city ward, students, magazine subscribers, or association members).

Unlike other information-gathering techniques (e.g., interview and direct observation), questionnaires can be used successfully only when the respondents are literate, and both willing and able to report the desired information. A further limitation of questionnaire surveys is that respondents may misinterpret some of the questions asked, and, similarly, the researcher may misinterpret the meaning of some of the responses. This is especially true for mailed questionnaires, or for questionnaires administered by persons other than the researcher since both the physical and the social distance between the researcher and the respondent is great. Under these circumstances, the researcher cannot resolve problems in the wording of questions or responses as they arise, and in many cases cannot resolve them at all. For this reason, great skill and care in the design of the research instrument, before it goes out to respondents, is critical.

Another potential disadvantage of questionnaire surveys is poor response rates. Part of the budgetary advantage of using written questionnaires may be offset if a relatively small proportion of the questionnaires are returned, which often happens when questionnaires are distributed through the mail or respondents are given several days to complete and return the survey instrument. Over the last few years, in our own research, we have seldom achieved a response rate of better than 50 percent for mailed questionnaires, and as many as 15 percent of respondents who have taken questionnaires home with them have failed to return them. When questionnaires are administered to an assembled group and collected immediately, higher return rates may be expected. Because the researcher anticipates low response rates, the questionnaire must be distributed to a large number of potential respondents in order to provide an adequate number of returned questionnaires. Low response rates also present data analysis and interpretation problems for the researcher because there may be important differences between those who did respond and those who did not, with respect to the research issues. The researcher's efforts to determine what those differences might be are often time-consuming. Both of these adjustments, larger sample size and response-difference analysis, add to research costs.

## Types of Questionnaires

Questionnaires range from highly structured, fixed-alternative instruments to open-ended forms. **Fixed-alternative questionnaires** require the respondent to choose an answer from a printed list of choices. Such questionnaires may include a simple "yes–no" or "true–false" response, a multiple-choice list, or a series of degrees of agreement or disagreement in relation to a variety of assertions. Fixed-alternative questionnaires are simple to administer, easy for the respondent to complete, and relatively easy to analyze. One major weakness is that respondents may feel compelled to select one of the alternatives provided by the researcher even when none really fits their position.

**Open-ended questionnaires** allow respondents to answer in their own words. This can mean greater detail and a broader range of responses.

However, it can also mean lower response rates because the respondent must think and write more than he would with a fixed-alternative instrument. Furthermore, the information the researcher does obtain may be very difficult to analyze and summarize. For example, a questionnaire concerned with the incidence of property crimes might contain questions like this:

- Has your home ever been burglarized? _____
- If yes, how often has your home been burglarized in the last six

  years? _____

Responses from different respondents might be "once in a while," "frequently," or "twice in the last year." Such responses are difficult to interpret and to compare. A fixed-alternative question might look like this:

- Has your home ever been burglarized? ____ Yes ____ No
- If yes, how often has your home been burglarized in the last six years?

  ____ Once ____ 2–3 times ____ 4–5 times ____ More than 5

  times ____ Not in the last six years

The responses given with this format will be much easier to manage when it comes time to analyze and summarize the data from the many questionnaires received.

When the researcher is seeking data, not about easily quantifiable phenomena, such as "how many times," but about opinions and feelings, open-ended questions can be much more effective. They are also very useful when all the possible answers to a question are either not known or very numerous.

Many researchers attempt to benefit from the advantages of fixed-alternative and open-ended questions by using both types in their questionnaires. This approach is sometimes advantageous, but it does not eliminate the weaknesses of either type of question, and it may greatly complicate analysis.

## Construction of Questionnaires

Once a researcher has decided that the questionnaire is the appropriate research instrument in a particular research project, he begins to construct the questionnaire. If other questionnaires on the same topic are available in the literature or from a colleague, they may be used (with the permission of the original developer) in whole or in part. If not, a researcher may begin by listing the various topics to be covered in the questionnaire. Once the topics are listed, their best order must be determined. For example, questions of a personal nature (e.g., concerning income or sexual behavior) should usually be placed toward the end of the questionnaire, for two reasons. First, if the respondent has already cooperated with the researcher in answering earlier questions, he is more likely to answer sensitive questions that come later. Second, should posing a personal question cause a respondent to discontinue the questionnaire, the researcher will at least have some useful information in the respondent's answers to earlier questions.

Next, the researcher must decide upon appropriate response forms. Is the questionnaire to be basically a fixed-alternative instrument, an open-ended instrument, or some combination of the two? If the researcher is examining a subject about which he or she knows a good deal, and if comparisons across respondents are to be made, fixed-alternative questions might be most appropriate. If the researcher is doing exploratory research on a subject about which little is known, and if comparisons across respondents are not critical, open-ended questions may well be employed. In many instances, both types of questions are used to provide respondents the opportunity to address in open-ended questions issues which the researcher failed to address in fixed-alternative questions.

After these issues are resolved, the researcher begins writing questions. Each question is reconsidered and rewritten until the researcher is satisfied that it will not be misunderstood and that it will provide the information sought. Appropriate alternatives must be listed for each fixed-alternative question, and space must be provided for answers to open-ended questions.

When fixed-alternatives are used, they must be mutually exclusive and exhaustive. A list of response categories is **mutually exclusive** if there is one and only one response category appropriate for each respondent. To illustrate, the categories in figure 5.1 are not mutually exclusive because a respondent who earns $15,000 could check either a or b. A set of responses is **exhaustive** if it includes all possible answers to the question posed. The categories in figure 5.1 are not exhaustive because there is no category for annual incomes under $10,000 per year or for incomes of more than $20,000 and less than $25,000.

Because the categories provided are neither mutually exclusive nor exhaustive, they constitute a very poor device for measuring income, and make meaningful comparisons and analysis almost impossible. In figure 5.2 are mutually exclusive and exhaustive response categories to that same question.

| Figure 5.1 | Figure 5.2 |
|---|---|

| *What is your annual income?* <br> *(check one)* | *What is your annual income?* <br> *(check one)* |
|---|---|
| _____ a. $10,000–$15,000 <br> _____ b. $15,000–$20,000 <br> _____ c. $25,000–$30,000 <br> _____ d. over $30,000 | _____ a. $10,000 or less <br> _____ b. $10,001–$15,000 <br> _____ c. $15,001–$20,000 <br> _____ d. $20,001–$25,000 <br> _____ e. more than $25,000 |

How many categories of response should there be? The answer to this question depends on how the information will be used. Essentially, response categories should generate as much detail as needed to shed light on the research question. If there were reason to believe, for example, that there may be important differences between individuals whose incomes differ by $2,500, response categories with that range should be created.

Suppose we were interested in the effect of marital status on certain attitudes of the study population. We could ask:

> What is your current marital status?
> (check one)
>
> _____ a. married
>
> _____ b. not married

These two response categories will give us information—perhaps enough for our research purposes. But compare the information they produced with that generated by the following:

> What is your current marital status?
> (check one)
>
> _____ a. single, never married
>
> _____ b. single, divorced
>
> _____ c. single, widowed
>
> _____ d. married for the first time
>
> _____ e. remarried

These five response categories generate much more detailed information about the respondent group.

One other point needs to be made about the advantages of fixed-alternative questions. The income question, for example, could be asked with an open-ended format:

What is your annual income,
rounded to the nearest $1,000?

$ _____

If respondents are willing to answer this question, the "raw" data generated by the question can be used to create whatever categories of income are useful during the analysis phase of the research. However, income is a sensitive matter for many respondents. Researchers have found that respondents are often more willing to identify a general range for their income than to state the exact amount. Hence, the likelihood of gaining at least some information about respondents' incomes may be increased by asking a fixed-alternative question with fairly broad income categories rather than an open-ended one. Pretesting the questions with different response categories, a technique discussed later in this chapter, is one way of choosing which question format is best for a given set of respondents.

Both the wording of questions and the response categories provided have an effect on the quality of the information collected in a survey. If the researcher wants to know the sex of the respondent, for example, it is generally best to present the question in a fixed-alternative form, such as:

Sex: \_\_\_\_male    \_\_\_\_ female

Experience shows that asking respondents the open-ended question:

Sex? _____

sometimes results in answers such as "sometimes," "yes," and so forth. Skilled researchers take into account not only their research topic but also the characteristics of the respondents in designing questions and response categories. We shall return to these and related matters when measurement of variables is discussed in chapter 7.

As a questionnaire is developed, a researcher also must decide what instructions are to be provided to respondents to assist them in completing it. Are they to fill in blanks, circle appropriate responses, check appropriate spaces, or use some special code to indicate their response? Are respondents to select only one or more than one of the alternatives provided? How often should instructions be repeated? When the format of the questions changes, are new instructions required? Again, the researcher has to consider the best form for the data to be collected and must provide clear-cut instructions to obtain the data in that form.

In addition, the proper length of the questionnaire is an important consideration for two reasons. First, all the information needed for the research project at hand must be collected, and if important questions are omitted, there may be little or no chance of asking them of the same respondents later. Second, although all relevant information must be included, the length of the questionnaire is an important factor because researchers are asking respondents for a valuable commodity—their time. The longer the questionnaire, the more time will be involved, and, as a result, the more likely it is that the response rate will be low. On the other hand, if a questionnaire is too short, valuable information may not be collected. Therefore, a compromise is often required to construct a survey instrument that allows a researcher to collect the necessary information while asking a minimum number of questions.

Two other considerations are essential to the construction of a good questionnaire. The first concerns the overall appearance of the instrument, for the more professional the questionnaire looks, the more likely respondents are to complete it. If you have ever received a mailed questionnaire which was mimeographed, difficult to read, crowded on the page, and printed on poor quality paper, you can understand the importance of this consideration. Easy-to-read print, proper spacing between questions, adequate margins, and enough space to answer open-ended questions are essential in the development of a good questionnaire.

Second, a cover letter or an introductory statement emphasizing the importance of completing the questionnaire should be prepared. Typically, this is done by briefly explaining the purpose and importance of the survey, and the significance of the respondents' opinions. To encourage participants to respond honestly, the cover letter or introductory statement may indicate that there are no right or wrong answers, that the respondents will remain anonymous, and that the results will be presented only in grouped, summary form, only to designated audiences, and will be used only for specifically stated purposes. The researcher is, of course, ethically bound to abide by these statements. Instructions for returning a mailed questionnaire are also included in the letter or statement, and these generally state that the questionnaire is to be returned in an enclosed, self-addressed, stamped envelope or that the group-administered questionnaire should be placed in a plain envelope or in a sealed box at a specified location. In most cases, a time frame for returning mailed questionnaires is also established. The researcher should identify himself clearly by using letterhead stationary, a complete signature block, and including a statement that indicates who he is and who is sponsoring and paying for the research. Finally, the researcher should always thank respondents for their time and cooperation.

## Pretesting the Questionnaire

Questionnaires should always be pretested before they are distributed to the respondents. A **pretest** is conducted by asking a small number of respondents similar in background characteristics to the target population to read the cover letter, listen to or read the introductory statement, and complete the questionnaire. As they complete the questionnaire, they should note any problem areas they encounter— unclear instructions, words that are unfamiliar or not clearly defined, embarrassing questions, spelling errors, and so forth. At the end of the pretest, the researcher can make any necessary revisions in order to eliminate problem areas before administering the questionnaire to the study group.

## Precoding the Questionnaire

A researcher who collects survey (questionnaire) data should, whenever possible, determine in advance how this information can be recorded or coded in a shorthand form suitable for systematic analysis with or without the aid of a computer. **Coding** is facilitated when fixed-alternative questions have been used, since these can easily be **precoded**; that is, code numbers can be assigned to each alternative response before the questionnaire is administered. When the questionnaires are returned, the preassigned code numbers, rather than the respondent's actual written responses, are recorded.

This procedure is sometimes used with open-ended questions as well. For example, the researcher might pose the question, "How would you evaluate the services of the public defender?" and then devise categories and assign code numbers as follows: positive rating (1), mixed rating (2), negative rating (3), and other (4). An open-ended question of this type might yield responses such as "rotten," "very good," "so-so," "in some respects good, in others bad," etc. In order to use these responses, the researcher must place the actual responses into the mutually exclusive and exhaustive categories he has prepared, assigning appropriate code numbers to each of the responses.

In either case, if a computer is to be used in the data analysis, the code numbers would be transferred to a computer tape or disk or to computer cards. Note that the question could easily have been asked in fixed-alternative form:

How would you evaluate the services of the public defender?

_____ very good      _____ good            _____ fair

_____ poor           _____ very poor

The questionnaires could then be coded easily by recording a "1" for every respondent who checked the "very good" category, a "2" for those who checked the "good" category, and so on.

## A Sample Questionnaire

Figure 5.3 shows part of a precoded questionnaire from an actual research project, and as you can see, the code value for every alternative is included in parentheses next to each question.

Typically, coding merely substitutes one set of numerical symbols for another set of either verbal or numerical symbols (the raw data). Because the code numbers assigned are usually not the same as the actual responses given, a researcher must create and maintain a master code sheet that specifies what each code designation represents.

Perhaps the best way to summarize the steps involved in constructing a questionnaire (all of which are interrelated even though we have discussed them separately), is to go through the process step-by-step. Let us suppose that we wish to know the attitudes of residents in our community toward the municipal police. Let us also assume that we have decided that a standardized, fixed-alternative questionnaire is the most desirable means of collecting the information we desire. As a first step, we might review survey instruments previously used to obtain this type of information. That review would probably indicate a number of topics that should be addressed. We might decide, for example, to examine the attitudes of the public regarding the police, in areas such as:

## Figure 5.3  Crime and the Police Questionnaire

**No information = 9**

*Background Information*—Please check the correct blank for each question.

Age (actual age in years)

Sex (1)___ Male   (2)___ Female

Marital Status (1)___ Single   (2)___ Married   (3)___ Widowed
(4)___ Divorced   (5)___ Separated

Type of Residence (1)___ Own Home   (2)___ Apartment
(3)___ Relative's Home   (4)___ Sr. Citizens Housing
(5)___ Nursing Home   (6)___ Other

Education (1)___ 8 years or less   (2)___ Some high school
(3)___ High school graduate   (4)___ Some college
(5)___ College graduate   (6)___ Some graduate work
(7)___ Graduate or professional degree

Approximate Annual Income for Your Household   (1)___ Less than $10,000
(2)___ $10,000–$20,000
(3)___ more than $20,000

*Police Contacts*—Please check the correct blank for each question.

1.   Have you ever contacted the Burlington Police
Department for assistance? (If no, check the
correct blank, and go on to question 2.)     (1)___ Yes  (2)___ No

1a.  If yes, were you satisfied with the services
provided?     (1)___ Yes  (2)___ No

2.   Have you ever contacted a Burlington Police
Officer on the streets for assistance? (If no,
check the correct blank, and go on to question
3.)     (1)___ Yes  (2)___ No

2a.  If yes, were you satisfied with the services
provided?     (1)___ Yes  (2)___ No

3.   Have you ever been arrested by the Burlington
Police?     (1)___ Yes  (2)___ No

4.   Have you ever been issued a traffic ticket by the
Burlington Police?     (1)___ Yes  (2)___ No

5.   Do you know any Burlington Police Officers
personally?     (1)___ Yes  (2)___ No

*Crime Information*—Please check or fill in the correct blank for each
question.

6.   Have you ever been the victim of a crime in
Burlington? (If no, check the correct blank, and
go on to question 7.)     (1)___ Yes  (2)___ No

6a.  If yes, how many times? (actual number)

1. traffic enforcement
2. police/community relations
3. police/juvenile relations
4. police as investigators
5. police as crime preventers
6. the trustworthiness, competency, and manners of police officers
7. police actions with respect to minority group members
8. police patrol practices
9. fear of crime among citizens
10. police handling of liquor and other drug violations

Although many other areas could be examined as well, these will suffice for the present. At this point, we would have to determine the proper form for the fixed-alternative questions and write one or more questions for each of these areas. For example, we might use a Likert-type scale for some of our questions. Respondents are asked to express the degree to which they hold certain attitudes by choosing among the response categories "strongly agree," "agree," "undecided," "disagree," and "strongly disagree" to a series of statements. Each of these categories is assigned a number ("1" for "strongly agree," "2" for "agree," and so on) and respondents are instructed to circle the appropriate number for each question. Sample questions might include:

The local police department puts enough emphasis on enforcing traffic laws.

| strongly agree | agree | undecided | disagree | strongly disagree |
|---|---|---|---|---|
| 1 | 2 | 3 | 4 | 5 |

or,

The local police department does a satisfactory job of handling juvenile problems.

| strongly agree | agree | undecided | disagree | strongly disagree |
|---|---|---|---|---|
| 1 | 2 | 3 | 4 | 5 |

After the respondents circle their choices, we could prepare the data for computer analysis by punching in the code number corresponding to each of the respondent's answers.

In addition to the general topics listed above, we would probably also want to find out something about the background characteristics of the respondents. A person's sex, race, social class, education, occupation, place of residence, number of times arrested, marital status, income, number of traffic tickets received, and a variety of other factors may be related to attitudes toward the police. We would request this type of information for each of the respondents so that we could cross-tabulate the specific items concerning police performance with each of these variables either singly or in combination. (We shall discuss the details of cross-tabulation in chapter 8.)

Finally, we might want to give respondents the opportunity to comment on other areas that they feel are important even though these areas were not included on the form. The questionnaire could be concluded with a statement such as: "Please feel free to make additional comments concerning the local police in the space below. Responses to this question will be categorized and included in our analysis."

A cover letter should be attached to mailed questionnaires that indicates who the researchers are and explains why responses to the questionnaire are important and in what form and to whom they will be made available. It also might indicate that the local police are quite interested in improving their services, and that they will have access to the results of the questionnaire in order to get a better feel for public attitudes concerning them. We should pretest the questionnaire and make appropriate modifications before distributing it to the sample we have selected.

Essentially the same steps are followed each time a survey instrument is designed. The research can often benefit by reusing sections of questionnaires previously used on the same topics, either by this researcher or by another. An advantage of using a question or a set of questions that is identical to one in earlier research is some measure of comparability. Again, if a substantial section of another researcher's survey instrument is to be used, permission must be secured.

## Increasing Response Rates

For reasons we have already discussed, good response rates are both important to survey researchers and often difficult to achieve. There are several strategies that can increase response rates during various stages of the research process. As was suggested earlier, well-designed and well-printed questionnaires with relatively few, clearly written, fixed-alternative questions are easier to complete than are longer ones with many open-ended questions, and usually produce higher response rates. Including a self-addressed, stamped envelope with mailed questionnaires also increases response rates. Where appropriate, it is helpful to publicize the study in the local news media; this underscores the legitimacy of the researchers and the study itself. Finally, whenever feasible, it is at least a good gesture to offer to share the results of the study with the respondents, at their request.

Once the first administration of the questionnaire has been completed, some follow-up techniques may be used to obtain questionnaires which have not yet been returned. Among these are sending one or more notes to respondents thanking those who have returned the questionnaire and reminding those who haven't of the importance of doing so; putting notices to the same effect in local newspapers; and phoning nonresponders, either to urge them to complete and return the questionnaire on their own time or to complete it now over the phone.

Great care must be taken, however, in using follow-up techniques. Some of them add substantially to research costs. Also, if a respondent has been promised anonymity and has not been asked to provide name and address on the questionnaire, sending him a reminder may make him feel deceived. In such circumstances, reminders should be sent to *all* persons on the original mailing list, a fact which should be clearly stated in the note itself. In general, monetary and other costs of follow-up procedures must be weighed against gains in response rates which may be achieved.

## *Interviews*

Like questionnaires, interviews can give a researcher access to information about respondents, including their experiences, their knowledge of events, their plans for the future as well as their opinions, attitudes, and motivations. Unlike a questionnaire, an interview is a person-to-person interaction, usually either face-to-face or over the telephone.

Like questionnaires, interviews fall into two general categories, depending on the types of questions asked. A structured, standardized, or **formal interview** has a fixed-question content and structure. Standardized interviews are generally used when the researcher has already determined what specific information she is seeking. In this type of interview, predetermined questions are asked in a prescribed order. As with the questionnaire, often a set of *fixed alternatives* or standardized responses are read by the researcher following each question, from which the respondent selects the one that most nearly describes his position. The parallel types of information obtained from all respondents enable the researcher to compare and analyze responses relatively easily.

*Unstructured* or **informal interviews,** while starting with planned areas of questioning, are more flexible in both the questions used and the directions taken. Informal interviews are generally used in exploratory studies, when the researcher needs more detailed or extensive information than can be given with structured interviews. In interviews of this type, the structure of the questions is often open ended, and the order of the questions to be asked may not be as completely predetermined. Rather, the interviewer explores preselected general question areas, follows up on particular responses and pursues additional topics suggested by the respondent.

While informal interviews may or may not generate responses that can be compared among respondents, they often give more insightful, extensive information about the research topics as well as the emotions and attitudes of the respondent. As a result, such interviews are often used both by sociological and anthropological field workers and by psychological and psychiatric clinicians.[1]

As with questionnaires, a given interview may include both highly structured questions and open-ended ones. Basically, the same advantages and disadvantages associated with fixed-alternative and open-ended questionnaire items apply to these types of interview questions.

Whichever type of interview the researcher selects, he must be concerned with three things: (a) establishing good rapport with respondents; (b) determining the meaning and truthfulness of their responses; and (c) using the type of questioning that will elicit the required information.

Establishing rapport means creating a situation in which the respondent feels comfortable and free to give his frank opinions, without fear of being laughed at or of having his opinions inappropriately passed on to others. An interviewer can take several steps to establish rapport effectively. First, he should produce credentials that legitimate his presence (normally, a letter of introduction and/or a simple identification badge stating who he is and who he works for will suffice). Second, the interviewer should answer reasonable questions about the research project posed by respondents. Third, he should assure respondents of confidentiality and anonymity. A thorough knowledge of the interview questions will enable the interviewer to be courteous and conversational, putting the respondent at ease.

The interviewer's personal appearance and presentation often determine his success in establishing and maintaining rapport with respondents. Sending a white, middle-class interviewer into a lower-class black neighborhood during a period of racial disturbance to conduct interviews on black attitudes toward whites, for example, would probably make it impossible for either the interviewer or the respondent to feel at ease. Likewise, the interviewer's remarks and attitudes have an effect upon the respondent. The interview is an interactive situation; the interviewer's actions and words serve as cues to the respondent. If, for example, an interviewer collecting data on attitudes toward abortion expresses or implies contempt for people who participate in abortions, he may lead the respondent to conceal or misrepresent his own attitude toward abortion. In short, the interviewer should maintain a neutral attitude toward the issues in question, even though he may privately have opinions about them.

The interviewer's second major concern is the meaning and truthfulness of the responses he obtains. As in day-to-day conversation, it is seldom sensible to take every statement at face value. The respondent may be unwilling to answer honestly for a variety of reasons—embarrassment, dislike of interviewers, and so on—or he may not remember accurately, or he may misunderstand the question, or simply tell the interviewer what he believes the interviewer wants to hear. Thus, the interviewer often may have to **probe** to learn the basis for, and truthfulness of, responses. One must do this without suggesting any particular response to the interviewee; for example, the interviewer can ask the respondent to explain his answer in a little more detail, or ask him what his answer means. It would not be appropriate, however, to probe by saying "I can't believe you really mean . . ." or "Did you mean. . . ." To determine the truthfulness of responses, the interviewer can ask the same question twice, but in different ways ("Have you ever voted for a Democrat for office?" and later, "How many Democrats would you say you have voted for?"). He can then compare the respondent's answers to see if there are discrepancies.

Attempts to determine the meaning and truthfulness of responses are of little value unless the interviewer accurately records the responses. The interviewer must always separate, insofar as possible, his interpretations of responses from the responses themselves. In some cases this may require tape recording the interview; in other cases, it may require note taking; and in others, simply marking an "x" in the appropriate column on the interview sheet. The latter, of course, may require the interviewer to make additional written comments about the respondent's answer, which can lead to interpretation problems; this should be kept in mind when training interviewers and analyzing the data they collect.

In considering what type of questioning will most likely yield the desired information, a researcher—regardless of whether he uses a formal or an unstructured interview—must phrase and order the questions carefully. The wording of the questions should be clear and concise, and should not suggest any particular response. Usually, a respondent must feel comfortable before she will answer personal questions. Since even a skilled interviewer needs some time to achieve rapport with his subject, personal questions should generally follow less sensitive ones.

Interviews can be used with virtually any kind of respondent (including those who are illiterate), and when probing is used intelligently, they can yield detailed information. Their disadvantage is their high cost if the interviewee group is large or the interview is long. When a researcher must gather information from a large, literate group, he may be able to collect the data less expensively with a questionnaire.

## Notes

1. For another discussion of specific types of interviews see Louise H. Kidder, in Selltiz, Wrightman, and Cook, *Research Methods in Social Relations*, 4th ed. (New York: Holt, Rinehart, and Winston, 1981), pp. 178–97.

## Review Questions

1. What are the advantages and disadvantages of using interviews compared with using questionnaires as research instruments?
2. What are the advantages and disadvantages of fixed-alternative and open-ended items on surveys?
3. Why is it important that fixed-alternative answers to survey questions be mutually exclusive and exhaustive?
4. Why should a researcher pre-test a survey instrument?
5. What purposes do a cover letter and instructions serve on a questionnaire?
6. How can questionnaire response rates be improved?
7. How might the personal appearance of an interviewer affect the willingness of a respondent to answer questions or the answers given?
8. Why is recognizing that an interview is an interactive situation important?

# *Exercises*

1. Write both a fixed-alternative and an open-ended question for measuring the following variables pertaining to a person:

   - sex
   - age
   - arrest record
   - income
   - education
   - opinion concerning equality of treatment in the courts of defendants of different ethnic groups
   - opinions concerning the performance of the local police force or campus security
   - reasons for coming to this college or university
   - reasons for studying criminal justice research methods

2. Compare the questions you wrote for (1) with those of another member of the class and discuss the strengths and weaknesses of the questions.

3. Pre-test the questions you wrote on 8 or 10 of your friends. Then make any revisions in the questions you think necessary and indicate why you changed them.

4. Ask the revised questions of 8 or 10 other friends or classmates. Compare the responses to fixed-alternative and open-ended questions and write an essay discussing the advantages and disadvantages of the two types of question.

5. Prepare a questionnaire, complete with cover letter, combining fixed-alternative and open-ended questions focused on determining the respondents' opinions concerning alternative ways of dealing with juvenile delinquency.

6. Prepare an interview schedule combining formal and informal interview styles focused on the issue of question 5.

7. Assume you were going door-to-door to interview respondents in a large city. Would you dress differently depending on which neighborhoods you were interviewing in? Why or why not?

8. Write an essay discussing what aspects of your own behavior you should be especially aware of and attempt to control during an interview if you wanted to improve the validity of your research.

9. Have someone observe you interview another person, looking for clues (head-nodding, smiling, frowning, etc.) you may be giving to the respondent during the interview. Discuss the results and their implications for the validity of your research.

# 6

## Research Tools and Techniques: Document Research, Physical Evidence, Observation, and Experimentation

While surveys may be the backbone of social science research, they provide a body of information very much controlled by the researcher, in both content and structure. The data result from the interaction between researcher and respondent. In spite of all precautions, the researcher faces one source of error that he can neither eliminate nor assess accurately when using interviews and questionnaires, as well as other types of research methods: the effects that the researcher's activities will have on the persons he is studying. The simple act of filling out a questionnaire, for example, may modify a respondent's view of himself and, in turn, his responses to subsequent questions. The mere presence of an observer may lead people to act in unaccustomed ways. A respondent who feels obliged to answer an interview question may hastily formulate opinions about issues he had not thought about before.

**Nonreactive** or unobtrusive data-collection methods remove biases introduced by the research process itself, by eliminating the subjects' knowledge that they are being studied. In this chapter several nonreactive research methods are examined, along with other data-gathering methods. These methods complement the quantitative approach of surveys, providing alternative ways to test ideas and hypotheses against the real world. Nonreactive techniques are document research, study of physical evidence, and complete observation, while more interactive methods include participant observation, disguised observation, and experimentation.

## Document Research

An investigator can obtain a great deal of information by analyzing written documents, mass media reports, or data kept by institutions for administrative or governmental purposes. Institutional data include the U.S. Census, which represents an attempt to collect data from every household in the country and which contains a wealth of demographic information about our population. Media reports include articles such as those appearing in *Time* and *Newsweek*, which might be used to assess the current state of public knowledge and concern about criminal justice issues. And the National Institute of Justice and other criminal justice agencies produce hundreds of written reports annually dealing with a variety of criminal justice issues. In addition, the researcher may rely upon personal accounts such as letters, memoirs, or diaries, or reports consisting of video or voice tapes covering events with historical significance. In short, if the researcher wants information about a past event, he can visit libraries or archives to request the use of personal and historical documents. If his concern is with ongoing events, he can often supplement his knowledge by collecting current documents prepared by or about the people he is studying. Research based upon analysis of existing sources of information is often referred to as archival or **document analysis.**

Let us consider the kinds of information that are routinely available in document form. For most individuals in our society, a great deal of biographical data can be obtained, including information about birth, schooling, marriages, divorces, military service, and death, as well as dates and causes of police arrests. Sources include official documents such as birth, death, and marriage certificates and school, military, and court records; they can be supplemented by unofficial sources such as newspapers, high school and college yearbooks, employment records, and personal documents such as letters and diaries. For well-known persons or well-publicized events, a wealth of information may be found in books, magazines, newspapers, films, and videotapes. Using these and other sources, both historical and contemporary data about the person, group, or event under study can be obtained without relying on the persons or participants themselves for answers, as is done in survey research.

A tool particularly useful to the document researcher is **secondary analysis**, in which the researcher reexamines the method, the data, and the results of earlier research. The researcher may analyze the data in new ways, or look for possible sources of error or bias in the data itself, the data analysis or in conclusions drawn by the original researcher. The researcher may also use others' research to shed some light on his own research problem.

As with all research, the investigator must be aware of potential errors or biases in the documents he is using as data sources. These errors stem from the fact that the documents being examined are created by persons other than the researcher for purposes other than that of the research project. First, the person who originally reported the information is likely to have been selective in both recording events and filing documents. The researcher's reliance on available documents means that his data sources are biased by the original recorder's selectivity. Second, there may be clerical or typographical errors or omissions in the documents or archives themselves. Although infrequent unsystematic mistakes such as clerical errors may have small effect on research findings, systematically incorrect or incomplete information can create a bias in research results. Third, much of the information contained in documents consists of the original recorder's reconstructions or interpretations of what the client, suspect, witnesses, or participants said or did. There is always a possibility that the original recorder misinterpreted what he heard, saw, or read. And, of course, the document researcher may compound the difficulty by misinterpreting the contents of the documents.

Perhaps an example will help clarify some of the dangers inherent in the use of preexisting sources of data. The Uniform Crime Reports (UCR), prepared and distributed by the Federal Bureau of Investigation (FBI), are the most commonly used official statistics on crime in the United States. However, researchers using these reports as data sources are confronted with a number of problems. *First,* they are incomplete. Reporting by the various police agencies is voluntary. Although approximately 97 percent of the total population is covered by agencies who do report to the FBI, the figure for rural areas is about 93 percent and that for cities with fewer than 50,000 residents is about 95 percent. If a researcher is investigating crime in rural areas based on UCR statistics, there is a greater possibility of error in drawing conclusions than if the subject population resides in cities with over 50,000 residents (about 99 percent of these cities are covered in the UCR). *Second* and potentially more serious than this bias is another dimension of incompleteness in the UCR. Independent surveys of crime victims consistently reveal that fewer than 50 percent of all serious crimes are reported to the police. Further, the extent of reporting varies by the type of offense. For example, most homicides are reported, but most burglaries, rapes, and assaults are not. Therefore, relying upon the UCR to provide an accurate picture of crime in the United States is unwise particularly when focusing on some types of offenses, because UCR data drastically underestimate the extent of many crimes. *Third,* errors in categorizing crimes undoubtedly occur since state codes may differ from the categories used by the FBI. *Fourth,* information may be biased. Motivations other than simply contributing to our knowledge of the extent and nature of crime may be involved in some cases. For instance, estimates of future crime by law enforcement agencies may be slightly higher than actually expected, in order to justify new budget requests; these possibly inflated estimates may be submitted to the FBI. The situation becomes even more complex if the researcher is interested in developing a profile of a certain type of offender based upon UCR data, since only about 20 percent of the serious crimes reported to the police lead to an arrest. As a result, our knowledge of the characteristics of rapists (based upon studies of arrested persons or convicted offenders) is quite incomplete, since we have studied only a small proportion of all persons who commit this offense. Some researchers suggest such studies focus on the least successful of these offenders—those who have been apprehended. Even the most widely used criminal justice documents, such as police records and reports and the UCR, then, have serious faults. In the case of the UCR, it should be pointed out that the FBI recognizes the biases in the data and cautions users of the UCR as a data source.

When a researcher collects documents from subjects he is studying (with their knowledge), he must be concerned about the possibility of deceit, misinterpretation, and misunderstanding. Some subjects may deceive the researcher by presenting him with documents that may make their performance look better than it actually is. Thus, a police officer providing the researcher with information detailing her career in law enforcement might present letters of commendation from citizens and superiors, but might not present the written reprimands contained in her file. Misinterpretation or misunderstanding occurs when subjects fail to understand the purpose of the research and so do not provide complete or correct information (in this case, that the researcher wants them to collect and present documents of both a positive and negative nature). Such misinterpretation and misunderstanding can also occur when a researcher tries to interpret unfamiliar material. For example, an investigator studying police crime-solving rates might note that according to police records 20 burglaries had been "cleared by arrest" and might assume that 20 burglars had been caught. In fact, however, only one burglar may have been caught, who was then persuaded by the police or district attorney to plead guilty to all 20 burglaries in exchange for a relatively light sentence.

## Content Analysis

In order to use a great many documents (such as newspaper or magazine articles and audio or video tapes) for research purposes, the researcher must employ **content analysis**. This technique systematizes the use of documents by providing a predetermined coding scheme and categories for tabulating the contents of the documents. The number of entries tabulated in each category indicates the direction or weight of the archival evidence.

The steps involved in a typical research project using content analysis are as follows. First, the material to be analyzed must be selected. Are all narrative police reports to be studied, or only those about certain kinds of incidents? Are all newspaper headlines from certain papers over a specified period of time to be analyzed? Are randomly selected sentences or paragraphs to be analyzed? Are certain radio or television broadcasts to be included? Second, a sample of the material to be used is analyzed in order to develop a coding scheme and a set of categories. These tell the researcher how to determine what material belongs in which category. Third, a panel of judges is selected and familiarized with the rules of the coding scheme and the categories to be employed. Using a panel of judges helps guard against the bias that might occur were the researcher to do the coding of the research documents herself. These judges are asked to evaluate one or more sets of materials, and their evaluations are compared. The judges then discuss discrepancies in their evaluations and attempt to resolve them. Finally, when the judges agree on categorization of the material most of the time (e.g., 80 percent), they are asked to evaluate the material selected for the research project. Perhaps some examples will help illustrate the manner in which content analysis may be employed.

Suppose we were interested in whether newspaper accounts of the residents of skid row during a certain time period were negative, positive, or neutral so that we could develop an effective campaign to convince the public to support a new alcohol treatment program designed to operate on skid row streets. If we found newspaper accounts to be basically positive, we could build on this image. If the accounts were basically negative, we could perhaps try to convince the public that the residents of skid row were worthy of our help. If the accounts were basically neutral, we would have to start a campaign to counter that image. First, we would select the newspapers and time period to be included in our sample. Then we would identify the kinds of words and their usages (in headlines, paragraph headings, the article narrative, etc.) which would be coded as positive, neutral, and negative (our three categories). Next we would impanel and train our judges and compare and discuss preliminary evaluations until the desired degree of agreement was reached. Finally, we would provide our judges with the newspapers we had included in our sample and ask them to evaluate those papers. Suppose our judges found a newspaper account referring to a skid row residence as a "house of horrors," to panhandling as "the touch of terror," and to the presence of skid row men as an "infection" or "blot on the city."[1] Other articles might include references to skid row men as animals who gather in packs, insects who swarm the city, demonic, and less than human.[2] Each of these references would be placed in the negative category and the total number counted. References which are neutral or positive would also be placed in appropriate categories and counted. The total number of references in each category could then be compared in order to enable us to answer our research question and help us make policy decisions.

If we were interested in understanding why the image of the police in America is what it is, we might go to the library and look at newspaper or magazine articles concerning the police to gain a historical perspective. Following the same procedure outlined above, we would evaluate articles such as the following from 1840: "It is notorious that the New York police is wretchedly inadequate to the arrest of offenders and the punishment of crime; as to *prevention* of crime, we might almost as well be without the name of a police, as we are all but without the substance." And, "Destructive rascality stalks at large in our city streets and public places, at all times of the day and night, with none to make it afraid—. . . ."[3] These clearly negative references would be counted and compared to the numbers of positive and neutral references in order to help us understand the image of the police as portrayed in the articles selected over the time period under study.

Document analysis can be used rather effectively to conduct research, especially when used in conjunction with other techniques. It is often the only way to collect data about past events, it is relatively inexpensive, and, with the exception of documents given the researchers by his subjects, the presence of the researcher has no effect on the content of the materials being analyzed. There are, of course, as we have noted, a number of potential sources of error in documents of which the researcher should always be cognizant.

## *Observation*

So far in our discussion of the three basic ways both laypersons and scientists gather information, we have considered communicating with others (through questionnaires and interviews) and examining the recorded reports of others (through document analysis). We come now to the final strategy: direct observation of the people or events by the researcher himself. As a data-collection technique, observation allows a researcher to record events as they occur, without having to rely on the introspective or retrospective powers of the subjects, or on records created by others. As we shall see, however, this strategy has its own weaknesses. Remember that the goal in research is to improve understanding while maintaining objectivity. Yet the closer researchers get to subjects in an attempt to understand them, the harder it becomes to maintain objectivity. If, on the other hand, researchers remain aloof from the subjects in the hope of remaining objective, they increase the danger of not understanding the meaning of what is observed or heard.

Three types of observational roles are employed by researchers, depending on the constraints and demands of the research purpose and setting: the complete observer, the participant observer, and the disguised observer. Each role has different implications for researcher objectivity and understanding.

The researcher who observes his subjects without their knowledge and without physically participating in their activities is called a **complete observer.** The complete observer studies his subjects from afar, so to speak. Examples are a researcher who sits, unknown to the observed, behind a one-way mirror, and the person who observes subjects through field glasses. The complete observer may be able to record the behavior he sees in great detail, and may concentrate on reporting these observations objectively. His interpretations of the meaning of that behavior, however, are quite another thing. He may misinterpret the meaning of what he has observed as a result of his own subjective biases about the behavior; or he may be unable to interpret what he sees at all because his personal repertoire of behavioral categories does not include the ones observed (a danger, for example, when observing cross-culturally). In either case, the complete observer cannot ask the subjects what their behavior means, and he may be so far removed physically that he cannot hear their comments on their behavior. Thus, while the complete observer may maximize objectivity, he may fall short of the goal of understanding.

A **participant observer** is one who identifies himself as an observer, states his purpose and physically participates in the activities of the observed. The extent of participation can vary greatly. It may be limited simply to being present among the subjects in order to observe (sometimes referred to as the role of ''observer as participant'') or it may extend to include complete participation in the activities of the subjects with observation a secondary concern (often referred to as the ''participant as observer'' role).[4] In either case, the participant observer has a much greater opportunity to understand the flow of events observed than does the complete observer, since through participation, the observer can use all his senses and can ask questions about events he does not understand.[5] At the same time, however, the participant observer finds it more difficult to be objective in reporting than does the complete observer. This is so because, in the process of participating, the observer makes friends (and possibly enemies), begins to feel more "at home" in the activities of the observed, and concentrates both on his role as observer and on his role as participant. Still, since the participant-observer role improves the possibility of understanding, while allowing the conscientious observer to work hard at being objective, it is an observer role frequently selected by social scientists.

Both the advantages and disadvantages of participant observation are illustrated in George Kirkham's book, *Signal Zero*. Kirkham accepted a challenge from a police officer who was among his students and actually became a policeman himself in order to determine to what extent his theories of policing applied on the streets. He became a complete participant by meeting the same requirements as other rookie officers and being assigned a regular beat; the police department was aware of his research. Initially, Kirkham attempted to keep an accurate, objective log of his observations and actions, but he soon found it impossible to maintain objectivity and difficult even to write daily logs. Kirkham concludes:

> I do not pretend that what follows [in *Signal Zero*] is an objective book about either the police or crime in our society. This could never have been such a work, although in the beginning I had thought it might be. But what happened to me in those months made it impossible for me ever again to view a policeman's world from the detached perspective of a social scientist. I realize that now.[6]

In fact, Kirkham had "gone native." When the time came for him to return to the classroom, he decided to continue working as a police officer on a part-time basis, and found himself accepted only marginally by his colleagues in academia, who found some of his comments concerning theoretical criminologists offensive.[7]

The third type of observer, a **disguised** or **secret observer**, misrepresents himself to his subjects, and observes them while participating as a group member. A researcher may adopt the disguised observer role if he would not otherwise be allowed to observe, as in the case of certain religious sects or criminal groups; or if he feels that being treated as one of the observed is essential to understanding them. Arguments against the use of disguised observation concern ethics and loss of objectivity. Many social scientists feel that it is unethical for a researcher to conceal his identity to gain inside information. Others feel disguised observation is ethical so long as the welfare of the subjects is protected.[8] Both groups agree that problems of objectivity are greatly compounded when the observer pretends to be a group member, because he may come to see himself as such ("going native") and be unable to report or analyze objectively the behavior he observes. A secret observer, of course, is engaged in a deception and must constantly be concerned with being discovered, a fear that compounds his difficulties.

Clearly, the problems of attaining understanding while remaining objective are inherent in the use of observation as a data-collection technique. A unique difficulty for observation is encountered when the investigator cannot predict when or where the event to be observed will happen (as with criminal activity or traffic accidents). Nevertheless, observation can be a valuable tool for the researcher who does not wish to interrupt unnecessarily the flow of events being studied by reading questions from a survey form.

## Recording and Coding

As in survey research and content analysis of documents, recording techniques usually must be decided before observation, for best use of the observation period. Questions such as how structured the observations are to be (is a suitable code scheme available?) and the effects the researcher anticipates his note-taking will have on subjects must be answered. If a set of categories has been prepared ahead of the observation period, the observer may need to do no more than place an "x" in the appropriate columns to indicate that a particular event occurred, initiated by a particular subject, at a particular time.[9] If no code scheme exists, he may make extensive notes on the events he considers to be important or video-tape the session. If recording procedures seem to interrupt the flow of events unnecessarily, the researcher may retire from the field of observation to make notes in private. Different research settings will provide variable opportunities for record keeping. For example, a staff meeting in a police department is a setting in which everyone present is taking notes, and the observer would be conspicuous only if he failed to do so. If, however, the observer were attending a confidential meeting where no one else present was taking notes, he might retire at convenient intervals to the office or the washroom to record observations.

## Accuracy of Observations

As with all research methods, observation has sources of error. Accuracy of observations often poses serious difficulties for the observer.

He may have been thoroughly trained to separate what he observes happening from what he expects to see happening, and may record observations in great detail. Still, the possibility exists that another observer viewing the same events might see and record them differently. One method of assessing observer accuracy is to employ more than one observer and compare their reports. Unfortunately, the presence of more than one observer may further disrupt the flow of events, especially in a small group of subjects, who may come to view themselves as outnumbered by outsiders. As described in chapter 3, another method for attempting to improve scientific accuracy, triangulation, is especially suited for use by observers.

## *Physical Evidence*

It is well known that **physical evidence** is often the key to solving criminal cases. Physical evidence is also sometimes used in scientific research, usually in conjunction with other research techniques. For example, if we wished to know whether police officers assigned to narcotics units are involved in narcotics use themselves, we might interview selected officers or send them a questionnaire concerning drug use. We might also collect physical evidence by giving them blood tests or asking them to provide samples for urinalysis. Such physical evidence could then be compared with the information collected by interview or questionnaire to provide a more complete answer to our research question. Both blood samples and urinalysis belong to a category of physical evidence referred to as **accretion evidence,** or evidence produced by the accumulation or deposit of materials.

**Erosion evidence** is another category of physical evidence which includes evidence of use or wear. As a supplemental method of determining which of a series of educational tapes for inmates are more frequently used, we might examine replacement records to determine which tapes must be repaired or replaced most frequently.

Other types of physical evidence are also available to the researcher. In order to help determine the validity of self-report questionnaires, we might give our subjects polygraph tests (see chapter 11). The polygraph measures changes in blood pressure and respiration, and sometimes the subject's electrodermal responses (alternations in the activity of sweat pores in the subject's hands), or changes in muscular pressures and movements. Such physical changes can be used under certain conditions to help us determine whether an individual is telling the truth and therefore can help us assess the validity of data collected through other research techniques.

## Experiments

The words *science* and *experiment* seem almost synonymous to most of us, because when we hear or read about science or scientists, experiments frequently are mentioned. While scientists engage in many scientific activities that are not experiments (and while many activities that are labeled experiments are not scientific), this linkage of science and experimentation is justified because an important part of scientific study is engaging in controlled observation under controlled conditions, the essence of experimentation.

A *scientific experiment*, as we use the term, has several identifying characteristics. It is bound by the perspective and rules of science discussed earlier and conducted according to a research design formulated by the experimenter before the experiment is undertaken. Moreover, it is performed in an environment that the experimenter can at least partially control, either through selection or through construction (e.g., the laboratory). The experimenter also has control over, and usually manipulates deliberately, at least some of the variables he regards as independent or causal.

The classic experiment conforms to the before-after-with-control type of explanatory research design, and involves comparing an *experimental condition* with a *control condition*. In the **experimental condition,** the researcher measures an experimental group on the dependent variable, exposes the group to the **experimental treatment** (the presumed independent or causal variable), and then measures the group again on the dependent variable. In the **control condition,** a control group is measured once, *not* exposed to the experimental treatment, and then measured again. While not all experimental designs conform precisely to this pattern, all do involve some form of control that permits the investigator to assess the effects of changes in the value of one variable on changes in the value of another variable under controlled conditions. We use controls because they help to eliminate alternative explanations for changes we observe in the dependent variable for the experimental group, and hence strengthen causal inferences.

In a classic set of experiments, called the Western Electric studies, a group of social scientists was hired by an industrial firm to study the effects of variables such as illumination and different forms of employee compensation (the independent variables) on the productivity (the dependent variable) of assembly-line workers.[10] To conduct these experiments, a special work environment was constructed and equipped so that the experimenters could control the conditions in the area. The research design called for changing these variables in an orderly fashion and observing the impact of these changes on productivity. Regular employees of the company were selected for participation in the study, and their work was performed inside the specially constructed area. The investigators then executed their research plan, systematically varying the environmental conditions in the work area while observing the number of articles the workers produced in a given time span under each variation in condition.

This type of experiment has some significant advantages. First, since the investigator controls the independent variables, it is possible to isolate and manipulate a single variable (say, illumination) while holding another variable (temperature) constant, thereby gaining information about the contribution of this single variable to changes in the dependent variable (productivity). Second, the interactive effects of the independent variables can be systematically explored. The investigator might discover, for example, that certain combinations of values of two or more of the independent variables produce greater effects than the sum of the separate effects of the two variables. In short, a scientist uses an experiment to reduce a situation that may be very complex in its natural setting to manageable proportions, and to do a controlled and orderly exploration of the relationships among the variable components of these simplified units.

The characteristics that give the experimental technique its strength, however, also carry with them significant hazards. The Western Electric researchers did observe a significant increase in the productivity of the workers as the experiment progressed. However, these changes bore practically no relationship to changes in the independent variables. Productivity increased greatly and stayed at a high level, despite the relatively extreme variations in conditions introduced by the investigators.

How can we account for such findings? The investigators concluded that the special treatment of the workers itself—being selected for participation in a scientific study, being closely observed by the scientists, etc.—rather than any of the particular experimental variations, led to the workers' increased productivity. The effect produced by special treatment of experimental subjects is now known in the social sciences as the **Hawthorne effect** (after the Hawthorne, Illinois, site of the Western Electric plant studied), a phenomenon likely to occur whenever people are aware of being given special treatment, whether the research setting is inside or outside a laboratory.

Apparently, the investigators introduced a variable into their experimental procedure that they had not taken into account in their research design. The assumption that all relevant variables were accounted for in the research design turned out to be inaccurate in this case, and that possibility exists in any experimental procedure. The effects of unknown or unrecognized variables cannot, by definition, be assessed, and their presence and influence are always a possibility. Even if we do discover relationships among the variables being investigated, we have no guarantee that the variables are related in a **causal** way. That is, relationships among variables may be **spurious,** in the sense that an unknown and unaccounted-for variable may be responsible for the observed relationship.

Although experiments have numerous advantages, since they enable us to select and isolate a small number of variables for careful study, the risks of error and impracticality are also great. The relationships that we observe in a simplified and purified laboratory environment may not hold in the complex natural settings of the real world that contain numerous variables affecting the flow of events. Some social scientists (especially those who emphasize the situational determinants of behavior) contend that all we learn about human behavior by observation in a laboratory is simply how people behave in the laboratory, and, furthermore, that there is no necessary connection between peoples' behavior in this situation and their behavior in any other situation that humans encounter in day-to-day life.

Of course, not all experiments are plagued by the artificiality of the laboratory, and one of the most interesting experiments in criminal justice was conducted *in the field* in Kansas City in 1972–73. The Kansas City Preventive Patrol study clearly illustrates a number of the problems we have just discussed.[11] The study was designed to determine whether routine preventive patrol, considered by most police administrators and officers to be the backbone of police work, was important in deterring crime, responding to crime, and citizen satisfaction with the police. This was to be accomplished by dividing the city into 15 beats that were further divided into five groups of three each— computer matched on the basis of crime data, calls for service, income, racial/ethnic composition, and other selected factors. Within each group of three, one beat was designated reactive, one proactive, and one control. In the reactive beats, there was no preventive patrol—officers entered them only in response to calls for service. In the control beats, the usual level of patrol (one car per beat) was maintained. In the proactive beats, the patrol was increased by two to three times its usual level. The results of the experiment indicate that, in Kansas City at least, increasing or decreasing the level of preventive patrol has no effect on crime, citizen satisfaction with police services, or response time.

As might be expected, the Kansas City experiment generated considerable controversy. First, there was a concern among many involved with the study about the ethics of removing patrol cars from some beats and possibly endangering the lives of citizens by increasing response time or failing to detect crimes in progress. Second, many people were (and some still are) concerned about whether experimental conditions were maintained and if the data collected can be generalized to all cities and patrol policies. Last, but not least, many police administrators remain convinced that preventive patrol deters crime in spite of the results of this experiment and other studies conducted later. It is difficult to admit that one of the assumptions upon which police administrators have based their operations over many years may be inaccurate. It is much easier to find fault with the research conducted and to continue to adhere to traditional beliefs. This is a common response to research that challenges such beliefs, in the criminal justice field and in other fields as well.

## *Entering the Field*

Some research strategies (especially participant observation, but also some types of interviewing) require that the researcher go to natural settings where his subjects live or work. The sometimes difficult process of beginning research in such settings is called "entering the field." What is the best way to enter the field? There is no simple answer to this question, but a researcher's first venture into the field can be less traumatic if he considers the following issues both prior to and during field research activities:

1. What questions do I want to answer?
2. Who can give me the answers I need?
3. How do I want subjects to view me?
4. How are subjects likely to view me?
5. What alternative strategies for entering the field are available?
6. Should I disclose my identity as a researcher?
7. What kinds of opposition might I expect and from whom?
8. What strategies might be effective in coping with this opposition?

Suppose we want to learn about the interaction among judges, prosecutors, and defense attorneys. We decide that the best way to understand this interaction is to observe it and to question members of each category of professionals about it. Although we want our subjects to view us as legitimate researchers, they are likely to view us, at least initially, as intruders. Because we anticipate that some judges and attorneys may oppose our presence at their meetings, we believe that authorization from the chief judge of the circuit will give legitimacy to our presence and reduce potential opposition from other judges and attorneys. Since some of the information we collect may be of a sensitive nature, we recognize that appropriate assurances of confidentiality will have to be made and kept. Therefore, we obtain the support of the chief judge (who may write a letter indicating her approval of our research to the other judges and attorneys) and guarantee our subjects anonymity and confidentiality at the outset.

This is, of course, only one strategy for entering the field. In some cases, identification with or support from administrators might make it extremely difficult for us to obtain the desired information, and we might need to use a different strategy. In any case, a clear, concise statement of our research problem coupled with careful consideration of the other seven issues mentioned above will usually enable us to begin translating our research plans into action.

Perhaps the most important thing for the prospective researcher to keep in mind is that he is entering an interactive setting that will be altered by his very presence, regardless of the techniques employed (with the exception of the complete observer). His entry into the field almost always disrupts the flow of events to be observed to some extent, and his personal values, techniques, and questions all affect his subjects to varying degrees. Therefore, the effects of a researcher's entrance and presence in the field, and his personal values (where appropriate) should be identified, assessed, and presented as part of his research documentation.

Jerome Skolnick's classic study of the police provides considerable insight into the process of entering the field. Skolnick explored the day-to-day behavior of the police and other individuals in the criminal justice system in an attempt to "learn how those who are charged with enforcing criminal law in a constitutional democracy come to interpret rules of constraint—thereby giving these life and meaning—and to analyze the practical dilemmas they face."[12] Skolnick's first entry into the field was as a participant in the "Westville" criminal courts community. His first observations were made in the public defender's office for several months, and then, as a result of contacts made with assistant prosecutors, a recommendation from the public defender, and a long interview with the prosecutor, he proceeded to observe the workings of the prosecutor's office. Through contacts developed in the prosecutor's office, Skolnick approached the chief of police, who proved willing to allow him to observe police officers in action, and a lieutenant was assigned to introduce Skolnick to the police officers to be observed. Skolnick proceeded to observe patrol officers as they performed their duties and to question them concerning their actions. Based on his belief that additional information concerning his specific topic might be collected by observing detectives, Skolnick eventually had the opportunity to observe the vice, burglary, homicide, and robbery squads. In the long run, Skolnick had entered the field so successfully that he was sometimes taken as a detective, and sometimes performed police tasks for the detectives (see our discussion above on the dangers of "going native"). Skolnick concludes that the more time an observer spends with his subjects, the more accustomed to his presence they become; that open, sometimes enlightening discussions frequently occur when an observer has good rapport with his subjects; and that the police are often not free to alter their behavior so as to deceive the observer. Successful entry into the field may help to minimize disruptions, while making it possible for the researcher to exercise "drop-in" privileges with those previously observed.

Another example of entering the field comes from Howard S. Becker's study of marihuana users, in which he took advantage of a special skill he possessed in order to gain access to his subjects:

> To develop and test my hypotheses about the genesis of marihuana use for pleasure, I conducted fifty interviews with marihuana users. I had been a professional dance musician for some years when I conducted this study, and my first interviews were with people I had met in the music business. I asked them to put me in contact with other users who would be willing to discuss their experiences with me.[13]

In addition, Becker's colleagues working with opiate users made available to him some interviews that dealt with marihuana as well as opiates: "Although in the end half of the fifty interviews were conducted with musicians, the other half covered a wide range of people, including laborers, machinists, and people in the professions."[14]

In concluding this chapter, we should caution the reader by noting that conducting research is an art as well as a science. Although we have separated the research steps here, we do not mean to imply that they constitute a recipe that, if followed faithfully, will result in successful research. As the example from Skolnick's research clearly indicates, the research process is an interactive one. Subjects and situations do not wait passively for the manipulations of the researcher. Rather, the researcher must always be ready to respond sensitively, flexibly, and creatively to the demands of the research situation.

## *Notes*

1. Howard M. Bahr, *Skid Row: An Introduction to Disaffiliation* (New York: Oxford University Press, 1973), pp. 59–61.

2. Ibid.
3. James F. Richardson, *The New York Police: Colonial Times to 1901* (New York: Oxford University Press, 1970), pp. 23–29.
4. For a comprehensive discussion of these and other observer roles, see Raymond Gold, "Roles in Sociological Field Observations," *Social Forces* 36 (March 1958): 217–23.
5. The possibility of misunderstanding is never eliminated for the participant observer, since his subjects may deliberately deceive him, or he may think he understands when, in fact, he doesn't.
6. George Kirkham, *Signal Zero* (New York: J. B. Lippincott, 1976), p. i.
7. Other good examples of participant observation as a technique for studying deviance and criminal justice include Albert J. Reiss, *The Police and the Public* (New Haven, Conn.: Yale University Press, 1971); Jerome H. Skolnick, *Justice without Trial* (New York: Wiley and Sons, 1967); Laud Humphreys, *Tearoom Trade: Impersonal Sex in Public Places* (Chicago: Aldine, 1970); Ned Polsky, *Hustlers, Beats, and Others* (Chicago: Aldine, 1967); and William F. Whyte, *Streetcorner Society* (Chicago: University of Chicago Press, 1943).
8. For a discussion of both sides of this issue, see Kai T. Erikson, "A Comment on Disguised Observation in Sociology," *Social Problems* 14 (Spring 1967): 366–73; and Norman K. Denzin, "On the Ethics of Disguised Observation," *Social Problems* 15 (Spring 1968): 502–4.
9. See, for example, Edgar F. Borgatta and Betty Crowther, *A Workbook for the Study of Social Interaction Processes.* (Chicago: Rand McNally, 1965).
10. F. J. Roethlesberger and W. J. Dickson, *Management and the Worker* (Cambridge, Mass.: Harvard University Press, 1939).
11. *The Kansas City Preventive Patrol Experiment: A Summary Report* (Washington, D.C.: Police Foundation, 1974).
12. Skolnick, p. vii.
13. Howard S. Becker, *Outsiders: Studies in the Sociology of Deviance* (New York: Free Press, 1963), p. 45.
14. Ibid, pp. 45–46.

## Review Questions

1. What are the advantages and disadvantages of non-reactive data collection techniques?
2. Of what possible problems in the accuracy of the data should a researcher who uses documents be aware?

3. Of what possible errors of interpretation should an investigator using physical evidence be aware?
4. What are the advantages and disadvantages of being a participant observer as compared with being a secret observer or a complete observer?
5. What questions should a researcher ask himself or herself before entering the field as an observer?
6. What are the advantages and disadvantages of being an observer compared with using non-reactive research methods?
7. What scientific advantages are there in experimentation as a research technique? What are its limitations?

## *Exercises*

1. Identify and discuss the usefulness in document analysis of at least three different sections of a daily newspaper.
2. What kinds of documents might one use to study:

   - criminal behavior
   - educational background
   - political philosophy of newspersons
   - citizens' views of police or court performance

3. Discuss how you might draw a simple random sample of newspaper editorials for a daily paper over a two-year period.
4. Develop a coding plan for at least one variable pertaining to newspaper editorials about the "law and order" issue.
5. Write an entering-the-field plan for doing an observational study of police encounters with juveniles.
6. Suppose you wanted to do an observational study of drug use on your campus. Discuss the advantages and disadvantages of being a:

   - participant as observer
   - observer as participant
   - secret observer
   - complete observer

Include in your discussion issues concerning recording observations, accuracy of observations and objectivity.

# 7

# *An Introduction to Descriptive Statistics*

Statistics are numerical tools used by researchers to help them describe and explain phenomena. Any numerical *datum* qualifies as a statistic (though the term is often employed in a more specialized sense), and most social-science data are presented in statistical form. Statistics appear in criminal justice textbooks and research reports, and government officials use a variety of statistical information in making policy decisions. Advertisers trying to convince us of the desirability of their product frequently present us with statistics to bolster their case, while consumer information groups use statistics to assess the relative merits of products. If we are to do research or to understand and assess the research of others, we must know something about statistics.

However, there are dangers here for the unwary, for in our number-conscious culture, "statistics" have almost become synonymous with "facts." Because statistics seem to have a hardness, an immutability, a finality to them, we are inclined to think that they are unquestionable. But just as facts do not speak for themselves, neither do statistics, for statistical data can be misused or misinterpreted, and in the discussion which follows, we will note some of the errors and ambiguities that sometimes emerge. A few of the more elementary statistical concepts and procedures will be discussed in detail, while several more complex statistical techniques will be introduced to give the reader a sense of their importance. For a more complete discussion, the reader should consult some of the suggested readings listed at the end of this book.

There are two basic types of statistics: descriptive and inferential. **Descriptive statistics** show relationships between variables or describe and summarize a particular data set. They will be the focus of this and the following chapter. **Inferential statistics,** considered in chapter 9, help us draw conclusions (make inferences) about the characteristics of populations, based on the characteristics of samples drawn from those populations.

## *Measurement and Scales*

We are all familiar with certain kinds of measurement and the procedures for obtaining them. If, for example, we wanted to find out if a piece of lumber was long enough to use for a particular purpose, we could hold a yardstick up to it and measure its length. To determine the sex distribution or age range in a given group of people, we can obtain data with a good degree of accuracy, by examining birth certificates. However, measurement of variables in social-science research is seldom so straightforward, and consequently we must often devise our own "yardstick" for obtaining required measurements. For example, psychological attributes such as stress can be measured only indirectly, for instance, through the administration of a questionnaire designed to assess stress for each member of a group. The respondent's answers could be converted to a score representing whether, or to what extent, the respondent "possessed" the particular attribute.

### Continuous and Discrete Variables

Scientists classify variables into two types—continuous or discrete—based upon the kinds of values the variables can assume. Suppose we were interested in the variable "length" of a piece of lumber. A particular piece of wood can have infinitely many measurements of length because we can always, at least theoretically, make the spaces between measurement units smaller (3.2 inches, 3.217 inches, 3.21795 inches, etc.). Continuous variables such as length, age, and time, can in principle assume infinitely many values. In contrast, discrete variables such as sex (with values of male and female), political party affiliation (values of Democrat, Republican, Independent, etc.), number of children in a family (values of 0, 1, 2, . . . but not of 1.2, 2.36), number of crimes committed by a person (values of 0, 1, 2, . . . but not 1.6), or type of crime (the concepts "misdemeanor" and "felony") can assume only a finite number of values. Understanding whether the variables under investigation are continuous or discrete is important because the variable type is related to both the *level* at which we can measure the variable and the statistical techniques available to describe and analyze our data.

### Nominal Level

The simplest level of measurement is called **nominal.** Data measured at the nominal level can be placed in exhaustive, mutually exclusive categories but cannot be ordered further. Examples of data measured at the nominal level include responses categorized as true or false; information about religious affiliation categorized as Protestant, Catholic, Jewish, and other; and information about ethnic affiliation such as Irish, Dutch, English, and so on. Variables measured at the nominal level are always discrete variables. In analyzing nominal data we can count the responses in each category (e.g., there were 6 males and 4 females) and cross-tabulate responses (relate responses given in one category to those given in another—e.g., there were 3 male Protestants, 2 female Catholics, etc.).

## Ordinal Level

Measurements at the **ordinal level** make it possible not only to categorize but also to rank elements in the population according to the degree to which a certain attribute is present. Like nominal level measurements, those at the ordinal level are always discrete. We would collect data at the ordinal level of measurement if we asked respondents to answer the question, "How do you feel about the president's views on crime prevention?" by choosing one of the following alternatives: "strongly agree," "agree," "slightly agree," "neutral," "slightly disagree," "disagree," "strongly disagree." We could then rank respondents according to the degree of agreement they had expressed. Several types of scaling have been developed for the analysis of ordinal data, including sociometric scaling, which measures degrees of friendship; Guttman scaling, which ranks respondents according to the patterns of their responses to a set of questions which measure attitudes; and social distance scaling, which measures respondents' degrees of acceptance of various categories of people.

For example, to measure the social distance between respondents and political radicals, we might ask respondents if they would (1) marry a political radical or accept one as a close relation; (2) have one as a close friend; (3) accept one as a next-door neighbor; (4) accept one in your church, school, etc; (5) accept one in your community, but have no contact; (6) accept one as a resident of your country, but not your community; (7) not accept one.[1]

Furthermore, if our assumption that these items form a continuum of acceptance is true, then a respondent willing to accept a political radical as a spouse or close relative also would be willing to accept one as a neighbor, church member, community member, etc. If, on the other hand, our respondent said he would accept a political radical as a resident of his community but would have no contact with him, we would expect that he would reject him on items 1 through 4 on the scale. So, a respondent's answer concerning the social distance he would put between himself and a political radical yields additional information about his level of acceptance. The same question could be asked about other types of nonconformists to learn if a respondent generally accepted or rejected nonconformity; or we could compare responses, for example male and female, to determine whether one sex was more accepting of political radicals. Note, however, that we could not say *how much* more with this level of measurement, because the difference between ranks has no quantitative meaning.

## Interval Level

With **interval level** measurement, we cannot only categorize and order, we can also specify the *quantity* of variation between responses. An interval scale has a fixed and constant unit of measurement, such that the difference between any two adjacent points on our scale is the same as the difference between any other two adjacent points on the same scale. Temperature, as measured in degrees, is an example of interval level data, and we can say that the difference (interval) between 50°C and 25°C is quantitatively the same as the difference (interval) between 40°C and 15°C. Interval data can be added and subtracted, but multiplication and division are theoretically inappropriate. For example, it makes no sense to say that 50°C is twice as hot as 25°C, because the zero point on the centigrade scale is arbitrary. To understand the effects of an arbitrary zero point on mathematical operations, consider what would happen if we moved the arbitrary zero point on the centigrade thermometer up 10 units. The point on the scale that was originally 25° would now read 15°, and the point that was originally 50° would now be 40°; 40 is certainly not twice 15, but the difference between 15 and 40 is still 25. Measures of intelligence, such as IQ, are also, technically, interval scales; a person with an IQ of 60, for example, is not regarded as being exactly one-half as smart as a person with an IQ of 120. Variables measured at the interval level may be either discrete or continuous.

## Ratio Level

**Ratio level** measurement has all the properties of nominal, ordinal, and interval measurement, and in addition, has an absolute zero point representing a complete absence of whatever is being measured. Because of the absolute zero point, we can legitimately multiply and divide ratio data. Age, time, weight, area, volume, length, the number of days in office (or jail), number of contacts between parole officer and parolee, frequency of coffee breaks and number of court cases are all examples of ratio level data.

It should be noted that data for variables measured at the nominal level can usually serve as the basis for data for a variable measured at the ratio level, by using proportions; for example, while male is a nominal value of the discrete variable sex, proportion of males is a continuous variable pertaining to a group of persons measured at the ratio level.

**Figure 7.1 Measurements of Students in Criminal Justice Methods Class**

| Sex as a nominal variable pertaining to persons | Sex as a ratio variable pertaining to group |
|---|---|
| Males: 6 | Proportion of males: 6/10 = .60 |
| Females: 4 | Proportion of females: 4/10 = .40 |
| Total: 10 | Total: 1.0 |

Furthermore, as Blalock points out, the distinction between interval and ratio scales is often academic. In most cases, a legitimate interval scale can at least theoretically be converted to and treated as a ratio scale, because once the size of a unit on the scale has been determined, an absence of units can be conceived, even though we may not be able actually to measure this condition.[2] The level at which we measure data is important because it will determine the type of mathematical and statistical procedures we can use in analyzing our data. In general, arithmetic operations (addition, subtraction, division, and multiplication) can be used only with interval and ratio data.

## Describing the Data

Once variable type (discrete and continuous) has been identified, measurement level has been determined, and data have been gathered, we must choose among several options for describing the data.

### Raw Numbers

Suppose, as a project for a law enforcement class, we asked a number of people who passed by on a street corner if they regarded crime as a serious problem in their city. After collecting their answers, we might report the results of our informal survey in several ways. We could say: 100 persons said they did consider crime a serious problem in their city, and 25 persons said they did not. In this case, the **raw num-**

**bers** that fell into each of the response categories were reported. These simple frequency counts are called "raw" because the numbers have not been "processed" in any way; that is, they have not been converted to ratios, percentages, etc.

Raw numbers, which are frequently indicated by the letter $n$ (in our example, $n = 125$), are the point at which any statistical description must begin, and these numbers have the advantages of being simple, straightforward, and easy to understand. Statistical descriptions should always include raw numbers, or at the very least should be presented in a way that enables a reader to derive the basic raw numbers involved. If you read a statistical report which does not include the raw numbers upon which the other statistics were based, be suspicious, for statistical data presented without raw numbers can be very misleading.

Let us add a further caution here. Returning to the data from the crime survey, note that the description includes only the responses of those people who answered the question. We said nothing about the number of people who refused to answer, or who answered "don't know." Perhaps no one fit into those categories, but unless the presentation of the data indicates that, we can't be sure. Maybe $n$ was really equal to 575, and 450 people said they did not know if crime was a serious problem. That would have a considerable impact on our interpretation of the raw numbers presented earlier. Whether the data are presented in raw numbers or in any of the other forms we will discuss, it pays to think about other response categories for which data may not have been presented. As with all descriptions, what is left out of a statistical description may be more important than what has been included.

Before we proceed to another way of presenting our data, think back to your days in junior high and high school math classes. You undoubtedly studied ratios, proportions, decimals, and percentages and you probably recall the way in which these statistics were expressed. You will also remember that any of these expressions can be transformed into any of the other forms; thus, 1 out of 5 = $\frac{1}{5}$ = .20 = 20%. Now, let us return to an alternative way of presenting the data from the crime survey; we could say 4 out of 5 (or $\frac{4}{5}$, .80, 80%) of the persons said crime was a serious problem while 1 out of 5 (or $\frac{1}{5}$, .20, 20%) said it was not. In this case, we have used ratios, proportions, decimals, and percentages to report the data and communicate the thrust of the raw number data. By examining these statistics alone, you know that considerably more people thought crime was a serious problem than did not, but you would not know *how many* people responded in a particular way. We might have talked to 5 people or 5,000. Consider the following statements: "Two out of three doctors recommend . . .''; "One out of four marriages ends in divorce"; "College professors are right at least 50 percent of the time." While these expressions may appear precise and scientific at first glance, they are, in fact, almost meaningless. To make sense of them we must know, among other things, the raw numbers involved.

The raw number of responses alone is not a reliable guide to the amount of trust one should have in a given set of statistics. A well-planned study reporting on a relatively small number of cases should elicit greater confidence than a poorly planned one reporting on a larger number of cases. So, while it is important to know the raw number basis for the calculation of ratios, proportions, etc., one cannot assess a statistic exclusively on this basis. In general, the method used to identify or select the cases is more important in the assessment of the data than is the raw number of cases studied.

Assuming that the raw numbers have been provided or can be derived and the cases for study have been carefully identified or selected, ratios, proportions, decimals, and percentages are very useful statistical expressions in certain circumstances. Since percentages are probably the most practical and widely used form of statistical expression in the social sciences, we will focus on them, though many of our observations apply to other types of statistics as well.

## Percentages

**Percentages** are standardized fractions, in the sense that they have a common denominator of 100. Since the common denominator is understood (percent means "for each 100"), only the numerator of the fraction is given, followed by the percent sign. Thus $80/100 = 80\%$. Given the fraction $x/100$ and any other fraction connected by an equals sign, you can solve the equation for $x$. The solution for $x$ is the percentage that the numerator is of the denominator in the second fraction. For example

$$\frac{x}{100} = \frac{1}{5}$$

$$5x = 100$$

$$x = 20$$

1 is 20% of 5. (In practice we can simply divide the numerator by the denominator and multiply the result by 100 to calculate the percentage: $1 \div 5 = .20$; $.20 \times 100 = 20\%$). Given the raw number of responses in a specific response category and the total number of re-

sponses for all response categories, we can calculate the percentage for that particular response category. The sum of all the percentages for all of the response categories should, of course, equal 100 percent, or the whole. We might say that percentages result when we treat a group of any number of cases for statistical purposes as if there were 100 cases.

Sometimes we hear an expression like, ''Service requests increased 200 percent this year compared to last.'' Percentage expressions that involve amounts greater than 100 percent can be interpreted in the same way as those involving amounts of 100 percent or less. Thus, 200 percent is twice the amount used as the base for the original calculation, and 150 percent is one and one-half times that base amount. Percentages of less than 1 percent are expressed as a decimal percentage; thus, 0.2 percent is two-tenths of 1 percent.

When should you go beyond the presentation of raw numbers to the calculation and presentation of percentages? Percentages can be used to deal with a large number of cases, or to compare two different sets of data about a given phenomenon when there are sizable differences in the number of cases involved. Suppose that instead of 125 people, we had asked 38,400 people whether they regarded crime as a serious problem, and 24,576 said they did. It is easier to grasp the meaning of these data by saying that 64 percent of the persons we talked to thought crime was a serious problem. Now let us further suppose that we had taken a similar survey a year ago, obtaining responses from 12,400 people, 7,936 of whom said they regarded crime as a serious problem. Has the tendency to regard crime as a problem changed? It is difficult to tell simply by comparing the raw numbers, but if we compare the two results in terms of percentages, we discover that in both cases 64 percent of the people surveyed felt crime was a serious problem in their city. Because percentages are standardized forms of numerical expressions, they should be used when raw numbers alone would be confusing.

However, when the raw numbers involved are small, percentages may be misleading. For example, if the total number of cases is 10, converting to percentages magnifies the differences in the numbers reported by a factor of 10. If there are 4 cases in one category of response and 6 in another, the raw number difference is 2, while the percentage difference is 20 percent. This magnification may well distort our interpretation of the data presented, and as a rule of thumb, we suggest that percentages not be used unless one is reporting on at least 30 cases.

Just as the conversion of very small raw numbers to percentages magnifies apparent differences, the conversion of very large raw numbers diminishes apparent differences. If 1,000,000 votes were cast in an election with a 490,000-to-510,000 candidate count, a raw number difference of 20,000 yields a percentage difference of only 2 percent. The difference created by such conversions is more dramatic if we consider another example. Suppose two different surgical procedures are available for repairing a damaged valve in the heart. One group of 50,000 patients is operated on using one procedure, and another group of 50,000 patients receives the other procedure. Suppose, further, that 9,500 patients in the first group and 9,000 patients in the second group die during surgery. Saying that the outcome of the two procedures differs by 1 percent may give the impression that there is very little difference between them, but stating that 500 more people survived the second procedure provides quite a different impression. Still, statistically these two presentations of the data are equally correct. Because there is no simple rule of thumb indicating the maximum number of cases for which conversion of raw numbers to percentages is appropriate, one should always know the raw numbers involved and bear in mind what the statistics are about. Finally, one must be very careful not to confuse decimals and percentages; remember that $.25 = {}^{25}/_{100} = 25\%$ and that $.0025 = {}^{25}/_{10,000} = .25\%$.

## Rates

Another statistical expression we may read or hear about often is rate—the crime rate, the rate of inflation, production rates, interest rates, and so forth. **Rates** express the frequency of an event in relation to a fixed unit or units of measurement, and time is usually one of the fixed units. A rate of speed, for example, is expressed in number of miles per hour; a crime rate is the number of crimes of a particular kind per fixed unit of population (say, 100,000) per fixed unit of time (say, one year). In the latter case, a fixed unit of population is added to the fixed unit of time.

Like percentages, rates can be very useful statistics for comparative purposes. As long as the fixed units are explicit and constant, existing differences or changes taking place can be compared and assessed. For example, crime rates for different societies or for different time periods in the same society can be compared as long as definitions of criminal acts are the same across societies or at different times.

In addition to expressing the frequency with which something occurs, rates can be used to calculate the extent to which that frequency is changing, that is, increasing or decreasing. Again, these are useful expressions, as long as you do not get tangled up in them. Consider, for example, the following statement: "The rate of increase in the nation's crime rate is decreasing." This means that while the crime rate is still going up, it is not going up as fast as it had been. The statement does make sense, but such statements must be interpreted carefully to avoid being misled.

In using or interpreting rate statistics, the units must be fixed, known, and remain unchanged from one citation to another. Furthermore, since percentage expressions are frequently combined with rate expressions (e.g., there was a 15 percent increase in the rate of felonies this year as compared to last), and since rates are also standardized forms of statistical expression, the cautions we raised about percentages apply here as well.

## Frequency Distributions

Another way to present data is to construct a **frequency distribution.** A frequency distribution indicates how many times a particular event or value of a variable occurs in the assembled data. In addition to counting and reporting the raw number of responses falling into each response category for a given variable, the researcher may want to represent the data graphically in the form of a *bar* or *line graph* (discussed further in chapter 10) that is derived from raw numbers.

Suppose that you are interested in the sex distribution of shoplifters. Sex is a variable with two values: male and female. You could begin your analysis by making two columns on a sheet of paper, one labeled "female shoplifters," the other labeled "male shoplifters," and listing the names of the shoplifters under the appropriate heading. Suppose your list looked like the one in figure 7.2. By counting the number of names in each list, you would find the frequency distribution of the sex of the shoplifters to be 7 males and 4 females. To convert this expression into a graph, you could create a two-dimensional space defined by a horizontal and vertical axis. Along the horizontal axis, you would provide space for each of the response categories (male and female). Along the vertical axis, you would provide space for each of the possible frequencies with which each response category might appear in the data. You would then create a rectangular space for each response category by raising a "bar" to the height corresponding to the frequency with which that category appears in the data. Figure 7.3 shows what a graphic representation of the data might look like. Note that the zero frequency category is located at the point where the horizontal axis intersects with the vertical axis.

**Figure 7.2  Sex of Shoplifters**

| Male Shoplifters | Female Shoplifters |
| --- | --- |
| Bob | Sally |
| George | Matilda |
| Tom | Joan |
| Richard | Francine |
| Henry | |
| Alphonso | |
| Beauregard | |

The advantages of graphic presentation of frequency distributions become more apparent when the number of response categories is large. Suppose, for example, that a test has been given to a class of 36 police recruits and that a perfect score on the test is 20. After scoring the exams, the tester might use a frequency distribution to provide herself and the recruits with a picture of class performance. To construct the frequency distribution, the tester must count the number of people who received a particular score on the examination. Again, a range of frequencies—in this case 0 to 9—is arrayed along the vertical axis, and the range of possible examination scores—in this case 0 to 20—is arrayed along the horizontal axis. Suppose our graph looked like the one in figure 7.4. The graph indicates that no one in the class scored lower than 8, and that one person scored 8, two scored 9, six scored 13, three scored 16, and so on.

Line graphs, sometimes called **histograms,** communicate essen-

**Figure 7.3  Sex of Shoplifters**

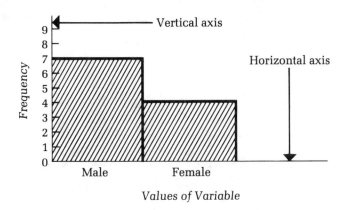

**Figure 7.4  Bar Graph Frequency Distribution of Police Recruit Test Scores**

tially the same information as bar graphs, though perhaps less vividly. A line graph is constructed by assigning each of the scores a point on the horizontal axis and each of the frequencies a point on the vertical axis. In contrast to the construction of a bar, a point is used to represent the intersection of a score and its frequency in the line graph. To locate this point in the graph, we draw an imaginary line perpendicular to the horizontal axis at the location of the score, and another imaginary line perpendicular to the vertical axis at the location of the frequency with which that score appears in the data. The point where these two imaginary lines intersect is the point we use. We repeat this procedure for each score and its corresponding frequency. We create the "line" in the graph by connecting the points we have located with a series of straight lines. The line graph corre-

**Figure 7.5  Line Graph Frequency Distribution of Police Recruit Test Scores**

sponding to the bar graph of police recruit test scores looks like the one in figure 7.5.

Statistics that are used to characterize frequency distributions are of two types: **measures of central tendency** and **measures of dispersion.** Bear in mind that in the following discussion we are no longer just considering the measurement of variables per se, we are describing measures of the *distributions* of those variable measurements.

## Measures of Central Tendency

There are three frequently used measures of the central tendency of a frequency distribution, the mean, the median, and the mode.

### The Mean

The **mean** (referred to as $\bar{x}$) is the arithmetic average of the individual numerical scores that make up a distribution. It is calculated by summing all the scores and dividing by the number of scores that went into the sum. If, for instance, there are five individual scores, and we call them $x_1$, $x_2$, $x_3$, $x_4$, and $x_5$, then the mean is

$$\bar{x} = \frac{x_1 + x_2 + x_3 + x_4 + x_5}{5}.$$

Using the summation sign (the Greek letter sigma) gives a shorter way to say this:

$$\bar{x} = \frac{\sum_{i=1}^{5} x_i}{5},$$

where $\sum_{i=1}^{5} x_i$ means "the sum of all the scores $x_i$ from $x_1$ to $x_5$"

($i$ is an index used to give each score a different label).

Using the test scores from our hypothetical police recruit exam, we calculate the mean as follows. We add all the scores achieved by each recruit and divide by 36, the total number of scores. The sum of the scores is 468.

$$\sum_{i=1}^{36} = 8 + 9 + 9 + 10 + 11 + \ldots + 19 = 468.$$

The mean is the sum of scores divided by the number of scores (n).

$$\bar{x} = \frac{\sum_{i=1}^{n}}{n} = \frac{468}{36} = 13.$$

Hence, the mean or arithmetic average score on this test is 13.

## The Median

The **median** of a distribution is the middle score, in the sense that half the recruits have made that score or less, and half have made that score or more. To find the median of a distribution, we must: (a) arrange all of the individual scores in numerical order, either from lowest to highest or from highest to lowest, and (b) find the score that is in the center of this array, by counting in from both ends of the array simultaneously. For example, if the police recruit test scores represented by the frequency distribution were arrayed in ascending numerical order they would look like this: 8, 9, 9, 10, 10, 10, 11, 11, 11, 11, 12, 12, 12, 12, 12, 13, 13, 13, 13, 13, 13, 14, 14, 14, 14, 14, 15, 15, 15, 15, 16, 16, 16, 17, 17, 18. Since there are 36 scores (an even number of scores), the center of the array falls between two scores, counting 18 scores from each end. In this case, we take the arithmetic average of these two scores: 13 + 13 = 26; 26 ÷ 2 = 13. Hence, the median of this distribution is 13. If the number of scores in the distribution was odd, a single score would occupy the point equidistant from each end of the array, and that score would be the median of the distribution.

## The Mode

The **mode** of the distribution is the score that occurs with the greatest frequency in the distribution. By inspecting the frequency distribution (figure 7.4), it is easy to locate the mode. Since the score 13 appears six times, and no other score appears more than five times, the mode of the distribution is 13.

In the example we have used, the mean, median, and mode all have the same value. These three measures of central tendency will all have the same value when the distribution is unimodal (has one mode) and is symmetrical. So long as one deals with unimodal symmetrical distributions, then, it is not a problem to select an appropriate measure of central tendency. However, the means, medians, and modes of other types of distribution are not usually equal to each other, and when distributions are not symmetrical, the measure of central tendency that will be most useful for the analysis should be selected and reported.

To further understand the issues involved in the choice among measures of central tendency, suppose that the distribution of police recruit test scores looked like the one in figure 7.6.

**Figure 7.6  Bar Graph Frequency Distribution of Police Recruit Test Scores**

Figure 7.7 shows how a line graph of this distribution would look. Distributions similar in shape to the one in figure 7.6 are called **skewed distributions,** which are characterized by a bunching of scores toward one end or the other of the horizontal axis.

**Figure 7.7  Line Graph Frequency Distribution of Police Recruit Test Scores**

Now suppose that we calculate the three measures of central tendency for this distribution. Again, we have 36 scores; the sum of the scores in this case is 400. The mean is 400 ÷ 36 = 11.1 (rounded to nearest tenth); the median is 14.5; and the mode is 15. Note that in this distribution, the mean, median, and mode have different values, and the value of the median lies between the values of the mode and mean. This is typically, though not always, the case in skewed distributions.

Choosing a particular measure of central tendency for this kind of distribution may seem a relatively arbitrary matter, but the measure we use may influence the interpretation of our data. If a tester wanted to demonstrate how well the class performs, he might choose to report the modal score, 15, and to play down the group's performance, he might report the mean, 11.1. In most cases the safest and most honest way to present the data is to report all three measures of central tendency, because there is less chance of misleading or being misled. Substantial differences among the reported mean, median, and mode are a sure sign that the distribution is highly skewed.

In some cases, not all the measures are appropriate because one or more may not be meaningful for the type of data collected. A variable, such as sex, measured at the nominal level has only one appropriate measure of central tendency—the mode—because it makes no sense to speak of "mean sex" or "median sex." For ordinal level data—those that permit the ranking of individual scores—both median and mode are appropriate. In the case of interval or ratio levels of measurement, any one or a combination of the measures of central tendency can be used.

The appropriateness of measures of central tendency also depends on whether the variable investigated is discrete or continuous. Modes and medians can be used with either discrete or continuous variables, but strictly speaking, a mean should be utilized only when the variable is continuous. In practice, demographers and other social scientists do calculate means for discrete data, telling us, for example, that "the average American family" has 2.3 children. A mode for discrete data cannot assume a fractional value, and a median can do so only when the distribution contained an even number of scores and the procedure for determining the median discussed previously was employed.

Finally, we must caution the reader that the three measures of central tendency are affected differently by extreme scores—that is, those scores in a distribution that are either very large or very small in comparison to the other scores in the distribution. A simple example will highlight the differential impact of extreme scores. Given the following scores: 4, 5, 5, 4, 6, 3, 4, and 1, the mean, median, and mode of this distribution have the same value: 4. If the highest score was 20 instead of 6, neither the median nor the mode is affected, but the mean is now 5.75. Because the calculation of the mean depends on summing all the scores, it is most affected by extreme scores. Extreme scores have a distorting effect on the mean; hence, when they are present, the mean is a misleading indicator of central tendency.

The three different measures of central tendency are computed to reflect somewhat different aspects of a distribution, and the meanings of their variant forms are quite important. Often, the terms *average* and *typical* are used imprecisely, for in some instances, they may refer to an arithmetic average (i.e., the mean), and in other instances to the value that occurs most frequently (i.e., the mode). In any case, measures of central tendency provide us with only a limited amount of knowledge about any particular distribution. To learn more about the nature of a distribution, we need to use one or more measures of dispersion.

## *Measures of Dispersion*

In addition to knowing the central tendency of a distribution, it is helpful to know the *dispersion* of a distribution; that is, how wide a range of values the distribution includes. Figure 7.8, where several symmetrical distributions (A, B and C) have been drawn on the same set of axes, illustrates the additional information that a measure of dispersion communicates.

**Figure 7.8 Three Different Symmetrical Distributions with Same Mean, Median, and Mode but Different Dispersion**

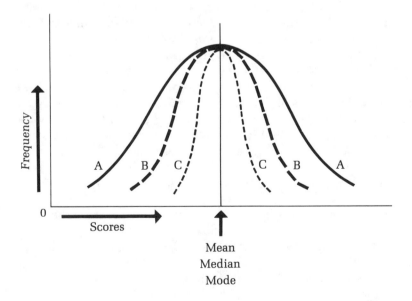

While each of the distributions is bell shaped, or symmetrical, and all have the same mean, median, and mode, they represent quite different arrays, some spanning most of the potential scores (A), and some encompassing only a small part of them (C). Measures of dispersion permit us to summarize these differences.

## Range

The **range** of a distribution is indicated by reporting the largest and the smallest scores that appear in the distribution. In the first distribution of police recruit test scores previously discussed, the lowest score was 8 and the highest, 18; therefore, the range of the distribution is from 8 through 18. Sometimes the range is indicated as a single number, arrived at by subtracting the smallest score from the largest one (in our example, 18 − 8 = 10). Note, however, that when the range is reported only as a single number, the reader has no way of knowing what the highest and lowest scores obtained were.

## Average Deviation

The **average deviation from the mean** is the arithmetic average of the differences between the distribution's mean score and each of the individual scores in the distribution. To find the average deviation from the mean, the mean must be calculated and then subtracted from each of the scores in the distribution. The **absolute value** of the differences (i.e., the value without regard to a plus or minus sign) is used in these calculations. The absolute value differences are then added and the total is divided by the number of scores in the distribution. Again, we shall use the first set of police recruit test scores to illustrate. The mean score was 13, and subtracting 13 from each of the 36 scores gives us the absolute values shown in column 3 of table 7.1. The sum of the absolute values of the differences is 70, and since there are 36 scores, the average difference, or deviation, is given by 70 ÷ 36 = 1.9 (rounded to the nearest tenth). The greater the average deviation from the mean, the more dispersed are the scores in the distribution.

## Standard Deviation

The **standard deviation** (referred to as *sd* or *s*) is probably the most frequently used and reported measure of dispersion. It is closely related to the average deviation from the mean, but differs from it in that the standard deviation of a distribution expresses differences from the mean in units of equal size for that particular distribution. The interesting and valuable uses to which we can put standardized units of

## Table 7.1 Deviations from the Mean of Police Recruit Test Scores

| Column 1 Score $(x)$ | Column 2 Mean $(\bar{x})$ | Column 3 Difference (Absolute Values) from Mean $(|\bar{x} - x|)$ | Column 4 Squared Difference or Deviation from Mean $(\bar{x} - x)^2$ |
|---|---|---|---|
| 8 | 13 | 5 | 25 |
| 9 | 13 | 4 | 16 |
| 9 | 13 | 4 | 16 |
| 10 | 13 | 3 | 9 |
| 10 | 13 | 3 | 9 |
| 10 | 13 | 3 | 9 |
| 11 | 13 | 2 | 4 |
| 11 | 13 | 2 | 4 |
| 11 | 13 | 2 | 4 |
| 11 | 13 | 2 | 4 |
| 12 | 13 | 1 | 1 |
| 12 | 13 | 1 | 1 |
| 12 | 13 | 1 | 1 |
| 12 | 13 | 1 | 1 |
| 12 | 13 | 1 | 1 |
| 13 | 13 | 0 | 0 |
| 13 | 13 | 0 | 0 |
| 13 | 13 | 0 | 0 |
| 13 | 13 | 0 | 0 |
| 13 | 13 | 0 | 0 |
| 13 | 13 | 0 | 0 |
| 14 | 13 | 1 | 1 |
| 14 | 13 | 1 | 1 |
| 14 | 13 | 1 | 1 |
| 14 | 13 | 1 | 1 |
| 14 | 13 | 1 | 1 |
| 15 | 13 | 2 | 4 |
| 15 | 13 | 2 | 4 |
| 15 | 13 | 2 | 4 |
| 15 | 13 | 2 | 4 |
| 16 | 13 | 3 | 9 |
| 16 | 13 | 3 | 9 |
| 16 | 13 | 3 | 9 |
| 17 | 13 | 4 | 16 |
| 17 | 13 | 4 | 16 |
| 18 | 13 | 5 | 25 |
| **Sums** 468 | 468 | 70 | 210 |

deviation from the mean in certain types of distributions will be discussed later. The standard deviation of a distribution is calculated by squaring the difference or deviation from the mean of each score (multiplying the deviation times the deviation), summing these squared deviations, dividing the sum by the total number of scores (the value obtained at this point is called the **variance** or $s^2$), and taking the square root of the result. The number thus obtained is the standard deviation of the scores from the mean. This process is given by the formula:

$$s = \sqrt{\frac{\sum_{i=1}^{n} (\bar{x} - x_i)^2}{n}},$$

where $s$ is the standard deviation, $n$ is the number of scores in the distribution, and $\sum_{i=1}^{n} (\bar{x} - x_i)^2$ indicates the sum of the squared differences of each individual score ($i$ = 1 to $n$) from the mean score. In the example from table 7.1:

$$s = \sqrt{\frac{(13-8)^2 + (13-9)^2 + (13-9)^2 + \ldots + (13-18)^2}{36}}$$

As with the average deviation from the mean, the greater the dispersion of the scores in the distribution, the larger the standard deviation.

Each measure of dispersion has its own strengths and limitations, and choosing the most appropriate measure depends on the particular situation. A range is seriously affected by relatively large or relatively small scores isolated at the extremities of a distribution; for example, if all the scores of a particular distribution fell between 35 and 50 except one that was 10, reporting the range as 10 to 50 does not summarize the actual dispersion of the scores in the distribution very well. The average deviation from the mean expresses how far, on the average, scores differ from the mean score, but it does not in itself tell us what the range of the scores is, and it is also greatly influenced by extreme scores, though less so than the range. The standard deviation, which is still less influenced by extreme scores, is preferable to the average deviation from the mean if a researcher is interested in more than a simple description of the dispersion of the data. However, neither the average deviation nor the standard deviation is very useful if one is dealing with a highly skewed distribution (i.e., one that is not a symmetrical curve).

Finally, while a range can appropriately be used with either discrete or continuous data measured at the ordinal level or above, both the average deviation from the mean and standard deviation assume that the data are continuous and are measured at least at the interval level. Again, as in the case of measures of central tendency, these measures of dispersion are often used with discrete data. When this is done cautiously and explicitly, little harm is done in this compromise with statistical rules.

We can use crime statistics to illustrate the application of many of the measures of central tendency and dispersion described here, and in the process we can also demonstrate how complex and tricky things can get even with these relatively simple statistical measures.

If someone tells you that the crime rate for city A was 4 per 1,000 in 1986, can any sense be made of such a report? For reasons which will become obvious, the answer is no. We need to know a great deal more about how that rate was calculated before we have any idea of what it "really" means.

The first thing that we need to ask is what was the population base used—per 1,000 what? The rate may have been calculated on the basis of:

1. the total population in the city;
2. only adults in the city (defined how?);
3. adults and juveniles (defined how?); or
4. only males, etc.

The rate means very different things depending on what "per 1,000" is involved.

When and how was the population counted? During the last census? If it was some years ago, has the population in the city changed very much? How do we know? If it has, was the population count used for the base adjusted? How and on what basis was the adjustment made? Was the count of crimes made in at least roughly the same period as the count for the population base? A rate calculated on the basis of a 1980 population census and a count of crimes in 1985 may be seriously misleading.

Furthermore, what was counted as a crime? How was crime defined? Felonies only? Misdemeanors and felonies? Consider also the following possible ways of counting crimes during a specified period of time:

1. crimes actually committed (the "real" crime rate);
2. crimes observed by others;
3. crimes reported to the police;
4. crimes recorded by the police (the basis for most official crime statistics);

5. crimes for which someone was arrested;
6. crimes for which someone was prosecuted; or
7. crimes for which someone was convicted.


Any of these could be used to arrive at the "4" of the 4 per 1,000 and a reasonable argument could be made that any one of them would be useful. In any event, it should be obvious that which of them is used is quite important in making sense of the reported crime rate.

In addition to crime rates, we might want to consider other crime statistics and determine what kinds of complications might enter into making sense of them. What proportion of crimes are cleared by arrest? What are the mean, median, and mode of the distribution of the lengths of sentences handed down by courts in a given jurisdiction? What is the average deviation and standard deviation of the distribution of the number of months persons convicted of felonies in your state actually spend in confinement? There are many other statistics that can be very useful to the student or practitioner of criminal justice.

## *Indicators of Location in a Distribution*

Suppose that you have just received a report on the results of a scholastic achievement test that you and 267,598 other students have taken. Suppose, further, you are told that your score on the test was 575. This information would not be very helpful to you, would it? In order to make sense of your score, you would want to know both the maximum score possible and how your score compared with the scores of the other students who took the test. In other words, you would want to be able to locate your score in the distribution of test scores.

If the report included a bar graph frequency distribution of the test scores, you could find the bar representing the frequency of your score in the distribution. By examining the location and height of this bar relative to the other bars in the graph, you could learn something about how you performed relative to others. Since this is a simple and straightforward procedure for communicating information, we recommend that you use bar graphs whenever feasible.

However, when the range of test scores is large, constructing and presenting a bar graph frequency distribution may be impractical. In the absence of the frequency distribution itself, it would be somewhat helpful if the measures of central tendency and dispersion for the distribution as a whole were reported. You might be told, for example, that the scores ranged from 100 to 800 and that the median for the distribution was 523. Given this information, you may conclude that your score was in the upper half of the scores in a distribution. But that is only a rough indication of the location of your score relative to the other scores in the distribution. How can we improve your ability to locate your score in the distribution?

The median, you will recall, is found by dividing the scores arrayed in ascending or descending numerical order into two groups, each of which contains the same number of scores. What if, by extending the principle used to determine the value of the median, the scores were divided into more than two groups? The greater the number of groups into which the scores are divided, the more division points analogous to the median would be available for reference in locating a particular score. In principle, we could divide the scores into any number of groups, each containing the same number of scores, as long as the number of scores is equal to or greater than the number of groups we chose to create. In practice, statisticians often use three different subdivisions of the scores in a distribution: quartiles, deciles, and percentiles. **Quartiles** (Q) are arrived at by dividing the scores into four groups, **deciles** (D) are based on a division of the scores into 10 groups, and **percentiles** (P) are determined by dividing the scores into 100 groups. As in locating the median, the scores must be arranged in numerical order before the values of these various **quantiles** (the general term used to refer to all of these measures) can be determined.

Since determining the value of the various quantiles depends on the division of the scores into more than two groups, some special procedures must be introduced. While there is only one median for a particular distribution, there are three quartiles, nine deciles, and 99 percentiles. Therefore, we need a procedure for distinguishing among the various quantiles of a particular type. The scores should be arranged in ascending numerical order and identifying numbers should be assigned to the quantiles, beginning with the first division point that occurs in the array. However, it is not always possible to find points that divide the scores into groups containing exactly the same number of scores. In such instances it is necessary to compromise with reality a bit and come as close as one can. Since the smaller the number of scores in the distribution, the greater the impact of this difficulty, it is best to restrict the use of quartiles, deciles, and percentiles to distributions that contain a relatively large number of scores.

Imagine that the line in figure 7.9 represents an array of scores listed from left to right in ascending numerical order. The line can be divided into various numbers of segments of equal length. The boundary points of these divisions correspond to the scores that are used to determine the values of the various types of quantiles (quartiles, deciles, and percentiles). To find the quartile division points we would divide the scores (the line) into four groups of (approximately) equal size and label the first division point from the left the 1st quartile, the second division point the 2nd quartile, and so on. For deciles, the scores would be divided into 10 equally-sized groups; for percentiles, into 100 equally-sized groups. Note that the median, the 2nd quartile, the 5th decile, and the 50th percentile all have the same value. Similarly, the 1st quartile and the 25th percentile have the same value, and so on.

If we know both the values of the various quantiles for a given distribution and a particular individual's score, we can locate that score approximately, relative to the other scores in the distribution, by saying it is less than, equivalent to, or greater than a particular quartile, decile, or percentile. Since percentiles provide more reference points in the distribution, they permit a more precise location of a particular score than do quartiles or deciles and are, therefore, the most frequently used quantiles, especially when both the number of scores in the distribution and their range are very large.

When we speak of a percentile, we refer to the percentage of scores in the distribution that are either equal to or less than the value of the given percentile. For example, if you are told that your score on a promotional test is equivalent to the 76th percentile, your score was higher than or equal to 76 percent of the scores, but 24 percent of the scores were higher than yours.

While quantiles are useful as indicators of location, we must be careful not to misinterpret them. First, the smaller the number of quantiles used as reference points in locating a particular score, the less apparent may be the differences in the scores reported by referring to their quantile values alone. Two scores may, for example, both be reported as "below the 1st quartile." But one may also be below the 1st decile, while the other is above the 2nd decile. Furthermore, one may be equivalent to the 2nd percentile, and the other may be equivalent to the 24th percentile. Obviously, the nature of the particular quantiles being used is critical when interpreting reports of scores made in terms of quantiles alone.

Other difficulties can be illustrated by examining a particular distribution of deciles, but the difficulties discussed apply to the use of quartiles and percentiles as well. Consider 20 scores ranging from 1 to 9 and the deciles for the distribution illustrated in figure 7.10. At the outset, we see that the 3rd and 4th deciles have the same value: 3.

# Figure 7.9 Quantiles

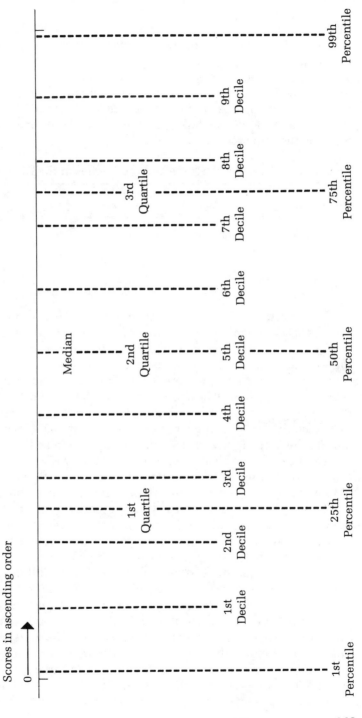

Now, suppose that your score on this test is 3. How would you report your score by reference to decile values? You must resist the temptation to identify the last 3 in the distribution as yours and contend that your score was above the 4th decile, because for the purposes of determining the decile values, it is irrelevant which of the 3's is yours. Surely, it would not be fair to a friend who also scored 3 to designate the first 3 as his and say it fell below the 3rd decile. After all, you both received the same score on the test.

**Figure 7.10  A Series of Scores and the Deciles of the Distribution**

| Scores: | 1 1 | 2 2 | 2 3 | 3 3 | 3 3 | 4 4 | 4 4 | 5 5 | 6 7 | 8 9 |
|---------|-----|-----|-----|-----|-----|-----|-----|-----|-----|-----|
|         | ↑   | ↑   | ↑   | ↑   | ↑   | ↑   | ↑   | ↑   | ↑   |     |
| Deciles: | 1st | 2nd | 3rd | 4th | 5th | 6th | 7th | 8th | 9th | |

| Values of Deciles: | 1.5 | 2 | 3 | 3 | 3.5 | 4 | 4.5 | 5.5 | 7.5 |
|--------------------|-----|---|---|---|-----|---|-----|-----|-----|

To be honest, you would have to say that your score (and your friend's) was equivalent to the value of the 3rd and 4th deciles.

Using the same distribution for illustrative purposes, suppose that your score is 4. What would be a conventional interpretation of a report indicating that your score is equivalent to the 6th decile? Your score would apparently be equivalent to or higher than 60 percent of the scores, but when we observe the actual distribution, your score is, in fact, equivalent to or higher than 70 percent of the scores. We hasten to note that the use of percentages here violates the aforementioned rule of thumb about having at least 30 scores before using percentages, but the general point is valid nonetheless: there is a margin of imprecision in the conventional interpretation of quantiles.

This imprecision arises because the procedures used to determine the values of the quantiles entail dividing the scores into groups that contain equal numbers of scores. Hence, it is quite true, for example, that 50 percent of the scores in the distribution fall below the 5th decile (and the 2nd quartile and the 50th percentile). But this procedure takes into account only the number of scores; it ignores the *values* of the scores themselves. Hence, the relationship between the values of the quantiles and the values of the scores is imperfect. A number of scores that have the same value may overlap quantile division points. When this happens, the conventional interpretation in terms of the percentage of scores equivalent to or below a particular quantile must be regarded as an approximation rather than a precise statement.

Finally, the range of values of scores encompassed between a pair of adjacent quantiles and any other adjacent pair of quantiles in a distribution can vary greatly. This is most apparent in highly skewed distributions. Quantiles, then, are most useful and least misleading as indicators of location when both the number of cases and the range of score values are large, and the scores are at least approximately symmetrically distributed.

# Distributions: Symmetrical and Otherwise

We have already become acquainted in a very general way with two types of distribution: symmetrical and skewed. Having discussed the measures of central tendency and dispersion of distributions, we can now extend our discussion of the different types of distributions. Remember that we create a curvilinear distribution by connecting the points which represent the corresponding frequencies of scores on a particular variable in our data.

## Unimodal and Multimodal Distributions

First, it is useful to distinguish between unimodal and multimodal distributions. A **unimodal distribution** has only one "hump," while a **multimodal distribution** has two or more "humps" (see figure 7.11). Another way of saying this is that if we traced the curve of the distribution with a pencil from left to right, in a unimodal distribution the pencil would move always up (as in distribution d) or always down (as in c) or change directions only once, from up to down (a, b); in a multimodal distribution, the pencil would change directions more than once (e, f, g) or change directions only once, but from down to up (h). Thus, although a particular distribution has only one mean, median, range, average deviation from the mean, and standard deviation, it may have more than one mode.

Both symmetrical and skewed distributions, as we have used these terms here, are assumed to be unimodal. They differ in that the symmetrical distribution is symmetrical with respect to the mean— that is, its shape on one side of the mean is the mirror image of its shape on the other side of the mean—while the skewed distribution is not, as shown by the distribution curves in figure 7.12. Skewed distributions may vary in their direction and degree of skewedness (note figure 7.13), but many distributions, though slightly skewed, closely approximate the symmetrical distribution, and can be treated as if they were symmetrical for most purposes.

# Figure 7.11 Unimodal and Multimodal Distributions

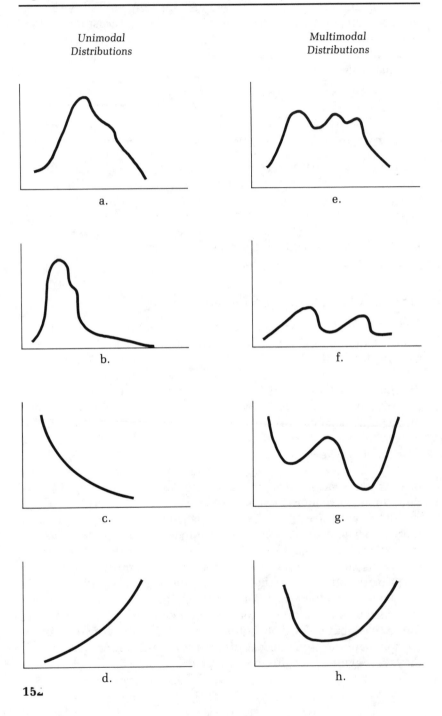

Unimodal Distributions

Multimodal Distributions

a.

b.

c.

d.

e.

f.

g.

h.

**Figure 7.12  Skewed and Symmetrical Distributions**

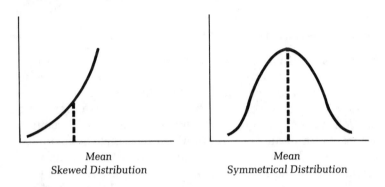

Mean
Skewed Distribution

Mean
Symmetrical Distribution

In the case of the central tendency of a unimodal, symmetrical (or approximately symmetrical) distribution, it is sufficient to state that the distribution is symmetrical (or nearly so) and report the mean, median, or mode, since all three measures of central tendency will be approximately equivalent. If the distribution is considerably skewed, however, all three measures of central tendency should be reported.

To know the mean and the standard deviation of a unimodal, symmetrical distribution is to have a fairly complete description of that distribution. Consequently, in many data reports, the actual graphic presentation of at least approximately symmetrical distributions is omitted, and these two statistics are reported instead. However, the less symmetrical a distribution is (for example, the more skewed is the distribution), the less reliable and useful are these statistics as descriptions of the distribution. Therefore, be suspicious of data reports that present only summary measures and not the distribution itself, unless it is clear that the distribution is unimodal and at least approximately symmetrical. If the distribution is highly skewed

**Figure 7.13  Skewed Distributions**

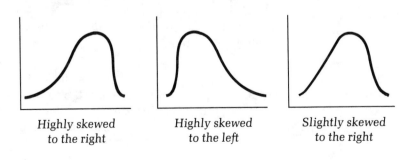

Highly skewed
to the right

Highly skewed
to the left

Slightly skewed
to the right

or multimodal, it is safest to present the distribution itself in addition to the summary statistics.

## The Normal Distribution and Standard Scores

The **normal distribution** is a unimodal, symmetrical distribution with especially useful statistical characteristics. To comprehend these special properties, we must understand the relationship between particular segments of the area encompassed by a graph and the proportion of times particular outcomes (e.g., test scores) occur in the distribution represented by the graph. Suppose that we calculated the area of each of the bars in a bar graph (such as the one in figure 7.14) by multiplying the width of a bar by its length. We could then determine the total area encompassed by the graph by summing the areas of the bars. Assuming that the bars have the same width, we could then express the area of any particular bar as a proportion of the total area of the graph. With a little effort you can demonstrate that the proportion of the total area of the graph included in a particular bar is equal to the proportion of times (the proportional frequency) the particular outcome represented by that bar occurs in the distribution. Suppose we superimposed a line graph over a bar graph, as we have in figure 7.14. Remember that these two graphs represent the same data.

**Figure 7.14  Bar Graph with Line Graph Superimposed**

*Police Recruit Test Scores*

Note that the area under the line (curve) is essentially the same as the area encompassed by the bars. We can, therefore, speak of the equivalence between proportions of area under the line (curve) and the proportions of times particular scores (outcomes) occur, just as we did when we referred to areas of the bars. Statisticians put to very effective use this relationship between areas under the curve of a particular kind of distribution and proportional frequencies of outcomes.

Suppose we have another unimodal curve, representing the frequency distribution of a continuous variable measured at the interval or ratio level. Let us assume that the distribution is symmetrical, and that it includes a very large number of cases. By using the procedures discussed earlier in this chapter, we can calculate its mean ($\bar{x}$) and standard deviation ($s$). Once we know the values of these two statistics for our distribution, we can use them to divide the area under the curve into segments. Consider figure 7.15. Using the mean as the point of departure, we can locate the points on the horizontal axis corresponding to ($\bar{x} + s$), ($\bar{x} + 2s$), ($\bar{x} - s$), and ($\bar{x} - 2s$). If we draw a line perpendicular to the horizontal axis at the points we have located, we will divide the area under the normal curve into segments.

**Figure 7.15  A Normal Curve**

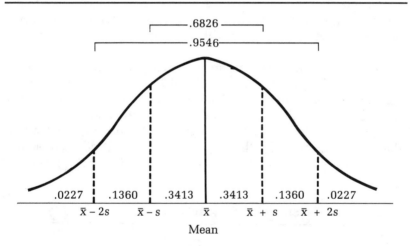

It is a special property of the normal curve that, of the total area under the curve, the proportion included between $\bar{x}$ and $\bar{x} + s$ is always .3413; the proportion between $\bar{x} + s$ and $\bar{x} + 2s$ is always .1360; and the proportion beyond $\bar{x} + 2s$ is always .0227.[3] Since the normal curve is symmetrical, the proportions of the area under the curve contained in corresponding segments below the mean ($\bar{x}$ to $\bar{x} - s$, $\bar{x} - s$ to $\bar{x} - 2s$, and beyond $\bar{x} - 2s$) are the same as those above the mean. Thus, 68.26 percent of the area under the curve (.3413 + .3413 × 100 = 68.26%) falls within one standard deviation of the mean, or between $\bar{x} - s$ and $\bar{x} + s$.

Using the same general principle we have been discussing, it is possible to construct a **standard normal curve** with a mean of 0 and a standard deviation of 1.0, as shown in figure 7.16, and to express the deviation from the mean of any actual score in a normal distribution in terms of standard or **z-scores.** We compute the z-score for a given raw score by subtracting the mean ($\bar{x}$) from the given raw score (x) and dividing by the standard deviation (s):

$$z = \frac{x - \bar{x}}{s}.$$

As indicated by the proportions between the dotted perpendicular lines under the normal curve in figure 7.16, 68.26 percent (.3413 + .3413 × 100 = 68.26 percent) of the area under the curve and, hence, 68.26 percent of the scores in the distribution fall within one standard deviation above and below the mean, or between points on the z axis of z = – 1.0 and z = + 1.0; and 95.46 percent of the area (and scores) falls between z = – 2.0 and z = + 2.0, etc. To put it the other way around, slightly less than 5 percent of the area (and scores) fall outside the area of the normal curve between z = – 2.0 and z = + 2.0.

Z is a continuous variable and can in principle assume infinitely many values between 0 and 1.0, 1.0 and 2.0, and so on. In practice, it seldom exceeds a value of 4.0. The table of z-scores (appendix B) permits you to determine the proportion of area under the normal curve (and, therefore, the proportion of scores in the distribution) between the mean and z, as well as the proportion of area beyond z corresponding to any z value between 0 and 4.0. The proportions of area under

**Figure 7.16  The Standard Normal Curve**

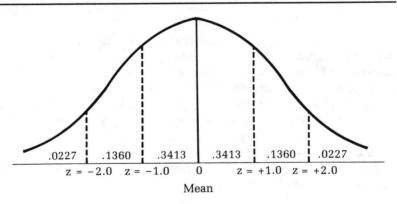

the curve included between the mean and any particular z-score are constant for any normal curve, regardless of the actual value of the mean and standard deviation of the distribution. Thus, z is an expression, in terms of standard units of deviation, of the area under the normal curve between it and the mean.

Suppose that the FBI has given a written entrance test to 3,410 applicants for entry level positions with the agency. You are charged with the responsibility of analyzing the scores. In doing so, you discover that the scores the applicants received on their tests range from 125 to 765 and are approximately normally distributed around a mean score of 445, with a standard deviation of 95. If one of the applicants writes you inquiring about her score on the test and how her performance compared to the others who took it, you could look up that person's test paper and determine that she received a score of 658. What will you tell her about the place of her score in the distribution of scores?

Actually, it will be very convenient for you to transform the raw score of 658 into a z-score, by using the following calculations:

$$z = \frac{x - \bar{x}}{s} = \frac{658 - 445}{95} = \frac{213}{95} = 2.24.$$

Consulting the z-score table in appendix B, you discover that the area under the standard normal curve beyond z = 2.24 (in column A) is .0125 (in column C). Hence, you can tell her that she scored in the top 2 percent of the applicants.

You might also use the z-score formula to set a passing score for the test. Suppose you were told that there were 341 actual openings in the FBI for this group of applicants. This is 10 percent of the applicant pool. You want to know what score on the test a person would have to receive in order to score in the top 10 percent of the applicants. What z-score corresponds with an area beyond z of .10? Going to the z-score table we look in column C until we find .10. Locating .1003 (which is the closest we can come) in column C, we read the corresponding z-score, z = 1.28 in column A. We now know the z-score which determines approximately the top 10 percent of scores. Hence,

$$1.28 = \frac{x - 445}{95}.$$

Solving this equation for x we have:

$$95\,(1.28) = x - 445$$
$$445 + 121.6 = x$$
$$566.6 = x$$

About 10 percent of the applicants received scores above 566, so you might set the passing grade as a score of 567. Z-scores are of considerable utility when questions about the location of one score relative to others in the distribution are the researcher's concern.

## Notes

1. This scale was presented by Jerry L. Simmons in *Deviants* (Berkeley, Calif.: Glendessary Press, 1969), p. 32. For a further discussion of scales at the ordinal level, see William J. Goode and Paul K. Hatt, *Methods in Social Research* (New York: McGraw-Hill, 1952).
2. See Hubert M. Blalock, Jr., *Social Statistics*, 2nd ed. (New York: McGraw-Hill, 1972), pp. 14–15.
3. Note that, as we might expect, if we sum the proportions on one or the other side of the mean, we get .5000, and if we sum the proportions on both sides of the mean, we get 1.000.

## Review Questions

1. What is the principal difference between descriptive and inferential statistics?
2. How do continuous and discrete variables differ?
3. What are the differences among nominal, ordinal, interval and ratio measurements?
4. What is a frequency distribution?
5. What are the most frequently used measures of central tendency and dispersion in a distribution, how are they arrived at, and what are their principal differences?
6. Which measures of central tendency and dispersion are appropriate for distributions of nominal data? of ordinal data? of interval data? of ratio data?
7. How do the various types of quantiles differ and how are they arrived at?
8. How do skewed and normal distributions differ?
9. How do unimodal and multimodal distributions differ?
10. Are all unimodal distributions normal distributions? Why or why not?
11. How does a normal distribution for data on a particular variable differ from a standard normal curve?
12. What are z-scores?

# *Exercises*

Use the following hypothetical data for the exercises below.

| Subject | Sex | Number of Arrests | Highest Level of Education Achieved* | | *Code | Category |
|---------|-----|-------------------|-------------------------------------|--|-------|----------|
| 1 | M | 2 | 3 | | | |
| 2 | M | 4 | 1 | | | |
| 3 | F | 5 | 1 | | | |
| 4 | F | 3 | 4 | | | |
| 5 | M | 1 | 4 | | | |
| 6 | F | 3 | 1 | | | |
| 7 | M | 2 | 4 | | | |
| 8 | F | 0 | 6 | | | |
| 9 | M | 3 | 2 | | | |
| 10 | F | 4 | 2 | | 1 | gradeschool or less |
| 11 | M | 5 | 4 | | | |
| 12 | F | 3 | 6 | | 2 | junior high school |
| 13 | M | 2 | 5 | | | |
| 14 | M | 1 | 1 | | 3 | high school |
| 15 | F | 4 | 1 | | 4 | community college |
| 16 | M | 6 | 1 | | | |
| 17 | F | 3 | 3 | | 5 | 4-year college |
| 18 | M | 4 | 5 | | 6 | more than 4-year college |
| 19 | F | 2 | 4 | | | |
| 20 | M | 3 | 4 | | | |

1. At what level of measurement is each of the variables measured?
2. Are the variables discrete or continuous?
3. Calculate appropriate measures of central tendency and dispersion for the distributions of each variable.
4. Construct a bar graph frequency distribution for each of the variables.
5. Are any of the distributions normal distributions?
6. Are any of the distributions skewed? multimodal?
7. Calculate quartile values for the number-of-arrests variable.
8. Calculate the z-score equivalent of the mean score, the lowest score, and the highest score in the number-of-arrests distribution.

# 8

*Descriptive Statistics:*
*Examining Relationships*
*Between Two or More Variables*

As we saw in chapter 7, frequency distributions and measures of central tendency and dispersion are useful when a researcher wishes to describe or analyze data concerning a single variable. Often, however, the researcher is interested in testing a hypothesis asserting a causal relationship between two or more variables. For example, is length of sentence related to recidivism? Is marital status related to support for police? Does changing the law produce changes in behavior addressed by the law? Answering such questions requires the researcher to consider at least two variables simultaneously. In this chapter we will consider three approaches to this problem: comparing frequency distributions, cross-tabulation, and correlation.

## *Comparing Frequency Distributions*

Suppose we are interested in whether there is a relationship between type of offense and sex of offender in a particular population of adult offenders, say the 26 adults convicted of petty theft, assault, or drug possession in the Horsetail Switch county court in the last six months. Clearly, a frequency distribution of the sex of these offenders alone would not give us sufficient information to answer this question. Nor would a frequency distribution of the type of offense. To find out if there is a connection between these two variables, we must find a way of considering both of the variables at once.

One strategy that could be employed is to construct two bar-graph frequency distributions of the type of offense, including only males in one and only females in the other, and compare them. Suppose the two graphs look like those in figure 8.1. A major difference in the two distributions is immediately apparent. The modal category for males is assault, while the modal category for females is petty theft.

Is there a relationship between the two variables? The answer may not be obvious, but generally speaking, if there are no differences between the distributions, there is no relationship between the variables; if there are differences, there may be a relationship (although not necessarily a causal one).

## Figure 8.1  Frequency Distributions of Type of Offense by Sex of Offender

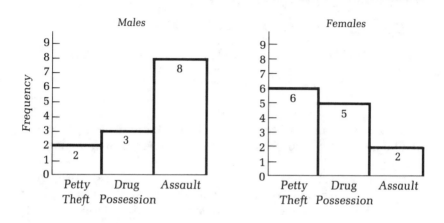

Why do differences in distributions suggest a relationship be- tween the variables? Consider what we have done in constructing the distributions. In each distribution, we have held the sex variable con- stant (i.e., we used only one value of the sex variable) and examined the distribution of the type-of-offense variable *within* that particular value (male or female) of the sex variable. We proceeded in this way (rather than holding the type-of-offense variable constant and exam- ining the distribution of the sex variable within each of these values) because we assumed that sex was the **independent** (causal) **variable** and type-of-offense was the **dependent** (effect) **variable**. Another way of saying this is that we constructed the distributions to answer the question: If we know what sex an offender is, what do we know about the type of offense he or she has committed? When, in comparing the two distributions, the data indicate that what we know about type of offense is different, depending upon the sex of the offender, we have some reason to believe that sex is related to type of offense. In our ex- ample, if we know the offender is male, we would be right 8 out of 13 times if we said that the person committed assault. If we know that the offender is female, we would be right 6 out of 13 times if we said that the offense committed was petty theft. This difference suggests that there is a relationship (though clearly not a perfect one) between sex and type of offense. Note, in this case, that both of the variables are measured at the nominal level and that we focused our attention on the modal type of offense category.

The basic idea of using differences between distributions as indicators of relationships between variables can be extended to include variables measured at other levels and to other summary statistics concerning distributions. With variables measured at the ordinal level, we might look for differences in the rank order of persons on the dependent variable, given particular ranks on the independent variable. For example, do persons of different social class (the independent variable) rank differently in their degree of support for the local police? For variables measured at the interval or ratio level, we could look for differences in the mean or standard deviation of two distributions. For example, is there a difference in mean age at time of first conviction for males and females?

These procedures have their uses, and they do help us answer some of the questions we might have. Nevertheless, the more frequency distributions you have to "eyeball" in order to make a judgment about the existence of a relationship, the more difficult it becomes. If you were dealing with two variables, each of which had four or five values, this method might be highly impractical. Fortunately, cross-tabulation provides a much simpler and more comprehensible alternative for handling many of these situations.

## *Fundamentals of Cross-Tabulation* ─────────

A **cross-tabulation** can be thought of as the intersection of two frequency distributions. Cross-tabulating data on two variables permits us to see relatively easily whether or not they are related to each other. The hypothetical data on sex and type of offense will be used again to illustrate the construction and uses of cross-tabulation.

### Constructing a Cross-Tabulation

The first step in constructing a cross-tabulation is to create a two-dimensional data grid, placing the values of the sex variable across the top of the grid and the values of the type-of-offense variable down the side (see table 8.1). We have now created a table, called a **contingency table,** that has two separate *columns* (corresponding to the two values of the sex variable) and three separate *rows* (corresponding to the three values of the type-of-offense variable). The spaces in the table defined by the intersections of the columns and rows are called **cells.** Note that we could have placed the type-of-offense variable across the top and the sex variable down the side, thereby creating a table with three columns and two rows. In this case, too, the order in which the males and females are listed could have been reversed, and the order of the types of offense could have been changed. The choice among these options is essentially arbitrary, because the variables with which we are dealing are measured at the nominal level. For a variable measured at the ordinal, interval, or ratio level, the values should be placed either in ascending or descending order on the grid.

**Table 8.1   Type of Offense by Sex of Offender**

| Type of Offense | Sex of Offender | |
|---|---|---|
| | Male | Female |
| Petty Theft | cell 1 | cell 2 |
| Drug Possession | cell 3 | cell 4 |
| Assault | cell 5 | cell 6 |

The next step is to place the data into the grid space by going back to the original data sheets or to the computer where the information has been stored and searching for the various combinations of the two variables represented by Horsetail Switch convicts. Individual A, who is a male and was convicted of petty theft, would be counted in the cell of the table corresponding to the intersection of the male column and the petty theft row. For this table, that means the individual is counted in the upper left-hand cell—cell 1. If the next person is a female convicted of assault, we find the female column and the assault row, or cell 6. If each person in the population of offenders was included, the table would look like table 8.2. The numbers that appear in each of the cells are called **cell frequencies.** Here, they indicate the number of persons in our population who possess the corresponding combinations of values of the two variables. Note that the two columns of the table correspond to the two frequency distributions presented at the beginning of this discussion.

We can now add the cell frequencies that appear in each of the rows and in each of the columns to get the results shown in table 8.3. The row sums 8, 8, and 10 are called **row marginal frequencies;** the column sums 13 and 13 are called **column marginal frequencies.** The number 26 in the lower right-hand corner of the table is the total number of cases included. This total (often referred to as n, as in n = 26) can be computed for any table by summing either the row or the column marginal frequencies. Because these two sums must be equal,

## Table 8.2   Type of Offense by Sex of Offender

| Type of Offense | Male | Female |
|---|---|---|
| Petty Theft | 2 | 6 |
| Drug Possession | 3 | 5 |
| Assault | 8 | 2 |

Sex of Offender

comparing them provides a simple (though not fail-safe) check on the accuracy of our table construction procedures and calculations. If the marginal row and column sums are different, a mistake has been made in one or more of the cell entries or in the additions of those figures. Furthermore, if the table total (n) is not equal to the total number of cases studied, some cases were either left out or counted more than once in the process of generating the cross-tabulation. Of course, any mistakes must be corrected.

## Table 8.3   Type of Offense by Sex of Offender

| Type of Offense | Male | Female | Total |
|---|---|---|---|
| Petty Theft | 2 | 6 | 8 |
| Drug Possession | 3 | 5 | 8 |
| Assault | 8 | 2 | 10 |
| Total | 13 | 13 | n = 26 |

Sex of Offender

We are now in a position to observe other connections between frequency distributions and tables. The row marginal frequencies constitute a frequency distribution of the types-of-offense variable while the column marginal frequencies are a frequency distribution of the sex variable. Hence, a byproduct of constructing a cross-tabulation of the sex and types-of-offense variables is the frequency distribution of each of the two variables. Again, this fact can be used to check the table, since the frequency distribution of each of the two variables must be the same as its respective marginal frequencies. If either is not, the process of cross-tabulation must be re-examined in order to correct the mistakes which have been made. Finally, the alert reader will have noted that the male and female columns of the table are the frequency distributions we constructed in figure 8.1, this time expressed in numerical frequencies rather than as bars in a bar graph.

It should not be inferred from our discussion of the connections between frequency distributions and cross-tabulation, however, that marginal frequencies determine cell frequencies. Consider table 8.4, whose marginal frequencies are specified, but whose cells are empty. Note that the marginal frequencies corresponding to a particular cell do impose some limits on that cell frequency. For example, the smaller of the two marginal frequencies corresponding to a given cell is the highest frequency that could appear in that cell. Still, many combinations of different frequencies could be entered in the cells of the table without changing the marginal frequencies. Therefore, knowing the frequency distribution of each of the two variables above does not tell us anything about the relationship between them.

**Table 8.4   Type of Offense by Sex of Offender**

| Type of Offense | Sex of Offender | | |
|---|---|---|---|
|  | *Male* | *Female* | *Total* |
| Petty Theft |  |  | 8 |
| Drug Possession |  |  | 8 |
| Assault |  |  | 10 |
| Total | 13 | 13 | n = 26 |

The final step in the construction of a cross-tabulation is creating a title for the table, which should describe briefly but completely what the table includes. Generally, the title should contain at least the names of the variables used to construct the table. In most circumstances, especially when the text that accompanies the table is not very explicit, it is advisable to include a brief description of the person (or cases) described in the table. For example, the tables illustrating this discussion are entitled "Type of Offense by Sex of Offender."

To be somewhat more descriptive, a phrase such as "Horsetail Switch County Court, May 1–30, 1986" might have been added to the title. Good titles specify clearly and completely what the cross-tabulation represents. An incomplete, vague, or missing title can be seriously misleading, since the reader can only infer what the table concerns.

All cross-tabulations are constructed according to the basic principles we have just illustrated; however, a few complications that may be encountered need to be considered.

## Collapsing Categories

Suppose we have a variable that we call "citizens' evaluation of police services." We have operationalized (measured) it on an ordinal scale of seven categories (values), beginning with (1) "police have provided excellent service" and ending with (7) "police have provided very poor service." We wish to examine the relationship of this variable to another variable (e.g., age) that we have operationalized with many more categories. In analyzing and presenting these data, we could construct a table having seven columns (for the seven values of the evaluation-of-police-services variable) and as many rows as we had ages in our study group. If the age variable ranges from 21 through 70 (having, therefore, 50 values) and there are seven values for the evaluation of services variable, a "7-by-50" table would be produced. It would have 7 × 50 = 350 cells, requiring a very large space for presentation. Making sense of the data might be very difficult, either because there are so many cells or because there might be numerous empty cells or cells containing very low frequencies, especially if we have relatively few subjects in our study.

Given these circumstances, the presentation of the data could be simplified by **collapsing categories.** By combining (collapsing) two or more of the original values of a given variable into a single new category, we can reduce the total number of cells in a table. For example, our evaluations variable could reasonably be treated as a three-category variable rather than a seven-category variable. The first two categories of our original scheme could be collapsed and include every person who scores either (1) or (2) (a "positive evaluation" score) on our scale. The next three categories of the original scheme might be collapsed to form a "neutral evaluation" category, and the remaining two categories could form a "negative evaluation" category. Now, the evaluation variable has three values rather than the original seven. Note that this is only one of several possible ways of collapsing categories for this variable.

The variable from which we can gain most by collapsing categories, however, is age. Again, the investigator must decide whether to collapse categories and, if so, into how many new values. The 50 values of the age variable could be reduced to two values; reducing it to one value—that is, putting everybody in the same age category—would, of course, be useless. We might create one new category of ages 21 through 45, and another of ages 46 through 70, or, we could create three new categories, or four, or five, or ten. If we decided on a three-category division of the evaluation variable and a five-category scheme for the age variable, we would then produce a 3-by-5 table that has 3 × 5 = 15 cells—a much more comprehensible table than one containing 350 cells.

What is at stake in deciding whether or not to collapse categories? Obviously, some possibly important detail is sacrificed if our variable is measured with a given number of possible values and the data are then analyzed and presented with fewer values. If, for example, there is a large difference between the evaluations of 35-year-olds and 38-year-olds, and we have lumped these two age groups into one new category, the difference will not show up in our analysis. One might also contend that some time and effort was wasted by measuring our variables in such detail if only a few more general categories were to be used anyway. Although there is no point in measuring a variable with greater detail and precision than is justified by the purposes at hand, it is also true that—short of doing another study—the researcher will never have a greater level of detail available for analysis than that recorded originally. In analyzing the data, the researcher can always reduce the number of categories in the analysis, but it is never possible to increase the number of categories. Within reason, then, the original raw data might deliberately be collected in more detail than the researcher expects to use for the analysis. If, in analyzing the data, the researcher encounters unexpected or otherwise intriguing results, the more detailed data may come in handy as he pursues these leads.

How can you decide which categories to collapse? You can, of course, simply try several different ways of collapsing the data on a trial-and-error basis. However, this procedure is only acceptable as an exploratory strategy. It is especially important, when choosing to collapse categories, not to select for presentation only the results of those collapsing strategies that make the strongest case for the author's point of view without informing the reader of the exploratory nature of the analysis. As a general rule, the researcher should decide on a collapsing plan *before* analyzing the data and apply as much reason, common sense, and ethical judgment as possible throughout the process.

A number of factors might be considered in deciding which categories to collapse. First, you could locate seemingly "natural" divisions of a variable; for example, an age variable might be broken down into categories corresponding to infancy, childhood, adolescence, adulthood, and old age—if those divisions make sense with respect to the problem being investigated. Second, divisions could be based on the categories included in a theoretical proposition or hypothesis, such as "middle-class people are more likely to support the police than are upper-class or working-class people." If the social class variable were operationalized in terms of annual income, it would be reasonable to break these data into three categories corresponding to the three social classes mentioned in the hypothesis. Third, by examining the frequency distribution of the variable, the original categories could be combined so that a sufficiently large number of cases is represented in each category to permit meaningful analysis. Caution is in order here. Categories should not be collapsed in a way that violates the theoretical substance underlying the study, even though they may be expedient. Finally, in the absence of a better rationale, arbitrary collapsing decisions can be made. Many investigators, for example, divide the age range into five- or ten-year intervals (e.g., 0–5, 6–10, 11–15 . . ., or 0–10, 11–20, 21–30 . . .), and proceed using those categories in their cross-tabulations.

Some or all of these considerations may be weighed in any decision to collapse categories in a particular way. You should remember, however, that the way data are collapsed may well influence the results which are produced. Consequently, collapsing should always be done honestly and in a way that is consistent with the variable categories implicitly or explicitly indicated by the research hypothesis.

## Use of Percentages in Cross-Tabulation

The cross-tabulations discussed so far have contained raw numbers (frequency counts) in the cells. In many cases it is easier to interpret the data if cell frequencies are converted to percentages; however, special complications may arise when converting to percentages.

The basic complication in using percentages in cross-tabulations becomes apparent if we attempt to answer the question: What base numbers shall we use in calculating the percentages? Consider the cross-tabulation in table 8.5 of data concerning the variables "position on police force" and "annual salary." Suppose we wanted to convert the cell frequencies in the table to percentages. The difficulty is that we could do so using three different base numbers, resulting in three different percentage figures for any given cell of the table.

**Table 8.5    Annual Salary by Position on Police Force**

| Position on Police Force | Annual Salary | | |
| --- | --- | --- | --- |
| | Below $15,000 | $15,000 and Above | Total |
| Sergeant | 30 | 60 | 90 |
| Patrol Officer | 86 | 24 | 110 |
| Total | 116 | 84 | n = 200 |

First, we could express each of the cell frequencies as a percentage of the total number of cases (n) included in the table and produce table 8.6. Percentages based on the total sample are useful to describe the proportion of cases falling into each of the categories of the table variables. Thus, table 8.6 indicates that 43 percent of all of the subjects studied are patrol officers earning under $15,000 per year, 30 percent are sergeants earning more than $15,000 per year, and so on. The sum of the cell percentages calculated in this way always equals 100 percent.

**Table 8.6    Annual Salary by Position on Police Force**

| Position on Police Force | Annual Salary | | |
| --- | --- | --- | --- |
| | Below $15,000 | $15,000 and Above | Total |
| Sergeant | 15% | 30% | 45% |
| Patrol Officer | 43% | 12% | 55% |
| Total | 58% | 42% | 100% |
| | | | n = 200 |

The two remaining possibilities for converting cell frequencies to percentages are to express them as percentages of the row or the column marginal frequencies. The choice between these alternatives is based on which of the two variables we have defined as the independent, or causal, variable in the research hypothesis.

You will recall that an independent (causal) variable must precede a dependent variable in time. Our analysis, then, should address the question: Given a certain value of the independent variable, what happens to the dependent variable? To answer this question, the cell frequencies should be converted to percentages with each value of the independent variable treated separately. Then the percentage distribution of the dependent variable within any one category of the independent variable can be compared to the percentage distribution of the dependent variable within any other category of the independent variable. If the independent variable forms the columns of the table, the column marginal frequencies are used to convert cell frequencies to percentages. If the independent variable forms the rows of the table, the row marginal frequencies are used. This practice is referred to as **percentaging in the direction of the independent variable.**

Consider again table 8.5. It seems reasonable to consider "position on the police force" the independent variable, since salary clearly does not "cause" position. The appropriate strategy, therefore, is to use the row marginal frequencies (90 and 110) as the base numbers to convert the cell frequencies in each row to percentages, as in table 8.7. Note that the sum of the percentages in each row (but not each column) equals 100 percent. This table permits us to compare positions on the police force in terms of the percentage of patrol officers whose salaries are in a particular range with the percentage of sergeants who earn salaries in the same range. Thus, while $30/90$ or 33 percent of the sergeants earn less than $15,000 per year, $86/110$ or 78 percent of the patrol officers earn less than $15,000 per year, and so on. Note that, in "reading" the table, we compare categories in the direction opposite from the one we used in calculating the percent-

**Table 8.7   Annual Salary by Position on Police Force**

| Position on Police Force | Annual Salary | | Total |
| --- | --- | --- | --- |
| | Below $15,000 | $15,000 and Above | |
| Sergeant | 33% | 67% | 100%<br>(n = 90) |
| Patrol Officer | 78% | 22% | 100%<br>(n = 110) |

ages. If the row marginal frequencies were used as the base for percentaging (as they were in our example), we compare figures in the same column. If the column marginal frequencies are used to calculate percentages, we would compare figures in the same row. As we might expect, the table as a whole shows that sergeants tend to earn more than patrol officers. In short, the table depicts a concomitant variation between these two variables; that is, that annual salary varies with position on the police force.

By observing that position on police force precedes salary in time and that the two variables do vary concomitantly, we have satisfied two of the three conditions for making causal inferences, as discussed in chapter 3. The third condition, eliminating other causal factors, remains to be met. If the researcher has used an experimental design to generate the data, considerable control has been exercised over possible alternative causal variables by the structure of the research design. In other cases, the analyst may *assume*, on the basis of common sense and in the absence of other data or controls, that the relationship revealed by cross-tabulation may be genuine and not spurious. This is, as we have seen, a risky assumption at best. In still other cases, especially in survey research, the investigator can examine the effect of a third variable (referred to as a **control variable** or **test factor**) on the relationship between the two variables that were the original focus of the analysis. This additional analysis of the data may assist the researcher in eliminating alternative causal variables, thereby strengthening his argument that the relationship between variables is causal. This procedure is called **elaboration analysis.**

## *Elaboration Analysis*

We can begin our discussion of elaboration analysis by considering once again the relationship we have observed between position on police force and salary. Suppose we are confronted by a skeptic who has examined table 8.7 but contends that, because females tend to occupy lower positions in an organization or to earn less than males even when they hold identical positions, sex is the real cause of the salary differentials observed. How could we test the contribution of the sex variable to the apparent relationship between position on the police force and annual salary?

By constructing two separate cross-tabulations, one for each value of the sex variable (male, female), we can consider all three variables at once. Suppose that tables 8.8 and 8.9 were the result. These tables are called **first-order partial tables** because each represents a

**Table 8.8    Annual Salary by Position on Police Force: Males**

| Position on Police Force | Annual Salary | | |
|---|---|---|---|
| | Below $15,000 | $15,000 and Above | Total |
| Sergeant | 14 | 46 | 60 |
| Patrol Officer | 58 | 12 | 70 |
| Total | 72 | 58 | n = 130 |

part of the original relationship and bears the following relationships to the original table 8.5 (called a **zero-order table**):

1. The sum of the total number of cases in the two partial tables (130 + 70) equals 200, the total number of cases in the zero-order table.
2. Each of the cell frequencies in the zero-order table can be recovered by adding the two corresponding cell frequencies in the partial tables (e.g., 28 + 58 = 86, and 46 + 14 = 60).
3. Similarly, the zero-order marginal frequencies can be obtained by adding the two corresponding marginal frequencies in the partial tables (e.g., 60 + 30 = 90; 58 + 26 = 84).

These relationships occur whenever first-order partial tables are constructed from the same data used to construct a zero-order table. If the zero-order table cannot be reconstructed by combining the partial ta-

**Table 8.9    Annual Salary by Position on Police Force: Females**

| Position on Police Force | Annual Salary | | |
|---|---|---|---|
| | Below $15,000 | $15,000 and Above | Total |
| Sergeant | 16 | 14 | 30 |
| Patrol Officer | 28 | 12 | 40 |
| Total | 44 | 26 | n = 70 |

bles in this way, a mistake has occurred; the reasons for any discrepancies must be sought and the tables corrected before proceeding with the analysis.

Again, we can convert the cell frequencies to percentages to facilitate interpreting the data, using the row marginal frequencies as in tables 8.10 and 8.11. In both tables, the proportion of patrol officers in the "below $15,000" category is greater than the proportion of sergeants in the same salary category, and the proportion of sergeants in the "$15,000 and above" salary category is greater than the proportion of patrol officers in the same salary category. Hence, the same general pattern or relationship between position on police force and annual salary found in the zero-order table holds for each of the partial tables as well. In elaboration analysis, this result is called **replication**.

Our skeptic can take some consolation in the data, however, since the relationship between these two variables seems to be considerably stronger among males than among females. That is, when the differences in percentages for sergeants and patrol officers within a given salary category are compared in the two tables, these differences are larger for males than for females. For example, in the "below $15,000" category for males the difference is 83 − 23 = 60 percent, while for females in the same category, the difference is 70 − 53 = 17 percent. It appears that sex is a factor here as well.

**Table 8.10   Annual Salary by Position on Police Force: Males**

| Position on Police Force | Annual Salary | | |
| --- | --- | --- | --- |
| | Below $15,000 | $15,000 and Above | Total |
| Sergeant | 23% | 77% | 100% (n = 60) |
| Patrol Officer | 83% | 17% | 100% (n = 70) |

The procedure we have just used to "test" the effect of the sex variable on the relationship between position on police force and salary can be repeated with all of the possible causal variables for which the researcher has data, in order to eliminate as many of them as possible. If the general relationship observed in the original zero-order cross-tabulation is observed in all the partial tables that are con-

**Table 8.11    Annual Salary by Position on Police Force: Females**

| Position on Police Force | Annual Salary | | |
| --- | --- | --- | --- |
| | Below $15,000 | $15,000 and Above | Total |
| Sergeant | 53% | 47% | 100% (n = 30) |
| Patrol Officer | 70% | 30% | 100% (n = 40) |

structed, we can tentatively infer that the independent variable is at least one of the causal factors involved.

## Explanation

Not all partial analyses result in the confirmation of the relationships observed in the zero-order table, however. In some cases, the relationship between the two zero-order variables will be substantially reduced, or even disappear, in *all* of the partial tables. Two accounts can be offered for this result in a partial analysis. The crucial factor which distinguishes between these two accounts is the time sequence of the variable. First, if the test factor precedes the independent variable, the zero-order relationship is called **spurious.** That is, what appears to be a causal relationship between the two original variables is a result of the causal relationship between a third variable (the test factor, which occurs before the independent variable) and each of the two original variables. This might be diagrammed as in figure 8.2, where x is the assumed independent variable, y the assumed dependent variable, and t the third variable (test factor). We are justified in concluding that the original relationship is spurious if the test factor (t) either precedes or coincides with the independent variable and precedes the dependent variable in time. In such cases, the test factor is said to **explain** the apparent but spurious relationship between x and y in the zero-order table.

**Figure 8.2**

## Interpretation

The second circumstance in which the original relationship is substantially reduced or disappears in all of the partial analyses occurs when the test factor intervenes (comes between) the x variable and the y variable in time. In this case, the results can be interpreted to mean that a developmental sequence exists in the relationship between the variables. This can be diagrammed as in figure 8.3.

**Figure 8.3**

$$x \longrightarrow t \longrightarrow y$$

When the test factor intervenes, the result is called an **interpretation** and t is called an **intervening variable**.

Again, the determination of whether the analysis has resulted in an explanation or an interpretation is entirely dependent on the time sequence of the variables—the numbers or percentages in the corresponding cells of the tables could be identical. Note further that in both explanation and interpretation, the test factor must be related to both of the original variables. To be sure that this latter condition has been met, we would have to construct two additional cross-tabulations, to determine that there is a relationship between t and x and t and y.

## Specification

It is also possible that when a test factor is introduced, the original relationship between the two variables may be substantially reduced or disappear in some but not all of the partial tables. When our analysis produces these results, we can specify those categories of the test factor within which the original relationship still holds and those in which it does not. This is called **specification,** for obvious reasons. We are justified in calling these results "specification" only if the test factor is not related to at least one of the original variables. If the test factor was related to both of the original variables, we would have an instance of either explanation or interpretation.

## No Apparent Relationship in Zero-Order Table

When the zero-order table shows no apparent relationship between two variables, a partial analysis may still reveal that a relationship between the original variables does exist within some or all of the categories of the test factor used to construct the partial tables. In cases of this type, the relationship between the two original variables within some categories of the test factor is the opposite of the relationship between the two original variables within other categories of the test factor. These opposing relationships tend to mask or cancel each other when combined in the zero-order table.[1]

We have summarized our discussion of elaboration analysis in figure 8.4, where x is an independent variable, y is a dependent variable, and t is a third, test variable.

## Some Examples of Elaboration Analysis

Suppose that we had conducted a questionnaire survey of the relationship between ethnicity and support for the police. We have measured the nominal ethnicity variable by asking our respondents to indicate in which of the following ethnic groups they belong: Black; White; Hispanic; Asiatic; American Indian; and Other. Moreover, the ordinal support-for-the-police variable has been operationalized as a five-point scale: (1) very supportive; (2) supportive; (3) neutral; (4) unsupportive; and (5) very unsupportive.

We hypothesize that ethnicity is the cause of support for the police; that is, ethnicity is our independent variable and support for the police is our dependent variable. As a first step to discovering whether a relationship exists between these two variables, we construct a cross-tabulation. Because there are so few respondents in some categories of both variables, we decide to collapse categories. We make our original six-category ethnicity variable a new three-category variable, taking black and white as two of the categories and using Other to combine the four categories of Hispanic, Asiatic, American Indian and Other to create the third category. For the support variable, the original categories 1 and 2 are collapsed into one new category, categories 4 and 5 into a second new category, leaving the original category 3 the same in our new category system.

Suppose that when we placed our data into the cross-tabulation, it looked like table 8.12.

We can now convert the cell frequencies in the table to percentages. Since ethnicity is our presumed independent variable we use the column marginal frequencies for the conversion. Our table would look like table 8.13 (with percents rounded to the nearest whole percent).

These data suggest that blacks are predominantly unsupportive of the police while whites are predominantly supportive. The others are about evenly divided in their level of support for the police. Hence,

# Figure 8.4

| If in the zero-order table | and | In the partial tables | and | The time sequence of the variables is | then | The tentative conclusion (inference) is |
|---|---|---|---|---|---|---|
| $x \rightarrow y$* | | $x \rightarrow y$ (in all partials) | | x before y | | x causes y |
| $x \rightarrow y$ | | $x \nrightarrow y$ [†] | | t before x before y | | Explanation:[‡] x not a cause of y; t explains relationship between x and y |
| $x \rightarrow y$ | | $x \nrightarrow y$ | | x before t before y | | Interpretation:[‡] x, t and y form a causal chain; x causes t causes y; t interprets relationship between x and y |
| $x \rightarrow y$ | | $x \rightarrow y$ (in some but not all partials) | | x before y; t occurs before y | | Specification:[§] t specifies causal relationship between x and y; x causes y only in some categories of t |
| $x \nrightarrow y$ | | $x \rightarrow y$ (in all partials, but direction of relationship differs in different partials) | | x before y; t occurs before y | | Relationships in partials cancel each other |

*Arrows read "is related to"
†Slashed arrows read "is not related to"
‡Assumes $t \rightarrow x$ and $t \rightarrow y$
§Assumes $t \rightarrow x$ or $t \rightarrow y$

**Table 8.12   Support for the Police by Ethnicity**

|                          | Ethnicity |       |       |             |
| ------------------------ | --------- | ----- | ----- | ----------- |
| Support for Police       | Black     | White | Other | Total       |
| Supportive               | 100       | 400   | 250   | 750         |
| Neutral                  | 150       | 100   | 150   | 400         |
| Unsupportive             | 400       | 200   | 250   | 850         |
| Total                    | 650       | 700   | 650   | n = 2,000   |

there appears to be a relationship between ethnicity and police support:

$$\text{Ethnicity} \longrightarrow \text{Support for Police}$$

Now suppose that we have also gathered data about whether our respondents have ever reported a crime to the police. We think that this might have a great deal to do with support for the police. Hence, we decide to perform an elaboration analysis. We divide our respondents into two categories (those who have and those who have not reported a crime to the police) and construct a cross-tabulation of our

**Table 8.13   Percent Support for the Police by Ethnicity**

|                    | Ethnicity          |                    |                    |
| ------------------ | ------------------ | ------------------ | ------------------ |
| Support for Police | Black (n = 650)    | White (n = 700)    | Other (n = 650)    |
| Supportive         | 15%                | 57%                | 38%                |
| Neutral            | 23%                | 14%                | 23%                |
| Unsupportive       | 62%                | 29%                | 38%                |
| Total              | 100%               | 100%               | 99%*               |

*Totals not equal to 100% are due to rounding error.

**Table 8.14   Percent Support for the Police by Ethnicity and Report of Crime**

| Support for Police | Reported Crime | | | Never Reported Crime | | |
|---|---|---|---|---|---|---|
| | Black (n = 325) | White (n = 350) | Other (n = 325) | Black (n = 325) | White (n = 350) | Other (n = 325) |
| Supportive | 16% | 59% | 38% | 15% | 56% | 38% |
| Neutral | 22% | 14% | 23% | 24% | 14% | 23% |
| Unsupportive | 62% | 27% | 38% | 61% | 30% | 39% |
| Total | 100% | 100% | 99% | 100% | 100% | 100% |

original two variables for each of these categories. Suppose the data looked like those in table 8.14.

In this case the relationship we observed in the original zero-order table (table 8.13) holds in both of the partial tables. Hence, reporting a crime to the police does not appear to affect the relationship between ethnicity and support. We are then still left with:

*Ethnicity* ⟶ *Support for Police*

But suppose the data appeared as in table 8.15. In this case, the relationship between ethnicity and support for the police observed in

**Table 8.15   Percent Support for the Police by Ethnicity and Report of Crime**

| Support For Police | Reported Crime | | | Never Reported Crime | | |
|---|---|---|---|---|---|---|
| | Black (n = 290) | White (n = 270) | Other (n = 290) | Black (n = 360) | White (n = 430) | Other (n = 360) |
| Supportive | 31% | 33% | 34% | 3% | 72% | 42% |
| Neutral | 34% | 33% | 31% | 14% | 2% | 17% |
| Unsupportive | 34% | 33% | 34% | 83% | 26% | 42% |
| Total | 99% | 99% | 99% | 100% | 100% | 101% |

the zero-order table (table 8.13) disappears in the "reported crime" partial table. In the "never reported crime" partial, however, the zero-order relationship remains; in fact, it is even stronger in this partial than in the zero-order table. Assuming that the report-of-crime variable is related to one (but not both) of the zero-order table variables (although we haven't done so here, we would have to construct the two tables—report of crime by ethnicity and report of crime by support for police—to determine whether this condition holds), this example of elaboration analysis has resulted in a *specification*. That is, we can now specify in which category of the test variable the zero-order relationship is maintained (in this case, the "never reported crime" category).

*Ethnicity*   →   ***Support for Police
(among those who have
never reported a crime)***

Let us look at another example of elaboration analysis. Suppose we have studied 500 16- to 18-year-old juveniles and examined the relationship between their social class (the independent variable) and the number of self-admitted delinquent acts in which they have engaged in the last year. We measured the social class variable in three categories (upper, middle, and lower) and the number of delinquent acts in three categories (less than two, three to five, and six or more). Suppose further that we have already constructed the zero-order table and discovered that there is indeed a relationship between these variables: the higher the social class, the lower the number of self-admitted delinquent acts. We then introduce the test factor of ethnicity, measured in two categories (white and nonwhite) and obtain the results in table 8.16.

In this case, the zero-order relationship disappears in both partial tables. Recall that when we get this result in an elaboration analysis, we have an instance of either *explanation* or *interpretation*. Which of these has occurred depends on the time sequence of the variables. If the test variable (in this case, ethnicity) occurs at the same time as or before the independent variable (social class) and before the dependent variable (number of delinquent acts), we have a spurious relationship in the zero-order table. It seems reasonable in our example to regard ethnicity as occurring simultaneously with the independent variable and prior to the dependent variable. That is, a person's ethnicity and social class are established at birth because a child's ethnicity and social class are determined by the ethnicity and social class of his parents, and both of these variables impact on the individual well before the delinquent acts being studied. Hence, assuming that our test factor (ethnicity) is also related both to the original independent variable (social class) and to the original dependent variable (number of delinquent acts), we may say that ethnicity is an *explanation* of the zero-order relationship. That is, the zero-order relationship is spurious.

Now suppose that instead of ethnicity, we introduced junior high school attended (measured in two categories for the two junior high schools our subjects attended) as our test variable and obtained the same cell percentages as those in table 8.16. In this case, we could reasonably argue that the school-attended variable occurs in time after the social class variable (our original independent variable), but before the number-of-delinquent-acts variable (our original dependent variable). The social class of juveniles is usually established at the time they are born; the delinquent acts in question are those committed by 16-to-18-year olds in the year prior to the study, which means that in most cases at least, they would have finished junior high school before they committed the delinquent acts in question. Hence, this result of our elaboration analysis is an instance of *interpretation*. The school-attended variable intervenes and interprets the relationship between social class and number of delinquent acts. The

**Table 8.16   Self-Admitted Delinquent Acts by Ethnicity and Social Class (in Percentages)**

| Number of Delinquent Acts | White | | | Nonwhite | | |
|---|---|---|---|---|---|---|
| | *Upper Class* (n = 42) | *Middle Class* (n = 108) | *Lower Class* (n = 100) | *Upper Class* (n = 25) | *Middle Class* (n = 95) | *Lower Class* (n = 130) |
| Less than 2 | 35% | 33% | 34% | 36% | 34% | 34% |
| 3 to 5 | 33% | 35% | 33% | 32% | 33% | 32% |
| 6 or more | 31% | 31% | 33% | 32% | 33% | 34% |
| Total | 99% | 99% | 100% | 100% | 100% | 100% |

relationships among the three variables as suggested by our analyses might be diagrammed as follows:

**Social Class** → **School Attended** → **Number of Delinquent Acts**

As a last example of the possible results of elaboration analysis, suppose that a study we did produced zero-order table 8.17. In this case, there is no apparent relationship between the type of defense attorney and trial outcome. We might nevertheless wish to explore this result through elaboration analysis. Suppose that we introduced sex of offender as a test factor and obtained the results shown in table 8.18. This result is interesting because, while there was no relationship between the variables in our zero-order table (table 8.17), there is a strong relationship in each of the partials. Note, however, that the relationships in the partials run in opposite directions. That is, males are more often found guilty when defended by a private attorney and innocent when defended by a public defender, while females are found guilty more often when defended by a public defender and innocent when defended by a private attorney. These two partial relationships cancel each other out, resulting in the absence of relationship in the zero-order table. No special name is given to this outcome in elaboration analysis.

Let us make one final observation about elaboration analysis. Which variable we begin with in our zero table is essentially arbitrary. That is, we could have begun our analysis with a zero-order relationship between ethnicity and reported crime and used our support-for-police variable as a test factor, or we could have begun with a zero-

**Table 8.17   Trial Outcome by Type of Defense Attorney (in Percentages)**

|   | **Type of Attorney** | |
|---|---|---|
| **Trial Outcome** | *Public Defender* (n = 50) | *Private Attorney* (n = 50) |
| Guilty | 54% | 56% |
| Innocent | 46% | 44% |
| Total | 100% | 100% |

**Table 8.18   Trial Outcome by Type of Defense Attorney and Sex of Offender (in Percentages)**

| Trial Outcome | Sex of Offender | | | |
|---|---|---|---|---|
| | Male | | Female | |
| | Public Defender (n = 24) | Private Attorney (n = 26) | Public Defender (n = 26) | Private Attorney (n = 24) |
| Guilty | 25% | 81% | 81% | 33% |
| Innocent | 75% | 19% | 19% | 67% |
| Total | 100% | 100% | 100% | 100% |

order table looking at the relationship between support for police and reported crime with ethnicity as our test factor. The point is that the researcher structures the analysis as he sees fit, being limited in his inferences only by the time sequence of the variables and whether the information actually shows relationships among the variables.

## *Measuring Relationships Between Variables*

So far in this chapter, we have written in very general terms about relationships existing or not existing between variables, based on "eye-balling" a table and comparing particular cell frequencies or percentages. You might well have asked yourself some questions as you read along: for example, How much of a difference in cell frequencies or percentages is enough to justify the conclusion that the variables are related? Is it possible to say more precisely how strong a relationship between variables is?

Fortunately, some statistical tools helpful in answering these questions are available to the researcher. These tools provide quantitative guides to the researcher in determining whether a relationship exists and, if it does, its direction and degree. The *degree* of a relationship is the strength of the association between the two variables. In general, the greater the degree of relationship between two variables, the more precisely one can predict values of the dependent variable when the values of the independent variable are known. The *direction* of a relationship refers to the way in which the values of variables change with respect to each other. In general, if the variables change in the same direction (i.e., if the data show that those who score high on one variable also score high on the other variable), they are positively related; if the variables change in the opposite direction (i.e., if the data show that those who score high on one variable score low on the other variable), they are negatively related. In the discussion that follows, we shall consider these and other aspects of relationships between variables and some of the statistics that have been developed for measuring (quantifying) relationships between variables.

## Correlation

Perhaps the most commonly used measure of degree and direction of a relationship is the **correlation coefficient** developed by Karl Pearson. It is a measure of the extent to which two variables vary together (concomitantly) and is denoted by r. While we will not describe the mechanics of computing the Pearson correlation coefficient, we will discuss some of the characteristics of this statistic.

Suppose that we have measured each individual in our study group on two continuous ratio variables. We shall call the independent variable Variable 1 and the dependent variable Variable 2. We are interested in determining the strength of the relationship, if any, between these two variables. We might proceed by creating a graph with the values of Variable 1 arrayed along the horizontal axis and the values of Variable 2 arrayed along the vertical axis. We could then locate each individual in our study group on this graph by placing a dot where his scores on Variables 1 and 2 intersect (see figure 8.5). (Note

**Figure 8.5 Locating an Individual's Score on a Scattergram**

**Figure 8.6  A Scattergram Showing No Relationship Between Variables**

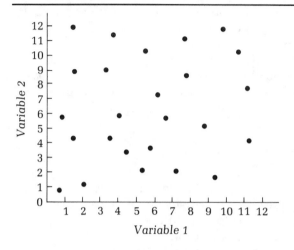

that this graphing procedure is different from the one we used in constructing frequency distributions.) The precise location of each dot in the space is determined as follows. Suppose respondent A scored 4 on Variable 1 and 6 on Variable 2. We would draw an imaginary line perpendicular to the horizontal axis at the point corresponding to a score of 4 and a line perpendicular to the vertical axis corresponding to a score of 6. At the point where these two perpendicular lines intersect, we place a dot (see figure 8.5). If we did the same thing for each individual in our study group, the result would be a graph scattered with dots representing the intersection of the scores on our two variables for the study group as a whole. This kind of graphic representation of the relationship between two variables is called a **scattergram**.

Suppose that when we finished this task our scattergram looked like the one in figure 8.6. Note that the dots are scattered fairly evenly over the graph. Consider again a question we asked earlier in our discussion of relationships between independent and dependent variables: If we know the value of the independent variable, what can we say about the value of the dependent variable? The scattergram in figure 8.6 would not permit us to say anything useful about the value of Variable 2 given a particular value of Variable 1. Choose any value of Variable 1 and examine the corresponding values of Variable 2 arrayed directly above it. They are as likely to be low as they are to be medium or high. Hence, the scattergram represents a situation in which the two variables are unrelated.

Now, let us suppose that our scattergram looked like the one in figure 8.7. In this case, the dots fall into a definable pattern, running

**Figure 8.7  A Scattergram Showing a Positive Correlation Between Variables**

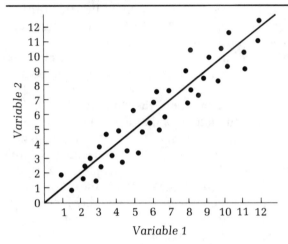

Variable 1

from the lower left-hand corner to the upper right-hand corner of the graphic space. Dots in the lower left-hand corner represent instances in which a low score on one variable was accompanied by a low score on the other variable; dots in the upper right-hand corner represent instances of a high score on one variable accompanied by a high score on the other variable. The dots (data) reflect a relationship between the two variables, in this case a **positive correlation.**

The scattergram in figure 8.8 represents a **negative correlation;** that is, the dots (data) reflect instances of a low score on one variable accompanied by a high score on the other.

**Figure 8.8  A Scattergram Showing a Negative Relationship**

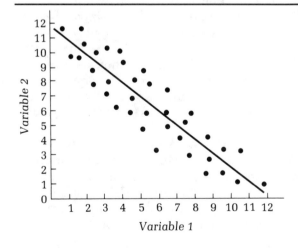

Variable 1

Both positive and negative correlations of the kind we have just discussed are examples of a **linear relationship**, for the pattern of the dots can be approximately represented by a straight line that runs diagonally across the graph (see figures 8.7 and 8.8). A correlation coefficient reflects how well the pattern of dots can be approximated by such a diagonal line. More precisely, a correlation coefficient expresses quantitatively how far the dots are, on average, from the line, often called a **regression line.**

Correlation coefficients indicate both the direction (positive or negative) and the degree of the relationship between two variables. They range from + 1.0 to – 1.0, the former (r = + 1.0) being generated if all of the dots in a scattergram fall precisely on a diagonal line similar to the one in figure 8.7, the latter (r = – 1.0) being produced if all the dots fall precisely on a diagonal line similar to the one in figure 8.8. The closer the dots fall to such diagonals, the higher the correlation coefficient generated by the data. The Pearson correlation coefficient can be used only with continuous data that have been measured at least at the interval level.

Of course, a scattergram can assume a variety of nonlinear forms as well. Suppose our scattergram looked like one of those in figure 8.9. In these the dots (data) clearly fall into a pattern, but not one well represented by a straight line. A curved line does much better, reflecting what is called a **curvilinear relationship.** A correlation coefficient measures only the extent to which there is a *linear* (i.e., straight line) relationship between two variables. When the relationship is curvilinear, a correlation coefficient is apt to be close to zero. For this reason, relying on the correlation coefficient alone may be misleading. Whenever possible, it is advisable to construct a scattergram of the data, since a scattergram gives the researcher a chance to discover curvilinear as well as linear relationships between two variables.

Correlation coefficients have predictive value. If r is positive, say, r = + 0.85, those who scored high on one variable also tended to score high on the other, and those who scored low on one variable also tended to score low on the other. A negative r indicates that those who scored high on one variable tended to score low on the other. However, if our correlation coefficient is close or equal to zero, knowing the value of one variable does not enable us to predict the value of the other.

Actually, the quantity $r^2$ (or r × r), called the **coefficient of determination,** is somewhat easier to understand statistically. Recall our discussion in chapter 7 of measures of dispersion of a frequency distribution. One of those measures was the variance $(s^2)$, which is calculated by squaring another of the measures of dispersion, the standard deviation (s). Again, without going into the details of the underlying

**Figure 8.9  Scattergrams Showing Curvilinear Relationships**

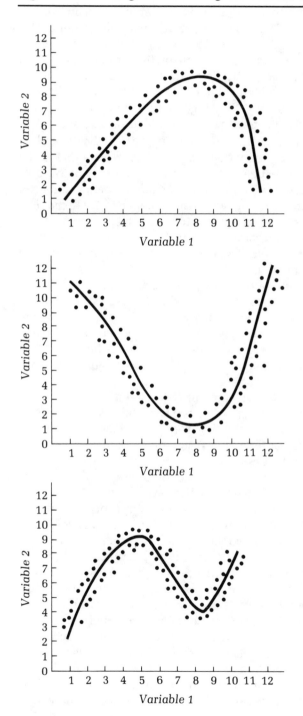

statistical rationale or the mathematical calculations, we can think of $r^2$ as a measure of the variance in the dependent variable accounted for by the independent variable. Consider the two scattergrams in figure 8.10, where the independent variables are on the horizontal axes and the dependent variables are on the vertical axes. We have raised a vertical dotted line above a given value of the independent variable in each scattergram and marked the range of values of the dependent variable which are associated with this value. This range can be taken as an indicator (a measure) of the amount of variance in the dependent variable accounted for by the independent variable. Note that in the scattergram above, the range of scores on the dependent variable (from about 5 to 14) for the given value of the independent variable (6) is larger than the corresponding range (from about 8 to 11) in the scattergram below. This can be interpreted to mean that the independent variable in the scattergram below accounts for more of the variance in the dependent variable. Note also that in both scattergrams, knowing the value of the independent variable does not permit one to predict perfectly what the value of the dependent variable will be. (Perfect prediction would result only if all of the dots fell on a straight line.) This can be interpreted to mean that some of the variance in the dependent variable remains unexplained by the independent variable. But we can say that the independent variable in the scattergram below "explains" more of the dependent variable variance than does the independent variable in the scattergram above.

Suppose the correlation coefficient (r) between crime rates and the proportion of the population who own handguns is $+0.6$, then $r^2$ $= 0.36$. In this case, variations in the proportion of handgun owners can be said to account for (or explain) 36 percent of the variations in crime rate. Of course, that means that 64 percent of the variation in crime rate remains unaccounted for. Remember that the use of the word *explain* here simply means statistical explanation. A causal explanation, as noted previously, requires an appropriate time sequence and the elimination of other potentially causal variables.

Although we have discussed the correlational technique as a way of measuring the direction and degree of the relationships between two variables, the same basic idea can be extended to a measurement of the relationships between a dependent variable and two or more independent variables. One of the statistics used for quantifying these relationships is called the **multiple correlation coefficient,** usually symbolized by R. The corresponding $R^2$ is called the **coefficient of multiple determination**, and its interpretation is analogous to that of $r^2$. That is, $R^2$ is the proportion of variance in the dependent variable accounted for by the combined effects of however many independent variables are included in the calculations. Suppose, for example, that

**Figure 8.10  Two Scattergrams Showing Different Amounts of Variance in the Dependent Variable Accounted for by an Independent Variable**

you are attempting to account for changes in the crime rate over time and assume that several variables contribute to these changes. If you can measure these variables at the interval or ratio level, you can use a multiple correlation analysis to determine the combined effects of all of your hypothesized independent variables. You could determine the combined contribution of, say, the proportion of the population owning handguns, the proportion of the population between the ages of 14 and 21, and the unemployment rate to the crime rate. As with r, R measures only *linear* relationships, so an R equal to or near zero means only that no linear relationship exists among the variables; however, nonlinear relationships may be present.

Because single or multiple correlation coefficients may have predictive value, a serious error in reasoning may occur in using them. That is, a researcher simply assumes that the existence of a correlation indicates causation. As we pointed out in chapter 3, correlation (or concomitant variation) is a necessary condition but not a sufficient condition for causation. High correlation coefficients alone do not permit us to make causal inferences.[2] The reader should keep this point in mind whenever correlation coefficients are presented as part of an analysis of data.

## *Correlation and Cross-Tabulation*

Our earlier discussion of cross-tabulation focused on the importance of specific rows and columns and their comparison. When a cross-tabulation involves two variables measured at the ordinal level or above, however, it is often useful to examine the diagonals of a table to determine whether or not the two variables are correlated.

### Diagonals

To gain a general understanding of the use of **diagonals** in reading a table, recall our earlier discussion of scattergrams and correlation. Figure 8.11 represents a scattergram with a data grid like the ones we used in constructing tables superimposed on it. Suppose we counted the dots included in each of the cells in the data grid, erased the dots, and entered the number of dots in the corresponding cells. We would then have a cross-tabulation of the two variables corresponding to the scattergram with which we began.

In converting the scattergram into a cross-tabulation, we have divided the range of the values (0 through 12) into four segments: 0.00–2.99, 3.00–5.99, 6.00–8.99, and 9.00–12.00. In the cross-tabulation, original scores ranging from 0.00 through 2.99 for each variable have been collapsed into a single new value, those from 3.00 through 5.99 form a second new category, and so on.

We can also approximate the pattern of the dots in a scattergram by drawing a straight, solid line to represent the general pattern of the data. In this example, the line would pass from the lower left-hand cell of the table to the upper right-hand cell, and its path would take it through several other cells in the table as well. The cells through

**Figure 8.11  Scattergram with Superimposed Data Grid**

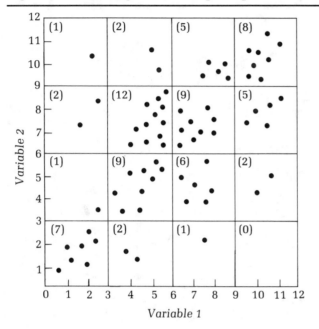

which the line passes constitute one diagonal of the table. Figure 8.12 shows that there are two diagonals in each table.

If the cell frequencies tend to be larger in the cells that lie on or near either one of the two diagonals than in those remote from it, we can conclude that a linear relationship exists between the two variables. (The reader should figure out which of the diagonals corresponds to a positive relationship and which to a negative relationship.) As in the case of correlation, the absence of a linear relationship (concentration of higher frequencies in the diagonals) does not necessarily mean that the variables are unrelated. If the cells we have connected with a dotted line in figure 8.12 contained the higher frequencies, a nonlinear relationship between the variables would be indicated.

## *Other Statistical Measures of Association*

The Pearson r assumes interval or ratio measurements of the two variables being correlated. There are other measures of association, some of which may be used with tables for variables measured at the nominal level, such as Lambda. Others can be used on variables measured at the ordinal level, such as the Spearman Rank Order Correlation Coefficient and Kendall's Tau. Like Pearson's r, they all rest upon cer-

**Figure 8.12  Linear and Nonlinear Relationships in Tables**

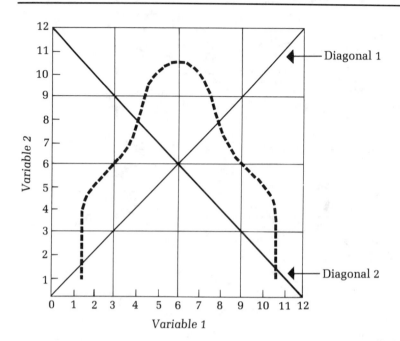

tain assumptions about levels of measurement, size of the study group, and so forth. Any good statistical manual will provide you with a list of these assumptions and the appropriate uses of these measures of association.[3]

## *Notes*

1. For a more complete discussion of elaboration analysis, see Stephen Cole, *The Sociological Method* (Chicago: Markham, 1972), especially pp. 106–32; and Herbert Hyman, *Survey Design and Analysis* (New York: Free Press, 1954), pp. 275–327.
2. Richard Runyon and Audrey Haber, *Fundamentals of Behavioral Statistics*, 2nd ed. (Reading, Mass.: Addison-Wesley, 1971), p. 125.
3. See, for example, Herman J. Loether and Donald T. McTavish, *Descriptive Statistics for Sociologists* (Newton, Mass.: Allyn and Bacon, 1974); and Theodore Anderson and Morris Zeldich, Jr., *A Basic Course in Statistics* (New York: Holt, Rinehart and Winston, 1975).

# Review Questions

1. What is a contingency table?
2. What is the relationship between marginal frequencies in a contingency table and frequency distributions?
3. What does it mean to say that the categories of a variable may be "collapsed"? What should be kept in mind by the researcher when collapsing categories for purposes of analysis?
4. When converting cell frequencies to percentages, which marginal frequencies should be used?
5. What is elaboration analysis?
6. What is the difference between zero-order tables and first-order partial tables?
7. On what basis might we conclude that an elaboration analysis has produced an explanation? an interpretation? a specification? a replication?
8. What is a scattergram?
9. What is a linear relationship between two variables? How does it differ from a curvilinear relationship?
10. What would an r of + 1.0 mean? an r of – 1.0? an r of + .50?

# Exercises

Use the following hypothetical data for the exercises below.

| Subject | Ethnic Group | Convicted of a Crime? | Social Class | Score on Criminal Justice Test | IQ Score |
|---------|--------------|----------------------|--------------|-------------------------------|----------|
| 1 | nonwhite | no | middle | 60% | 101 |
| 2 | white | no | lower | 54% | 98 |
| 3 | nonwhite | yes | lower | 63% | 112 |
| 4 | white | yes | lower | 57% | 100 |
| 5 | white | yes | middle | 72% | 115 |
| 6 | nonwhite | no | lower | 70% | 130 |
| 7 | white | yes | middle | 59% | 99 |
| 8 | nonwhite | no | middle | 60% | 100 |
| 9 | nonwhite | no | middle | 68% | 126 |
| 10 | nonwhite | yes | lower | 64% | 118 |
| 11 | white | no | middle | 64% | 107 |
| 12 | white | yes | middle | 65% | 113 |
| 13 | nonwhite | yes | middle | 80% | 121 |
| 14 | nonwhite | no | lower | 55% | 99 |
| 15 | nonwhite | no | middle | 48% | 92 |
| 16 | nonwhite | no | middle | 68% | 119 |
| 17 | white | yes | lower | 61% | 101 |
| 18 | nonwhite | no | middle | 85% | 140 |
| 19 | white | no | lower | 92% | 132 |
| 20 | nonwhite | no | middle | 40% | 123 |

1. Construct a zero-order table relating ethnic group to conviction of a crime. Is there a relationship?
2. Construct first-order partial tables for the two variables in 1, using social class as the third variable. Is there a relationship between social class and ethnic group? between social class and conviction record? How would you interpret the results of this elaboration analysis?
3. Collapse the IQ scores into three categories and construct a table for examining whether there is any relationship between social class and IQ. Is there a relationship?
4. Construct a scattergram for examining whether there is a relationship between IQ and score on the criminal justice class test. Is there a relationship? Would the r be positive or negative?

# 9

## An Introduction to Inferential Statistics

Suppose a researcher is interested in the distribution of some characteristic (i.e., variable) concerning the police officers (or offenders or crimes committed) in a major U.S. city during a specified period of time. As we noted in our discussion of populations and samples in chapter 4, the population being studied would consist of *all* of the officers (or offenders or crimes) in the particular city during the specified time period. The researcher's goal is to make descriptive statements about the entire set of persons, events, or other units included in the defined population. Because the amount of confidence we can have in these descriptive statements depends in large part on how many of the units in the specified population we have relevant information about, collecting data on every unit might seem to be the ideal research strategy.

For many reasons, however, it is often either impossible or impractical to study an entire population. In such circumstances, the best strategy is to select and study a sample and then use the data from the sample to learn something about the population as a whole. **Inferential statistics** are the tools that enable us to generalize from a sample to the population from which it was drawn with some specifiable degree of confidence that the generalizations are correct.

Once a sample is selected and the data assembled, the distribution of any particular measured variable can be described by calculating a proportion, percentage, mean, standard deviation, or other measures of central tendency or dispersion discussed in chapter 7. When these measures are calculated for distributions of sample data, they are called **sample statistics.** The corresponding measures for the population—that we do not know, but want to estimate by using sample statistics—are called **population parameters**.

If we could be certain that the sample accurately represented the population from which it was drawn, this task would be easy, for we would know that the values of the population parameters were the same as the values of the corresponding sample statistics. Unfortunately, when we take advantage of the convenience of sampling, we cannot avoid some uncertainty about the representativeness of our sample. We might draw a sample whose statistics are exactly like the population parameters. But we might also get a sample whose statistics are very different from the population parameters. Furthermore, the degree of correspondence between statistics and parameters will vary from sample to sample drawn from the same population. In short, some samples will be more representative of the population than will others.

When there are differences between the sample statistics and the parameters of the population from which the sample was selected, we say that these differences are due to **sampling error**. The less representative the sample, the larger the sampling error, and the greater the difference between our sample statistics and the corresponding population parameters. Whenever we use a sample to represent a population, then, we run some risk of sampling error.

The researcher's uncertainty, created by the possibility of sampling error, is enhanced by another troublesome consideration: we do not know and have no way of finding out exactly what the population parameters are. Therefore, it would appear that we have no way of knowing exactly how much, if any, sampling error has occurred. However, we can reduce these uncertainties and increase our confidence that samples can be used effectively if we do two things: (a) select our sample in the best way possible; and (b) use inferential statistics to make inferences about the population parameters from our sample statistics.

First, which methods of sampling are "the best"? A sample should be selected that has the best chance of being representative of the population, in order to minimize sampling error. As noted in chapter 4, perhaps the most important sources of potential bias or error in a sample are the researcher's own conscious or unconscious biases during the sampling process itself. In our discussion of sampling techniques in chapter 4 we pointed out that the best—that is, most representative—sample is achieved through probability sampling and that a simple random sample is the most basic type of probability sample.

In a simple random sample, each unit in the population has the same chance (or probability) of being included in the sample, and each selection of a population unit is *independent* of the selection of every other unit from the population. To draw a random sample we must have a complete list of all elements in the population. Each element must be "tagged" with a unique number, and then the sample is drawn with the aid of a random numbers table. Remember that we use this carefully planned and controlled process to ensure that each element in the population has the same *probability* of being chosen for the sample. By drawing a sample in this way, we eliminate any conscious or unconscious biases of the researcher during the sample selection process. As a result, a random sample is much superior to a quota, accidental, purposive, or any other type of nonprobability sample where we have no control over the probability of an element being selected and where the conscious or unconscious biases of the researcher may be involved. In short, a probability sample is more likely to be representative of the population from which it is drawn than is any other type of sample. We can reduce the uncertainty in sampling by using a probability sampling technique.

An alert reader may very well agree with our argument so far, but point out that we have not yet solved the basic sampling issue. Probability samples may be better (i.e., more representative of the population) than other types, but they too are subject to sampling error. The truth is that the possibility of sampling error cannot be eliminated, but by drawing a probability sample, some limits and, therefore, some control can be imposed over the sampling error uncertainties which remain through the use of inferential statistics.

It is beyond the scope of this text to consider in detail the mathematical theories upon which inferential statistics are based. In the sections of this chapter that follow, however, the general ideas involved will be introduced. Inferential statistics are based on a branch of mathematics called probability theory, and, although we did not mention it explicitly at the time, we used some elementary principles of probability theory to define a random sample. With probability principles built into the sampling process, probability-based inferential statistics can be used to estimate the amount of sampling error.

Before proceeding to a more technical discussion, let us introduce a rather simple example to describe what we are trying to accomplish through the use of inferential statistics. Suppose you spot a friend standing on the street corner outside the student union, idly flipping a quarter. Broke, as usual, you would like to have his quarter to buy a cup of coffee before returning to your study of research methods in criminology. While you know that your friend does not like to lend money, you also know that he is a sucker for weird bets. Being a bit of a risk taker yourself, you decide that you might bet him a quarter that in 10 flips of his quarter, he will get no more than 4 heads. How would you determine your chances of winning the bet?

You recognize, of course, that if your friend accepts your bet and flips the coin 10 times, any number of heads, from zero to 10, might turn up. Furthermore, the outcome of the bet will be determined by the sum of the outcomes of 10 separate flips of the coin. Hence, your chances of winning the bet are tied in some way to the chances of getting a head in a single flip of the coin. You are also aware that once your friend flips the coin 10 times, you will either win or lose the bet. Nevertheless, if you had some way of estimating the likelihood that your friend would turn up 4 heads or less in a sample of 10 tosses of the coin, you could estimate your chances of winning the bet.

## *Calculating Probabilities Empirically*

One way you might attempt to determine the likelihood that a given proportion of heads will turn up in 10 tosses of the quarter is to try it yourself. If your friend will let you borrow his quarter, you could flip it 10 times, noting the number of heads that came up. Suppose you found that the coin landed heads 8 times. Would you be willing to infer that you would get 8 heads in the next set of 10 tosses? Might you not observe 3 heads in the next set of 10 tosses, 6 in the next, and so on? In short, if you relied on the sample statistic (in this case, the number or proportion of heads) from any *single* sample of 10 coin tosses to estimate the corresponding parameter (in this case, the number or proportion of heads in all possible samples or sets of 10 flips of the coin), you would clearly be in danger of making an incorrect estimate because of sampling error.

Suppose, however, you took a large number of samples, each consisting of 10 tosses of the coin, and recorded the proportion of heads that turned up in each sample. To help you evaluate the data you have assembled regarding the proportion of heads in 10 tosses of a coin, you could construct a bar graph frequency distribution of your sample statistics. Table 9.1 shows our results when we took 100 samples consisting of 10 coin tosses each, while figure 9.1 shows the bar graph distribution of our sample statistics.

The distribution in figure 9.1 can be used to estimate the probability that any given proportion of heads will occur in 10 tosses of a coin over the long run. Our distribution suggests, for example, that the most likely outcome, in proportion of heads, is .50 (occurring 27 percent of the time), followed closely by .60 (22 percent of the time), and .40 (19 percent of the time). Outcomes of 0.0, .10, .90, and 1.00 appear highly unlikely. In fact, these outcomes did not occur in any of our samples.

From the information provided by our distribution of sample statistics we could estimate the likelihood of getting more than four heads by observing that in 36 (6 + 11 + 19 = 36) of the samples we took, 4 or fewer heads turned up, while in the remaining 64 samples, more than 4 heads occurred. Hence, we might infer that, over the long

**Table 9.1  Record of Results from 100 Samples of
10 Coin Tosses Each***

| Proportion of heads obtained in ten tosses of a coin | Number of occurrences |
|---|---|
| 0.00 | 0 |
| .10 | 0 |
| .20 + + + + + + | 6 |
| .30 + + + + + + + + + + + | 11 |
| .40 + + + + + + + + + + + + + + + + + + + | 19 |
| .50 + + + + + + + + + + + + + + + + + + + + + + + + + + + | 27 |
| .60 + + + + + + + + + + + + + + + + + + + + + + | 22 |
| .70 + + + + + + + + + + | 10 |
| .80 + + + + + | 5 |
| .90 | 0 |
| 1.00 | 0 |
| | n = 100 |

*Note: Each ( + ) represents one sample of ten tosses.

run, you will win your bet 36 percent of the time and lose it 64 percent of the time. Those are not very good odds. Even though you might be lucky and win your bet this particular time, you had probably better offer to make a different kind of bet or plan on that coffee another day.

Let us review what we have done in this example. We began with a bet concerning the proportion of heads that would turn up in 10 flips of a coin, noting that the bet would be won or lost in a single set of 10 flips and that a risk was involved in making the bet. We reasoned that if we could determine how often, in the long run, we could expect any given proportion of heads to turn up, we could use that knowledge to estimate our chances of winning the bet. Aware that sampling error might occur, we took a relatively large number of samples from the population consisting of all possible sets of 10 flips of a coin and examined the distribution of the sample statistic, proportion of heads, in these samples. From that distribution we estimated our chances of getting 4 or fewer heads.

Now suppose we change our perspective a bit about the distribu-

**Figure 9.1 Bar Graph Frequency Distribution of Proportions of Heads in 100 Samples of 10 Tosses of the Coin**

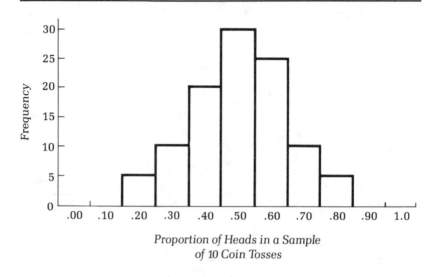

Proportion of Heads in a Sample
of 10 Coin Tosses

tion in figure 9.1. Given an ordinary coin, we assume that each time we flip it "honestly" a head is just as likely to turn up as a tail. We might assume, therefore, that in any even number of flips, we should get exactly 50 percent heads and 50 percent tails. However, we also recognize that, in a given series of flips (say 10), we will not always get exactly 5 heads and 5 tails. We are aware that there is a chance factor involved. When we flip a coin 10 times and do not get exactly 5 heads and 5 tails, we assume that an "error" of some kind—in effect, an error due to chance—has occurred. Another way of looking at the distribution in figure 9.1, then, is that it represents a distribution of errors due to chance, which occurred in our samples of 10 flips of the coin. This chance variation in our sample statistic is another way of defining the concept of sampling error, introduced at the beginning of this chapter. As we shall see later, the general idea of errors due to chance—sampling error—is extremely important in the use of inferential statistics.

## *Calculating Probabilities Mathematically*

While the betting example illustrates what we are trying to accomplish through inferential statistics, it is impractical and unrealistic as a general procedure for estimating the likelihood of particular outcomes. Usually, because of time and money limitations, we can only investigate 1 sample drawn from our population. Besides, if we had to take many samples to learn something about the distribution of our sample statistic, the usefulness of sampling as an alternative to studying the entire population would quickly diminish. We must be able to infer something about a population on the basis of data from a *single* sample. To do that we must determine the characteristics of the distribution of our sample statistic without actually taking a large number of samples.

## Sampling Distributions

Fortunately, a solution to this problem is provided through the application of certain mathematical procedures derived from probability theory. These procedures are commonly referred to as *inferential statistics*, because they are statistical ways of inferring some characteristics of a population from sample data.

Remember that we need a distribution of our sample statistic so that we can estimate sampling error. Instead of actually taking a large number of samples and deriving a distribution of sampling error empirically (as we did when we flipped our coin and created figure 9.1), a hypothetical or theoretical distribution of a sample statistic can be derived mathematically. To do so, three specific theoretical (mathematical) steps must be taken. First, all of the mathematically possible outcomes (values) of the measurement of a variable pertaining to a particular unit of the population must be specified and a probability assigned to each (that's what we did when we said that the possible outcomes of flipping a coin were a head and a tail, and that a head was as likely as a tail). Second, all of the mathematically possible outcomes (values) of a series of such measurements must be specified (as we did in the left-hand column in table 9.1). Third, probabilities must be assigned to each of the outcomes (values) specified in step two (we arrived at the figures in the right-hand column of table 9.1 empirically, by actually flipping a coin; now we will create the right hand column by mathematical calculation). The result of these procedures is a mathematically constructed distribution of the sample statistic. This theoretical or hypothetical distribution is called the **sampling distribution** for that particular sample statistic.

The sampling distribution serves the same purpose as the empirically derived distribution in figure 9.1. That is, it permits us to make quantitative statements about the probabilities associated with getting a particular outcome in a single sample. (We used the distribution in figure 9.1, you will remember, to tell us what the probability was of getting no more than 4 heads if we toss a coin 10 times.) The difference, again, is that our sampling distribution is created not empirically, but mathematically. Let us see now how we might construct a mathematically derived sampling distribution.

Suppose that we are interested in an event that has two possible outcomes, such as a decision made by an officer to arrest or not to arrest a juvenile stopped for questioning. Mathematically, this is equivalent to flipping a hypothetical coin—heads, let us say, represents a decision to arrest and tails represents a decision not to arrest. To make comparisons with what we have described in our betting example easier, we will use the hypothetical coin flip in the discussion that follows and call each single flip of the coin a *trial*. If we ignore the possibility that the coin may get lost or land on its edge, a trial has two possible outcomes: no heads (i.e., 1 tail), and 1 head.

We begin by assuming that the two possible outcomes of a single trial are equally probable. Expressed in probabilities, then, our initial theoretical assumption is that we expect to get no heads 50% of the time (probability of no heads $p_t$ = .50) and one head 50% of the time (probability of one head $p_h$ = .50). Note that the sum of the probabilities associated with the possible outcomes of this event is 1.00. This is always the case, no matter how many possible outcomes of an event there are, according to probability theory.

Now suppose we consider a series of trials consisting of a specified number of flips of the coin. We assume that for each trial in the series, $p_t = p_h$ = .50. Here, too, we could identify all of the possible results, expressed in terms of the proportion of heads that could turn up in the series. The number of possible results would depend on the number of flips we assume to occur in the series; for example, there would be 11 possible results in a series of 10 trials (0, .10, .20, . . . 1.0), 101 possible results in 100 trials (0, .010, .020, . . . 1.0), 1,001 in 1,000 trials, (0, .001, .002, .003, . . . 1.0), and so on.

While the probabilities of the two possible outcomes in a single trial are equal, the probabilities associated with the possible results of a *series* of trials are not equal. That is, in a series of trials we would not always expect to get exactly .50 heads and .50 tails; we might get .40 heads in some, .80 heads in others. But if our initial assumptions about the equal probabilities of each of the possible outcomes in a single trial are correct, probability theory tells us something more about what we can expect. For example, we can expect to get .40 or .50 or .60 heads more often than we can expect to get .10, .20, or .90 heads. In fact, we can use a mathematical probability model known as the

**binomial distribution** to determine the *exact* probability associated with each of the possible outcomes.

## The Binomial Distribution

The binomial distribution can be used as a sampling distribution whenever we are investigating a series in which each trial has two possible outcomes. For example, it can be used as the sampling distribution for determining the chances of winning the coin toss bet, or for analyzing an officer's decision to arrest or not arrest a juvenile. The major difference is that our sampling distribution is hypothetical, generated mathematically on the basis of the assumption that the coin is unbiased—that is, that in each flip of the coin a head is theoretically just as likely to turn up as a tail. (A real coin, of course, may or may not be unbiased, or a real coin flipper may or may not flip the coin honestly.) Table 9.2 shows the mathematical probabilities of obtaining various results in 10 tosses of a theoretical, unbiased coin, and figure 9.2 is a bar graph distribution of the results in table 9.2. Along the horizontal axis in this graph, we have placed all of the possible results (expressed as proportion of heads) in any single sample of 10 tosses of a coin—0, .10, .20, etc.—found in the left-hand column of table 9.2; the vertical axis of the graph has been converted to proportions as

**Table 9.2  Probability Sampling Distribution of Outcomes (in Proportion of Heads) for Ten Trials (Flips of Coin), from Binomial Distribution**

| Proportion of Heads | | Probability (p) |
|:---:|:---:|:---:|
| .00 | | .001 |
| .10 | | .010 |
| .20 | | .044 |
| .30 | | .117 |
| .40 | | .205 |
| .50 | | .246 |
| .60 | | .205 |
| .70 | | .117 |
| .80 | | .044 |
| .90 | | .010 |
| 1.00 | | .001 |
| | Total | 1.000 |

**Figure 9.2 Bar Graph Frequency Distribution of Probabilities of Proportion of Heads in 100 Samples of 10 Tosses of a Hypothetical, Unbiased Coin (from the Binomial Distribution)**

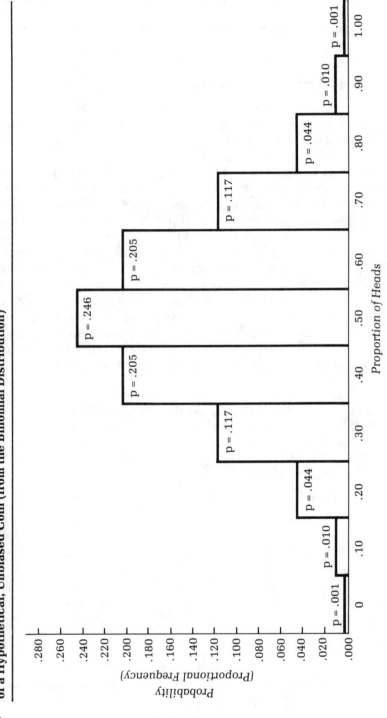

well. That is, instead of representing the raw frequency with which a particular proportion of heads occurs, it indicates the proportion of times in a series of trials a particular proportion of heads is *likely* to turn up. The height of each bar in the graph is derived from the probabilities in the right-hand column in table 9.2. We can use this sampling distribution to determine the likelihood of obtaining any particular proportion of heads, providing we assume that tails are just as likely as heads in any single flip of the coin. Because (according to probability theory) the probability of obtaining any one of a *set* of possible results equals the sum of the probabilities associated with each of the results in the set, the probability of getting 4 heads or less—that is, the probability of winning our bet—can be determined by summing the probabilities associated with getting zero, 1, 2, 3, and 4 heads. The probability of winning our bet, then, is .001 + .010 + .044 + .117 + .205 = .377. Note how close this mathematically derived estimate is to the empirically derived estimate (.36) obtained by actually flipping a real coin 10 times on 100 occasions.

By this summation method, we can determine the probability of obtaining any specified range of results—say, of getting a proportion of .40 through .60 heads. Adding the respective probabilities associated with each of the results (from table 9.2) would give us: .205 + .246 + .205 = .656. Thus, according to the binomial distribution, we have a .656 probability of getting 4, 5, or 6 heads, if the probability of a head is equal to the probability of a tail in a single trial.

Now, look at the bar graph distribution in figure 9.2 again. By converting this bar graph to a line graph, we would have the distribution in figure 9.3. Note the shape of this distribution and compare it to the shape of the normal curve in figure 7.13. They are remarkably similar, aren't they? It should not be difficult to imagine that, had we chosen to consider 1,000 samples of 10 tosses and then 10,000 samples of 10 tosses of our hypothetical coin, we would get a distribution increasingly like the normal curve. For practical purposes, we can say that if our sample size is large, say over 50, the binomial distribution is essentially equivalent to the normal curve. Another way of saying this is that the normal curve is an approximation of the binomial sampling distribution when the sample size is large.

Recall that we began our discussion of the binomial sampling distribution by assuming that the probability of heads was equal to the probability of tails in a single toss of our theoretical coin; that is, $p_h$ (heads) = $p_t$ (tails) = .50. Note that the distribution of probabilities in figure 9.3 has a mean proportion of .50. Probability theory tells us that, if a head and a tail are equally probable in a single toss of the

**Figure 9.3  Line Graph Frequency Distribution of Probabilities of Proportion of Heads in 100 Samples of 10 Tosses of a Hypothetical, Unbiased Coin**

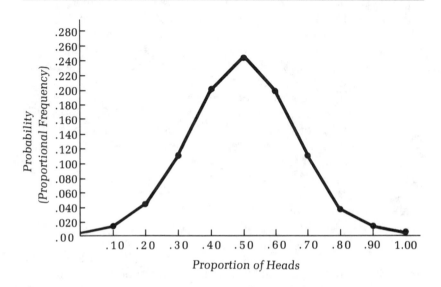

*Proportion of Heads*

coin, the sampling distribution of proportion of heads in a series of tosses has a mean proportion of .50. If we were actually flipping a real, unbiased coin, .50 is the proportion of heads that we would expect to get in the long run if we flipped it many times, keeping track of the number (and proportion) of heads that turned up as we flipped. Note that .50 is also the mean proportion of heads we would expect to get if we took many actual samples consisting of 10 or 100 or 1,000 flips of the coin and averaged the results from all the samples we took. In the absence of other data, then, the best guess or estimate that we could make of the proportion of heads that would come up in any single trial or in any series of trials is this mean—.50.

One additional important point should be made about probability theory and the binomial sampling distribution. While we will not provide the mathematical proof here, when probability principles are built into the sampling process (as in random sampling), the sampling technique itself provides an important part of the theoretical justification for using sampling distributions. By taking a random sample, for example, probability theory can tell us how our sample statistic (e.g., proportion of heads) will "behave"—that is, how the proportion of heads will be distributed around the mean proportion of

.50—in our sampling distribution. Any sampling distribution, whether it is normal, skewed, or has some other shape, tells us how sample statistics will be distributed if we have used a probability sampling technique. As we shall see, knowing how a statistic from a random sample behaves—that is, knowing the shape of the sampling distribution—is extremely useful in making estimates of population parameters.

Having established that the binomial sampling distribution we have been considering can be approximated by the normal curve, we can take one further preliminary step. As we noted in chapter 7, any normal curve can be converted to a standard normal curve, which has many important properties that can be used in our discussion of inferential statistics. It would be helpful to you to review the discussion of normal and standard normal curves and z-scores in chapter 7 before reading further.

As previously discussed, the standard normal curve may be described as a unimodal curve, symmetrical about the mean, with a mean of zero and a standard deviation of 1. Recall, too, that areas under the curve can be expressed in standard units called z-scores.

In inferential statistics, a sampling distribution is considered a distribution of probabilities. Some sampling distributions, as we have noted, are normal distributions. Areas under a sampling distribution curve correspond to probabilities. Normal curve sampling distributions, then, can be converted to a standard normal curve of probabilities with a mean of zero and a standard deviation of 1. In order to distinguish it from the standard deviation of distributions based on actual data, the standard deviation of a theoretically derived normal sampling distribution is called its **standard error**, reminding us that a sampling distribution is, as we have seen, a distribution of sampling error.

We said at the beginning of the chapter that there were inevitable uncertainties about the representativeness of samples, and we described certain steps we could take to reduce those uncertainties. The first step was taking a probability sample. For illustrative purposes, we chose the random sampling technique because, in the absence of any other guide, it gave us our best chance of getting a representative sample. We noted that, in a random sample, elements in the population are equally likely to be included in the sample. The second step was to determine the sampling distribution of our sample statistic. The sampling distribution indicates the probabilities of securing a particular result (or range of results), given the probability assumptions we make in creating the sampling distribution. We noted that many probability sampling distributions have the shape of the normal curve, whose properties would be useful in making *estimates* of population parameters. In particular, these properties help specify (in probabilities) the amount of sampling error that may occur.

If we take probability samples and use inferential statistics, we have gone as far as we can in reducing the uncertainties associated with using samples to represent populations. We have not, of course, completely eliminated all uncertainties—it is, in fact, not possible to do so. Using inferential statistics on our sample data requires us to be content with *estimates* of population parameters and statements about the *probabilities* that these estimates are correct. But both the theory upon which inferential statistics are based and years of experience by researchers in using these statistics testify to their usefulness.

## *Sampling Distributions for Other Sample Statistics*

As noted, the binomial distribution is useful for creating a sampling distribution when there are two equally probable outcomes in a single trial. It produces a normal sampling distribution, and we can use the properties of the normal curve to great advantage when those proportions are the sample statistics being used.

We can use this same general argument in constructing sampling distributions for many other, although not all, sample statistics. For example, the distribution of the mean salaries calculated from many large samples of police officers on a large urban police force (such as Chicago's) would be normally distributed very near the actual mean salary for the entire population of officers. Samples where the mean salary would be at least close to the actual population mean would be more frequent than would samples whose mean salary was quite different from the population mean salary and so on. In short, the sampling distribution for sample means is also a normal distribution. Furthermore, if we continued to sample Chicago's Police Department, the mean of the distribution of mean salaries from the various samples would come closer and closer to the actual population parameter, that is, the actual mean salary of all C.P.D. officers. But it is not necessary to actually draw a large number of samples to arrive at a sampling distribution of means for the C.P.D. Just as a mathematically derived binomial distribution can be used as a sampling distribution for proportions, a mathematically derived distribution of sample means can be generated and used as a sampling distribution for sample means.

Not all sampling distributions are normal distributions, however; for example, standard deviations have a skewed sampling distribution. When the sampling distribution is not normal, it may be possible to determine the shape of the distribution through the application of other mathematical models. If that is not possible, the sampling distribution may be created by having a computer simulate the empirical method we used to construct the distribution in figure 9.1. That is, the computer would simulate taking many samples from the same population, calculating the sample statistics in question for each sample, and then making a distribution of these sample statistics. Statisticians have used mathematical models or computer simulations to create sampling distributions for many sample statistics.

However it is derived, the sampling distribution is typically presented in the form of a table that gives the probabilities associated with the various values of the particular sample statistic being used. Regardless of the shape of the sampling distribution or the technique used to create it, however, the sampling distribution always serves the same basic purpose: it permits us to say how probable a particular result from a single sample is, given the initial assumptions used to create the sampling distribution.

## *A Few Words about Nonparametric Statistics*

In discussions of inferential statistics and sampling distributions, two types of statistics—parametric and nonparametric—are usually differentiated. The type we have been concerned with primarily in this chapter is called **parametric inferential statistics.** Although there are disagreements among statisticians about the importance of the distinction between the two types of inferential statistics, for our purposes, we shall simply note the two differences between them that are commonly cited.

The first difference concerns the level of measurement of a variable that is appropriate for each type (for a review of levels of measurement, see chapter 7). Parametric statistics assume the measurement of a variable at the interval or ratio level; **nonparametric inferential statistics** may be used with nominal or ordinal level data.

The second difference between parametric and nonparametric inferential statistics has to do with assumptions concerning the shape of the distribution of the values of the variable being studied. Parametric statistics are appropriate when the values are distributed normally in the population. Nonparametric statistics, on the other hand, are said to be "distribution free." That is, to use nonparametric inferential statistics, it is not necessary to assume anything about the shape of the distribution of the variable in the population.

While parametric and nonparametric statistics may be distinguished in the ways we have discussed, there is one important similarity, which should be mentioned. The sampling distributions for both types are based on the assumption that a probability (usually a random) sample has been chosen.

When a variable is measured at the nominal or ordinal level and when it seems inappropriate to assume that the variable is normally distributed in the population, nonparametric inferential statistics may be the best choice. Discussions of the most popular nonparametric statistics may be found in many inferential statistics texts.

We can now return to the issue with which we began this chapter: How can we use sample statistics to learn something about the parameters of the population from which the sample is drawn?

## *Point and Interval Estimation*

Suppose we want to estimate a population parameter, say a population mean such as the mean IQ of police recruits. If we have taken a simple random sample, we could simply estimate that the mean IQ of the population is equal to the mean IQ of the recruits in our sample. In effect, we are making what is called a **point estimate** of the population parameter. It is called a point estimate because, while we recognize that the sample mean may vary from the population mean to some extent, only one value (or "point") is used—namely, the numerical value of the sample mean—as our estimate. Point estimates have a desirable simplicity and specificity and are, in fact, our best "single value" estimate of the population parameter. However, these attractive characteristics must be weighed against the fact that the probability of our sample mean being exactly the same as the population mean is relatively small. In short, the probability that the point estimate is in error to some extent, is relatively high.

We could make a safer estimate of the population parameter if we used an **interval estimate** instead of a point estimate. That is, we could specify a range around the sample statistic and estimate that the population parameter falls within that range. Returning to our example of mean IQ scores, suppose we observe that the sample of recruits has a mean IQ of 120. Instead of saying that the estimate of the mean IQ in the population is 120 (a point estimate), we could say that it is somewhere between 115 and 125 or between 100 and 140 (interval estimates). Obviously, the wider the range we specify, the greater the likelihood that the specified interval will include the population mean. The increased confidence we gain by specifying a wide range, however, must be balanced against the decreased precision of our estimate.

## Confidence Intervals and Confidence Limits

The interval around the sample statistics that we specify for the purpose of estimating the population parameter is called a **confidence interval.** The end points of the specified range are the **confidence limits** for the interval.

How do we establish a confidence interval and specify the confidence limits? Suppose, again, that we are interested in making an estimate of a population's mean IQ. Because we know that the sampling distribution of means is a normal probability distribution, we can use the special properties of normal curves and z-scores to create intervals of various sizes. By choosing a particular value of z, we can specify the probability that the interval we create includes the population mean.

To understand the process by which these intervals are created, we must introduce some additional mathematical symbols. Remember that we are using sample statistics to estimate population parameters. To distinguish between the mean IQ score for the population and the mean IQ score for our sample, we use the symbols $\bar{X}$ and $\bar{x}$. Likewise, $S$ and $s$ represent the standard deviation of IQ scores for the population and for our sample, respectively. $\sigma_{\bar{x}}$ refers to the standard error of the mean (i.e., the standard deviation of the sampling distribution of means for a large number of random samples drawn from the same population) and $S_{\bar{x}}$ refers to an estimate of the standard error of the mean. As before, $n$ is the number of police recruits in our sample.

Expressed in these mathematical terms, then, we want to make an interval estimate of $\bar{X}$, the mean IQ score of the population of police recruits that we have sampled. To do so, we will make use of the sample statistics $\bar{x}$, $s$, and $n$ (which we can calculate from our sample data), as well as our general knowledge about sampling distributions for means, to make estimates of $\bar{X}$, $S$, and $\sigma_{\bar{x}}$. These estimates will be used in conjunction with the standard normal curve (z-scores) to create the interval estimate of $\bar{X}$.

To establish the center point for the interval, the sample mean IQ score ($\bar{x}$) is used as the estimate for the population mean IQ score ($\bar{X}$). Next we need an estimate of the standard error of the mean ($\sigma_{\bar{x}}$). At first it might seem that the standard deviation of our sample statistic ($s$)

could be used for this estimate. But think for a moment about the dispersion of scores in the two relevant distributions—the distribution of IQ scores in our sample of recruits and the distribution of the mean IQ scores from a large number of samples of a particular size (n) drawn from the same population. Suppose that the distribution of individual IQ scores looks like figure 9.4.

**Figure 9.4 Distribution of Individuals' IQ Scores for a Sample of Size *n*, Showing the Standard Deviation (s)**

*Individuals' IQ Scores*

The distribution of means from a large number of samples of size n drawn from the same population (i.e., the sampling distribution) might look something like figure 9.5. That is, the standard error of the mean ($\sigma_{\bar{x}}$) shown in figure 9.5 would be considerably smaller than the standard deviation (s) of scores (figure 9.4) in our sample. If we used the sample standard deviation to estimate the standard error of the mean, our estimate would be too large.* Hence, we need to adjust or "correct" our estimate of the standard error of the mean.

To arrive at a corrected estimate, we must consider the relationship between the standard error of the mean ($\sigma_{\bar{x}}$) and the standard deviation of the individual scores in the population (S). Without going into the details of its derivation, there is a constant relationship between these two quantities which is represented by formula 9.1.

$$\text{Formula 9.1} \qquad \sigma_{\bar{x}} = \frac{S}{\sqrt{n}} \; .$$

---

*Note that, in constructing the distribution in figure 9.5, we have assumed for illustrative purposes that the mean of the sampling distribution has the same value as the sample mean (120)—an assumption that may, of course, be incorrect. In general, however, sampling distribution standard errors are smaller than sample standard deviations.

**Figure 9.5  Distribution of Mean IQ Scores of Large Number of Samples of Size *n*, Showing the Standard Error ($\sigma_{\bar{x}}$)**

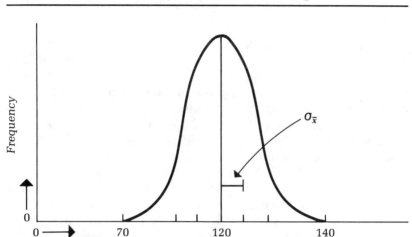

Here, $\sigma_{\bar{x}}$ is the standard error of the mean, S is the standard deviation of the individuals' IQ scores in the population, and *n* is the size of the sample. You may have noted that we still have not arrived at our goal of estimating the standard error of the mean. We do not know the value of S because we have observed only a sample statistic, not the entire population. We can, however, use our sample standard deviation (*s*) as an estimate of the standard deviation in the population (S).

Hence, we can use formula 9.2 to estimate the standard error of the mean:

$$\textbf{Formula 9.2} \quad S_{\bar{x}} = \frac{s}{\sqrt{n}}$$

where $S_{\bar{x}}$ is our *estimate* of the standard error of the mean ($\sigma_{\bar{x}}$), *s* is the standard deviation of the individual scores of our sample statistic, and *n* is the size of our sample.

One other minor adjustment in our formula has to be made because the standard deviation of individual scores in samples tends to be somewhat smaller than the corresponding standard deviation of individual scores in the population. The conventional means of making this correction is to subtract one from the sample size. Thus, to calculate the final estimate of the standard error of the mean, we use formula 9.3.

**Formula 9.3**    $S_{\bar{x}} = \dfrac{s}{\sqrt{n-1}}$ .

It is useful at this point to review our progress. Our basic objective is to use a sample statistic (in this case, mean IQ, $\bar{x}$) to estimate the corresponding population parameter ($\bar{X}$). We know that some sampling error is likely whenever we sample, and that as a result, $\bar{x}$ probably will not have exactly the same value as $\bar{X}$. We also know how the means of random samples of a fixed size ($n$), drawn from the same population, are distributed; that is, we know that the sampling distribution for means is a normal curve. We know, too, that there is a constant relationship between the standard error of the sampling distribution for means ($\sigma_{\bar{x}}$) and the standard deviation of the distribution of individual scores in the population ($S$), expressed in formula 9.1. We know that the sampling distribution can be treated as a probability distribution; that is, that an area under the curve defined by specifying a range of values of the mean corresponds to the probability that a particular sample mean will fall within that range. We don't know the value of $\bar{X}$, but we can put together the statistics we calculate from our sample data, with what we know about sampling distributions of means, to make an interval estimate of the population mean. To do so, we make a number of estimates. We use $\bar{x}$ to estimate $\bar{X}$, and we use $s$ and $n$ to calculate $S_{\bar{x}}$, which, when factored into formulas 9.2 and 9.3, gives us our estimate of $\sigma_{\bar{x}}$.

Having determined our estimate of the standard error of the mean, we can now turn to a discussion of the use of z-scores in creating confidence intervals for estimating population parameters from sample statistics. Remember that, in the absence of any other data, our best estimate of the population mean is the mean of our sample data. To improve our chances of making an accurate estimate of the mean IQ score for the population ($\bar{X}$), we want to create a range or interval around the sample mean ($\bar{x}$) within which we will estimate the population mean ($\bar{X}$)to fall. Furthermore, we want to state the probability that our population mean ($\bar{X}$) actually falls within the range we specify.

The general formula for constructing a confidence interval around our sample mean with a specified confidence level that the population mean falls within the interval is

**Formula 9.4**    $cl = \bar{x} \pm z\,(S_{\bar{x}})$

In formula 9.4, cl stands for confidence limits, $\bar{x}$ is the sample mean, and $S_{\bar{x}}$ is the estimate of the standard error of the mean for samples of size n from formula 9.3. The confidence interval is the range between $\bar{x} - z\,(S_{\bar{x}})$ and $\bar{x} + z\,(S_{\bar{x}})$. We calculate the values of $\bar{x}$ and $S_{\bar{x}}$ for our sample data. Then, by entering different values of z in this formula, we can construct confidence intervals of different sizes, with corresponding differences in our level of confidence that the range we have determined includes the population mean.

As we learned in chapter 7, the proportion of area under the standard normal curve between z = –1.96 and z = + 1.96 is .95 (see figures 9.6 and 7.16). If we wanted to be 95 percent confident that the specified range will include the population mean we would enter a z value of 1.96 in formula 9.4. If we wanted a 99 percent confidence interval, we would substitute 2.575 for z in formula 9.4.

**Figure 9.6 Using the Standard Normal Curve as a Probability Curve for Establishing Confidence Levels**

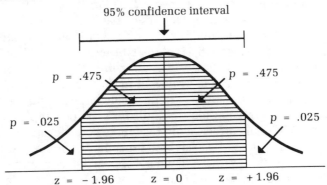

95% of the area under the probability curve is included in the interval z = - 1.96 to 1.96.

95% confidence interval

p = .475

p = .475

p = .025

p = .025

z = - 1.96        z = 0        z = + 1.96

Returning to our example of police recruits, recall that our sample mean IQ ($\bar{x}$) is 120. Suppose our sample size (n) is 100, the standard deviation of IQ scores in our sample (s) is 16, and we decide to establish a 95 percent confidence interval. Our estimate of the standard error of the mean (from formula 9.3) is given by:

$$S_{\bar{x}} = \frac{s}{\sqrt{n-1}} = \frac{16}{\sqrt{100-1}} = \frac{16}{\sqrt{99}} = \frac{16}{9.95} = 1.61$$

Our 95 percent probability or confidence limit formula would then give us

$$cl = 120 \pm 1.96 \, (1.61).$$

The confidence limits would then be:

$$120 + 1.96(1.61) = 123.16$$

$$\text{and}$$

$$120 - 1.96(1.61) = 116.84.$$

Hence, given our sample data, we can say that there is a .95 probability that the population mean IQ will be included in the interval between 116.84 and 123.16. By using the general formula and the table of z-scores in appendix B, we can determine the confidence limits for any confidence level we wish, simply by substituting different values of z in formula 9.4. The confidence interval that we establish constitutes our interval estimate of the population parameter (in this case, the mean IQ) in which we are interested.

Note that in specifying an interval within which we estimate our mean to fall, we are, in effect, making an allowance for sampling error. The larger the interval we specify, the larger the sampling error for which we allow and the safer our estimate.

Note also that the formula we used to obtain our estimate of the standard error of the mean $(S_{\bar{x}})$ included the term, $\sqrt{n\text{-}1}$. Hence, sample size plays an important role in establishing confidence limits, but the size of the population is irrelevant in these calculations. This is true so long as we are dealing with relatively large samples of at least 30 cases. Calculating confidence limits for smaller samples requires the use of additional correctional procedures in the formulas we have discussed. We will not discuss these procedures here. Nevertheless, an examination of formulas 9.3 and 9.4 shows that as sample size (n) increases, the confidence interval associated with a particular confidence level (e.g., 95 percent or 99 percent) gets smaller. This, in turn, means that as the sample size increases, our estimates of population parameters from sample statistics become more precise.

A few words of caution about inferring population parameters from sample statistics are in order. First, when you encounter a statistic, such as a crime rate, that purports to refer to the characteristics of a large population, you should ask yourself whether the data reported are actual population data, or whether they are sample statistics used as point estimates of population parameters. It is permissible to make point estimates of population parameters, but it is important to indicate that this is what has been done.

Second, confidence limits should be interpreted with care. A confidence level of 95 percent, for example, means that if we took a large number of random samples and used each of the sample means to construct a confidence interval, approximately 95 percent of those confidence intervals would include the mean and approximately 5 percent would not. This suggests the usefulness of *replication*—repeating the study by drawing a different sample from the same population and calculating new confidence intervals at the same confidence level. The two confidence intervals can then be compared. The chances of getting *two* confidence intervals that do not include the population mean are much smaller than the chances that a *single* confidence interval does not include the mean.

Third, inferential statistics are based on probability theory principles that assume probability sampling, and enable us, therefore, to estimate sampling error. However, they do not enable us to assess the influence of other types of bias that may have entered into our research procedures, such as poor research design, careless operationalization of the variables, and so forth.

Finally, while some sampling distributions, such as those for proportions and means, are normal, some are not—for example, the distribution of chi square $(\chi^2)$, which we will consider later in this chapter.

## *Testing Hypotheses*

A hypothesis is a hunch or proposition that a researcher hopes to confirm or reject by assembling and analyzing relevant data. Whatever particular variable or variables the hypothesis may be about, it can usually be translated into an assertion about a population parameter or a relationship between population parameters. When we gather data on an entire population, we can confirm or reject our hypothesis by examining the population data directly. Frequently, however, we must rely on sample data to test a hypothesis about a population; in this case, we can use what we have just learned about probability and sampling distributions to help us.

A hypothesis that asserts that different values of a particular independent variable will cause differences in a dependent variable will be referred to here as a **research hypothesis.** We cannot test a hypothesis that asserts a difference in results directly, however, because any differences that we observe in our sample data may have resulted from sampling error. Suppose, though, that we formulate an alternative hypothesis, or a **null hypothesis**, that asserts that there will be *no* differences in the results except those resulting from random (sampling) error. We can then construct a sampling distribution based on the assumption that there are no differences in the probabilities associated with the possible results. This hypothetical distribution permits us to determine the probability that any given result will occur if the null hypothesis is correct. Hence, we can test the research hypothesis indirectly by testing the null hypothesis directly. If our actual results have a very low probability under the null hypothesis, we have some empirical support for an alternative hypothesis—our research hypothesis. We must remember, though, that in rejecting the null hypothesis when our observed results have a low probability, we are still taking a risk. Even though the results that we obtain are quite unlikely to have occurred by chance when the null hypothesis is correct they may nevertheless have occurred by chance in this particular instance. Again, this possibility illustrates the importance of replication studies.

## Type I and Type II Error

Actually, in making a decision to accept or reject a null hypothesis, we always risk making one of two possible types of error. The first, called a **Type I error**, occurs when we reject a null hypothesis that is, in fact, correct. The second, a **Type II error**, happens when we fail to reject a null hypothesis that should be rejected. Estimating the probability of making a Type II error is a complicated procedure beyond the scope of this text. Estimating the risk of making a Type I error, however, is considerably less difficult. In fact, this is what we do when we construct a sampling distribution and use it to test the null hypothesis.

Suppose our research hypothesis is that children who watch a violent television program will be more violent in their play after the program than children who watch a nonviolent program. This research hypothesis might be translated into an assertion that the mean level of violence in play will be higher for children who watch a violent television program than for those who watch a nonviolent one. This is, in effect, an assertion about a population parameter: the mean level of violence of children in play. To assemble the relevant data, we select a sample of children and randomly assign them to one of two groups. One group is shown a violent television program, and the other group a nonviolent one. In a play period following the television program, the level of violence each child displays is measured (naturally, what constitutes violent behaviors has been determined in advance). We then construct frequency distributions of the violence data for each of the two groups, and calculate the mean level of violence for each of these distributions.

A null hypothesis in this case asserts that there will be no difference between the mean levels of violence for these two groups; that is, in effect, the two groups came from the same population. To test the null hypothesis, we need the sampling distribution for the differences between two sample means, assuming that the samples were selected at random from the same population. The shape of this sampling distribution, called **Student's *t*** or simply t, varies with sample size, but approximates a normal distribution if n (the size of the sample) is large (30 or more) and can, therefore, be treated as a distribution of z-scores.

The formula for calculating t is available in most advanced inferential statistics textbooks. For our purposes, it will suffice simply to observe that we could calculate t for the particular difference between the means we have observed. Then, referring to a sampling distribution of t in a t table (also available in most advanced textbooks), we could determine the probability of obtaining (by chance) a difference in mean level of violence as large as the one observed, if in fact the two sample means came from two different samples drawn at random from the same population.

Certain values of our sample statistics—in this case, the difference between means—will cause us to reject the null hypothesis. Values that are highly improbable, assuming that the null hypothesis is true, are called **contradictory values.** These contradictory values constitute the **rejection region**, or *critical region*, for the null hypothesis.

## Significance Level

Which values of our sample statistics will lead us to reject the null hypothesis? Regardless of the sampling distribution to which we are referring, researchers often adopt a 5 percent level as the cutoff point in deciding whether to reject the null hypothesis. For a normal sampling distribution, for example, the .05 level yields a z value of 1.96. For any sampling distribution, regardless of its shape, the cutoff point is referred to as the **significance level**. This level can be set at any level the researcher chooses in advance of the research, though the 5 percent and 1 percent levels are most commonly adopted. Establishing a significance level of .05 means that we run the risk of making a Type I error 5 times out of 100; a significance level of .01 reduces that risk to 1 in 100. See figure 9.7 for an illustration of a normal hypothesis testing probability curve with a .05 significance level.

Consider, again, our study of the effects of television violence on the violence of children's play. Suppose the data show a difference in the mean violence levels between the two groups that has a probability level of .03. Remember that we are testing the null hypothesis (i.e.,

**Figure 9.7 The Normal Curve and Hypothesis Testing at the .05
Level: The t-test for Differences between Means (Large Samples)**

Sampling distribution for differences between means from two samples
drawn from the same population, treating $t$ as a $z$ score.

The probability that this interval includes the difference between the two
means we observed if the two samples were drawn from the same
population is .95

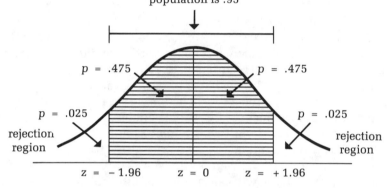

The probability that our observed difference between means is in a
rejection region is .025 + .025 = .05 or less.

that there is no significant difference between the mean levels of violence in our two groups). A probability of .03 means that only 3 times
in 100 would a difference as large as the one observed occur if, in fact,
there was no difference in the mean level. Another way of saying this
is that we run a 3 percent risk of making a Type I error, that is, rejecting the null hypothesis when it is true. If the significance level was set
at .05, we would, on the basis of our findings, reject the null hypothesis, leaving our research hypothesis as an alternative: watching television violence is related to levels of violence in play. Note, however,
that if we had set the significance level at .01, we could not reject the
null hypothesis. Where we set the significance level is essentially arbitrary; the governing factor is dependent upon what consequences
may flow from making a Type I or Type II error. What significance or
confidence level would you set, for example, if the study concerned
differences in mean death rates between two samples of patients, one
of which was exposed to a controversial new drug?

Finally, some words of caution about interpreting levels of significance and confidence intervals are in order. Significance levels and
confidence intervals tell us the *probability* of obtaining a particular

result (e.g., difference in means) by chance when we draw different samples from a population. They do *not* tell us whether any *particular* sample statistic is the result of chance or nonchance factors. In addition, in large samples, a small difference may be statistically significant; therefore, the attained significance level is directly related to the size of the sample we use.

Finally, the differences between the random assignment of members of a study group to two research conditions (as we described above and in chapter 3) must be clearly understood. Random assignment is essentially a method of randomizing any differences that might exist between two or more subgroups of the total study group. When we randomly assign a group of subjects to different subgroups, we are actually taking two random samples, without replacement, of the population consisting of the total group of study participants. The whole group may or may not itself be a random sample of some other population; that is, the whole group may have been selected at random from the population of all youngsters in a particular school, city, or state. Usually, however, participants are selected from these other populations using a purposive or some other nonprobability sampling technique. Random assignment *within* nonprobability samples can be used to measure the probability of differences between the randomly assigned groups in, for example, mean levels of violence observed. But in such cases inferential statistics do not permit us to make estimates of parameters or test hypotheses pertaining to a larger population from which the subjects were selected using nonprobability sampling techniques. Unless the study group as a whole has been selected randomly, we have no way of knowing how typical it is of the larger population of which they are a part. Randomly assigning members of the study group to two different study conditions does nothing to ensure their typicality as far as the population of all children or even children in a particular city or school is concerned. Unless we have selected a probability sample of some larger population, then, the population to which we may legitimately generalize our results is limited to the study group we selected and from within which we made random assignments.

## Assessing Relationships Between Variables in Tables

In an earlier chapter, cross-tabulation in a contingency table was discussed as a technique to determine if two variables are related. In some cases, however, relationships between variables are not that apparent, particularly when the variables include a large range of values. Inferential statistics provide a systematic way of determining if variables are related by enabling us to compare our observations of actual distributions of characteristics with expectations derived from probability theory. Here, a frequently used and easily understood statistic for assessing relationships between variables in tables will be considered.

## Chi Square

**Chi square** $(\chi^2)$ is a statistic used *only with relatively large, random samples* to test for a relationship between two variables measured at the nominal level and cross-tabulated in a contingency table. Through its calculation, we can determine if empirically obtained cell frequencies differ significantly from those we would have expected if no relationship existed between the variables. In short, chi square is a sample statistic that has a known sampling distribution, and, therefore, it can be used to test a null hypothesis. If the observed cell frequencies and the expected cell frequencies are identical, the chi square has a value of 0. The greater the difference between the observed and expected cell frequencies, the larger is the value of chi square. By setting a significance level in advance, we can compare the value of the chi square we compute with the chi square distribution (appendix C) and determine if the null hypothesis can be rejected.

Suppose we are interested in the effects of the sex of juvenile delinquents on court dispositions. Our null hypothesis states that there is no relationship between the sex of delinquents and court dispositions. We collect the sample data shown in table 9.3.

**Table 9.3 Court Disposition by Sex (Observed Cell Frequencies)**

| | Court Disposition | | |
| Sex | Jail Time | Released to Parents | Total |
| --- | --- | --- | --- |
| Male | 84 | 16 | 100 |
| Female | 30 | 20 | 50 |
| Total | 114 | 36 | n = 150 |

Assuming that sex (the independent variable) and disposition (the dependent variable) were unrelated, we would expect that since males account for two-thirds of our sample (100/150 = 2/3), they should also account for two-thirds of the jailed delinquents and two-thirds of those released to parents. Two-thirds of 114 (the number of delinquents jailed) is 76. (Note that this procedure is analogous to percentaging in the direction of the independent variable.) Two-thirds of 36 is 24. Subtracting the figures from their respective column totals in our table of sample data, we can compute the **expected frequencies (E)** for each of the cells in the table. The results are shown in table 9.4.

**Table 9.4  Court Disposition by Sex (Expected Cell Frequencies)**

| Sex | Court Disposition | | Total |
| --- | --- | --- | --- |
| | Jail Time | Released to Parents | |
| Male | 76 | 24 | 100 |
| Female | 38 | 12 | 50 |
| Total | 114 | 36 | n = 150 |

We can now compute chi square to see if the difference between the observed and the expected frequencies is statistically significant by using formula 9.5,

**Formula 9.5** $$\chi^2 = \sum \frac{(O - E)^2}{E},$$

where $\chi^2$ is chi square, O is the observed frequency in a given cell of the observed data table, E is the expected frequency in the corresponding cell of the expected frequency table, and $\Sigma$ represents the sum of the ratios calculated for the cells. Doing the calculation, we find that

$$\chi^2 = \frac{(8)^2}{76} + \frac{(8)^2}{24} + \frac{(8)^2}{38} + \frac{(8)^2}{12} = 10.5$$

After obtaining a chi square of 10.5, we must calculate the degrees of freedom (df) associated with this particular table because the sampling distribution of chi square is different for each different table size.[1] For any particular table, we can calculate the degrees of freedom (df) according to formula 9.6:

**Formula 9.6**   $df = (r - 1)(c - 1),$

where r is the number of rows and c is the number of columns. In our example, the table has two rows and two columns, so degrees of freedom equal one. Using one degree of freedom, then, we can look up the value of chi square in the chi square table and find that a chi square of this size could have come about by chance less than 1 percent of the time. Thus, we can reject the null hypothesis. The table provides evidence that there is, indeed, some relationship between sex of delinquent and court disposition. It is important to note that while chi square tells us whether or not a relationship exists between variables, it does not indicate how strong the relationship is. It is extremely important to remember this point when we recall that the significance level attained is related to the size of the sample used. With very large samples, it means little to say that we have a significant chi square; and with extremely small samples, it also means little to say that we have an insignificant relationship. A more important question concerns the strength of the relationship.

## Correlation Coefficient

The correlation coefficient r, you will recall from chapter 8, is a measure of the strength of association between two variables, which can be used to describe the relationship between two variables. It may also be used to test hypotheses on sample data, since the correlation coefficient (r) and the difference between correlation coefficients have known sampling distributions. Therefore, we can use the sampling distribution of r to determine the statistical significance of a sample r.

## Other Statistical Tests for Cross-Tabulations and Correlations

When a table containing sample data is presented, it is often accompanied by a statistic—perhaps $\chi^2$ (chi square), $\tau$ (tau), $\tau_b$ (tau$_b$), $o$ (rho), t (tee), $\gamma$ (gamma)—and an indication of the probability level, such as p < .001. While it is beyond the scope of this work to consider these statistics in detail, two comments are in order. First, all of these statistics are used to determine if a relationship between the cross-tabulated variables exists and/or to assess the strength of such a relationship. As discussed earlier, the probability level (p) indicates the proportion of times observed results can be expected to have occurred by chance alone. Thus, $p < .001$ means that the chances are less than 1 in a 1,000 that the results would occur by chance if a null hypothesis were true. Second, each of these statistics makes certain assumptions about the characteristics of the data, such as the level of measurement used, whether samples are independent, random, etc. Each statistic has its strengths, limitations and peculiarities. Applied to the same set of data, one test may produce a statistically significant result while another may not. Therefore, it is important to know if the data meet the assumptions of the statistical tests employed. Discussions of the assumptions on which various statistical tests rest, the techniques used to calculate the statistics, and their limitations can be found in any good statistics textbook.

Third, statistical significance should not be confused with what we might call fundamental significance. *Statistical significance* is a term that refers only to the application of probability theory in the testing of hypotheses; fundamental significance refers to something that is important in a practical or ethical way in human life. Statistically significant results from an analysis of data say nothing at all about the fundamental significance of the topic being investigated or, for that matter, of the results obtained.

## Notes

1. For a thorough discussion of degrees of freedom, see William Mendenhall, Lyman Ott, and Richard F. Larson, *Statistics: A Tool for the Social Sciences* (New York: Duxbury Press, 1974), p. 218.

## Review Questions

1. Compare and contrast population parameters and sample statistics.
2. What is sampling error?
3. What is a sampling distribution?
4. What are the principal differences between parametric and nonparametric inferential statistics?
5. Compare and contrast point and interval estimates of a population parameter.
6. Compare and contrast standard deviations and standard errors.
7. Why is the standard deviation of scores in a distribution larger than the standard error of the sampling distribution for the mean of those scores?
8. How and why can z-scores be used to create confidence intervals and establish confidence levels?

9. Compare and contrast null hypotheses and research hypotheses.
10. How are inferential statistics used in testing hypotheses?
11. Why do most inferential statistics permit only the testing of a null hypotheses?
12. Compare and contrast Type I and Type II errors. Why do the inferential statistics we have discussed permit us to estimate only a Type I error?

## *Exercises*

1. Take your own 100 samples of ten flips of a coin, recording the proportion of heads that occur in each sample of ten. (Be sure the coin is tossed so that it turns over several times in the air before you catch it.) Then construct a frequency distribution of sample results and compare it with table 9.1.
2. Suppose you have selected a random sample of 40 persons from a population of 2000 and measured their ages. Suppose further that the ages in your sample are normally distributed with a mean of 26 and a standard deviation of 2.5 years. Make a point estimate of the population mean. Calculate .50 percent, 95 percent and 99 percent confidence intervals for estimates of the population mean. Write a paragraph interpreting the results.
3. Using the same sample statistics, calculate 50 percent, 95 percent and 99 percent confidence intervals for a sample of size 200. Compare these with the results you obtained above. What do the differences in results tell you about the effects of sample size on interval estimates?
4. Calculate $\chi^2$ for the following hypothetical table and interpret the results.

**Number of Days in Jail by Sex of Offender
for First Offense, Theft over $150.00**

| Sex of Offender | Number of Days in Jail | | |
|---|---|---|---|
| | *4 days or less* | *5 days or more* | |
| *Male* | 32 | 148 | 180 |
| *Female* | 15 | 5 | 20 |
| | 47 | 153 | 200 |

# 10

## Common Sources of Error in Presenting Research Findings

Most people have heard of "loaded" questions—questions that, because of the way they are asked, tend to elicit the response the asker favors. It is less well recognized, but no less important, that answers may be loaded as well.

We have argued that researchers always conduct research in the context of their own values and collect data because either they or their employers recognize some issue as important. Because values affect the problem investigated (and perhaps also the conclusions or solutions proposed), it is always possible that others viewing the same problem may see it from a different, even opposite, value position. The researcher following the rules of the scientific perspective must, therefore, strive to present data in as "pure" a form as possible; that is, with as little distortion or falsification based on personal values as possible. The researcher may—and in most instances should—provide the reader with his honest interpretations of the data, including any inferences he believes are justified. However, the researcher also has an obligation to keep the presentation of the data separate from the inferences and speculations he or she draws from them.

The reader, the consumer of research, should also be aware of the distinction between the data the researcher presents and the interpretations the researcher generates. This distinction is particularly important when data are presented in written form because the reader is ordinarily not in a position to ask clarifying questions of the researcher. In this chapter, we want to indicate some of the principles and pitfalls of data presentation and analysis, and suggest some ways to avoid deceiving and being deceived.

## The Popular Misuses of Science

Science is a highly valued activity in American society. There are, of course, the humorous and pathetic stereotype of the scientist who cannot see the obvious, and the sinister image of the "mad" scientist, but most people look upon science and scientists with great respect.

**229**

Consequently, if one has something to sell—be it an underarm deodorant, a biochemical theory, or a program for reform of the truancy laws—the likelihood of having the product accepted is greatly increased if it can be linked to science. But the nature of the connection between science and the product may vary from extremely tenuous to very direct. Therefore, you should be both aware and critical of some of the aspects of this effort to have the prestige of science rub off on the product. We shall describe four commonly used means of connecting science with a product.

## Scientific Costumes and Props

Many attempts to connect science with a product are based upon a reversal of the commonly known phenomenon of guilt by association. We might call it the attempt to establish credibility by association in which the presenter tries to give the product a scientific aura by associating it with some of the trappings of science. Where visual images are used—in newspapers, magazines, journals, television, motion pictures—the presenter may appear in a white lab coat in a setting that includes a collection of scientific instruments: microscopes, test tubes and beakers, computers, questionnaires, shelves full of books, and so forth.

Now, it is true that some scientists do wear lab coats, many depend upon well-equipped laboratories, and most have offices well stocked with books related to their work. Nonetheless, when the relevance of these props for the data and conclusions being presented is not obvious, the consumer should question whether the props are, in fact, related in any reasonable way to the message being presented. Is the man in the white lab coat who is talking about headaches someone who really knows about headaches? Does the drab-looking person with heavy rimmed glasses and elbow on the lie detector machine really know how to read and interpret a polygraph record, and the pitfalls involved in its use?

## Quoting or Relying on Authorities

Many individuals, including scientists, like to quote or otherwise rely on authorities to increase their own credibility. References to authorities, such as ''Dr. X has found . . .,'' ''Several physicians interviewed contend . . .,'' ''A review of the psychological research on this topic indicates . . .,'' and ''Professor Y believes . . .,'' are frequently found in the text of research reports. Research reports and theoretical articles are usually accompanied by extensive footnotes and bibliographies, which indicate to the reader the context of the research being presented and the source of the cited literature. Thus, if the researcher relies on authorities to support a particular argument, enough bibliographic information should be provided for the reader to decide whether such support exists. Careful consumers should demand such documentation and attempt to appraise the expertise of the cited authorities in relation to the issue under consideration. Since scientific training is quite specialized, one cannot expect a scientist trained in one field to have much knowledge about another. Most physicians are not experts on psychology, for example, and few political scientists are knowledgeable about the biochemistry of water pollution. When people see titles such as "Doctor" or "Professor," or abbreviations for degrees such as Ph.D., M.A., or J.D. after a researcher's name, they may be especially prone to accept the researcher's expertise in many fields, not just the one in which he or she was trained. When titles are used, the researcher should indicate the field or discipline specialty in which the title was earned.

## Using Technical Vocabulary

While everyday language is adequate for ordinary social communication, it often lacks the precision required for scientific purposes. Consequently, scientists have developed specialized, technical vocabularies, inventing new terms and attributing specialized meanings to ordinary ones. To work in a particular field, then, one must be familiar with its "jargon," or specialized language. A presenter may try to give a scientific flavor to a presentation by suggesting or demonstrating familiarity with the jargon. For example, a reference to a PCV (pollution control valve in an automobile exhaust system) or dementia praecox (a medical term for a type of mental disorder) suggests that the presenter is an expert and knows all there is to know about the matter at hand. The use of disciplinary jargon can be roughly equivalent to name dropping. That is, the presenter may mention a few technical words—often in a deliberately offhand fashion—to give the impression of expertise or to suggest that scientific techniques have verified the quality of the product. Advertisers, scientists, lawyers, and social reformers alike sometimes do this. For example, a creme rinse is advertised as being "pH controlled," and a product for asthma sufferers is alleged to "relax tense bronchial muscles fast." Similarly, advocates select names for theories, reforms or programs that may promise more than can be delivered—"Scared Straight," "wholistic health," "officer-friendly," and "equitable justice" are examples. Laypersons as well as scientists must keep in mind that the use of a few technical words or catchy titles by themselves do not necessarily indicate either expertise or scientific support for claims.

The layperson often has little choice but to rely on a "translator" to put the theory and research of the discipline into more generally understood terms. Translation is, of course, a tricky business. Translators can overgeneralize the results of research, add inferences or interpretations not warranted by the data, or distort the inferences and interpretations of the original presenter. Consequently, although all of us will probably be forced to rely upon such translations to a greater extent in the future, we should be cautious in evaluating them. Does the translator have expertise in the area in which he is translating? Are other translations of the data available for comparison?

There is a second characteristic of the language used by scientists that is worth noting. One rarely finds a statement containing a personal pronoun, such as "*I* interviewed 24 subjects . . ." or "*We* think this information indicates . . .," in research reports. Researchers often consciously avoid using these pronouns in describing research and its results, preferring passive statements such as "Twenty-four subjects were interviewed . . ." or "The data indicate. . .," because they (or their editors) believe it is good article writing style or because it lends a detached, objective air to their scientific reports. The reader should note, however, that a researcher's use of the passive voice in reporting on research does not make either the research or the researcher more objective. Regardless of the writing style used to communicate the findings, the researcher is still a human being who may indeed fall victim to any or all of the pitfalls discussed in this book, even though he attempts to adhere to scientific perspectives and methods.

## Presenting Numbers, Percentages, Rates

Because numbers are directly associated with science, many people attach some degree of objectivity and precision to the study, evaluation, or other activity that produces such numbers. That is why presentations of the form, "Two out of three doctors recommend . . .," "Fourteen percent of the respondents said . . .," and "Only 4.2 milligrams of tar . . .," are so popular. Compare the following pairs of sentences.

- Joe has three brothers and two sisters.
- Joe has only two brothers and three sisters.

- The Defense Department estimates that about 50 percent of the young men who become 19 years old in 1973 will be drafted in 1974.

- The Defense Department estimates that as few as 50 percent of the young men who become 19 years old in 1973 will be drafted in 1974! (Try substituting ''as many as'' in this sentence.)

- The crude birth rate in country A is estimated to be 2.5 per 100.

- The crude birth rate in country A is estimated to be as high as 2.5 per 100. (Try substituting ''as low as'' in this sentence.)

- In this experiment, 15 percent of the male subjects manifested serious psychiatric symptoms, while 13 percent of the female subjects did so.

- In this ''experiment,'' 15 percent of the male subjects manifested serious psychiatric symptoms, *while only 13 percent of the female subjects did so!*

As these examples show, such presentations can be potentially misleading in several ways. First, words such as ''just,'' ''only,'' ''as few as,'' ''as many as,'' ''as high as,'' ''as low as,'' ''more,'' or ''less'' often have the effect—intentional or unintentional—of distorting the data being presented. Second, underlining, italicizing, capitalizing, or otherwise emphasizing certain words or phrases can also color the meaning. Third, percentages and rates calculated on either small or very large base numbers may be extremely misleading: 1 out of 3 is 33 percent and 3,000 out of 3,000,000 is .001 percent; a change from 2 to 6 is a 300 percent increase and a change from 5,000 to 3,000 is a 40 percent decrease. We cannot really make sense of these percentages (or any other rates) without knowing what the base numbers are.

As a final note, the procedures for associating science with a particular ''product'' can be used singly or in combination, and while none of them is inherently misleading, each may be. In short, every effort should be made to keep the data separate from those aspects of its presentation that, attractive as they may be, are irrelevant to the issue at hand. The consumer should ask the following questions to help separate the data from the props used in their presentation:

1. What value position is at stake in the presentation?
2. Do the data presented support the conclusions offered?
3. Are there alternative ways to interpret the data?
4. How reliable and valid are the data?

5. Is the presenter using any tricks to convince the audience of the truthfulness of the conclusions presented?

## *Graphs: Their Uses and Misuses*

Graphs are spatial representations of numerical data. They are among the most vivid means of communicating descriptive data to an audience. They come in many shapes and sizes and, if constructed with care and interpreted with caution, they communicate very well indeed. To the unwary, however, their striking visual characteristics may mask more than they reveal about the data upon which the graphic representation is based.

### Bar Graphs

In addition to vertical bar graphs presented earlier, bar graphs can be horizontal. A *horizontal* bar graph is constructed by putting the frequency dimension of the graph on the horizontal axis and the response categories on the vertical axis, as in figure 10.1.

**Figure 10.1  A Horizontal Bar Graph: Sex of Shoplifters**

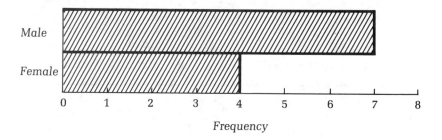

Both horizontal and vertical bar graphs can also be segmental. A *segmental* bar graph uses the basic format of the bar graph but adds information by partitioning each bar into segments. Each segment represents a part of the whole, with the whole represented by the bar's total length. For example, a bar graph representing the amount of cocaine produced by five cocaine-producing countries could have the bars divided into segments representing the proportion of cocaine consumed domestically and the proportion exported, as in figure 10.2. While each bar in this graph has only two segments, a bar can include as many segments as needed.

**Figure 10.2    Cocaine Production and Disposition in Five Countries**

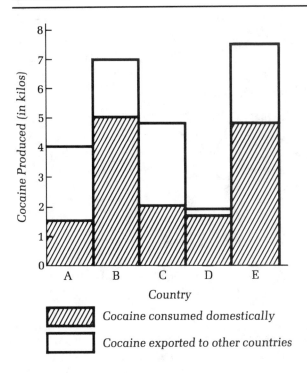

**Pie Graphs**

Pie Graphs are constructed by drawing a circle, representing a whole, and dividing it into wedges, representing its component parts. The size of each wedge is proportional to the part of the whole that that particular segment represents. See figure 10.3.

**Pictographs**

A pictograph uses symbols to represent data, usually in one of two ways. In one type of pictograph, a symbol of fixed size represents a specified number of objects, and several such symbols represent the total number. The number of law enforcement officers in three countries, for example, might be depicted with a graph as in figure 10.4.

**Figure 10.3   The Distribution of the Police Department Budget Dollar in City A**

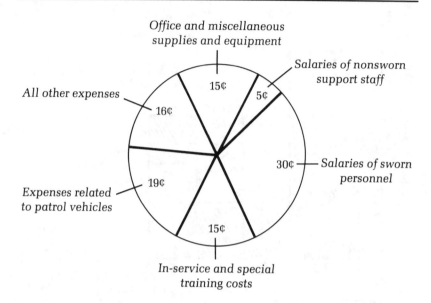

A second type of pictograph uses a single symbol, and varies the size of the symbol to represent variations in the quantity of the objects represented. Thus, the number of dollars spent by two countries for law enforcement in a given year might be represented as in figure 10.5.

**Figure 10.4   Law Enforcement Officers in Three Countries**

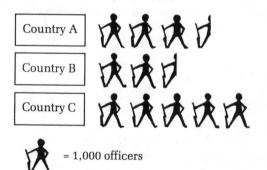

**Figure 10.5    Number of Dollars Spent for Law Enforcement**

Country A       Country B

      ($12,550,000)                           ($7,525,000)

## Hazards in Interpreting Graphs

Because graphic presentations of data are powerful communicators, they may seriously mislead an observer who is not alert. What should the designer or the reader of a graph look for? First, the designer chooses the scale to which the graph is drawn. The scale that is chosen affects the appearance of the graph, and may affect how the graph is interpreted. Consider, for example, the bar graphs shown in figure 10.6. Is it possible that all of these bar graphs are representations of the same data? The answer is yes. By changing the distance allocated to each frequency on the vertical axis and/or each category on the horizontal axis, very different visual impressions can be created. Changes in the radii of pie graphs can have the same effect. The scale can minimize or maximize the impression of differences. For this reason, the reader should watch for possible discrepancies between the visual impression created by the graph and the actual data. Such discrepancies cannot be detected, of course, unless one knows what the actual data are. Hence, the frequency dimension of bar graphs should be clearly marked and the raw data for pie graphs and other spatial representations of data should be clearly indicated. Graphs for which no raw data are provided should be ignored, since it is impossible to interpret their significance.

**Figure 10.6    Vertical Bar Graphs**

**Figure 10.7  Number of Deaths by Homicide in City A, 1982–85**

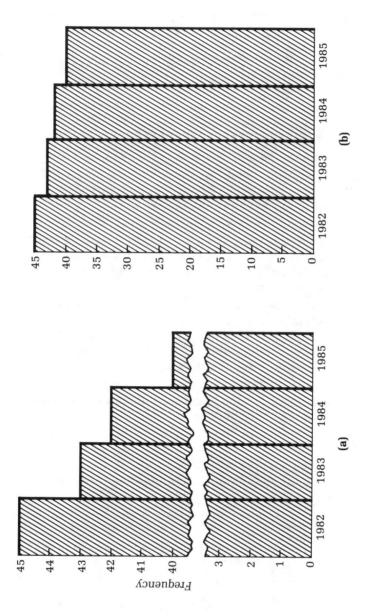

(a)

(b)

Occasionally, one encounters a broken bar graph like the one in figure 10.7(a). The separation of the bars demarked by wavy lines indicates that not all of the graph is shown. Note that the frequency designations in figure 10.7(a) jump from 3 to 40 over the gap, and that all the variation occurs between 40 and 45. When the graph is sized down so that the break is not necessary, as in figure 10.7(b), the differences among the bars become visually very small. While a broken bar graph is preferable to one whose initial frequency mark is greater than zero, it is interesting to ask yourself why the distance for each unit on the frequency dimension in graph (a) was not reduced so that the complete graph would fit into the space available. There may be good reasons for not doing so, but one should not automatically assume that there are.

Pictographs can present a related problem. Suppose you wanted to represent the change in handgun sales for a given state in the United States from one year to the next. Suppose, further, that handgun sales doubled, and you chose to represent this change in pictograph form, using a handgun silhouette for each year as a graphic symbol. You might represent the first year's production as in figure 10.8, but now you need to indicate the next year's sales. How do you

**Figure 10.8 Handgun Sales in State A, 1987**

10,000 handguns sold

proceed? You could double the height, or you could double the width of the gun. But either of these guns might look funny. To keep the gun proportional, you might choose to double both the height and the width to produce the gun shown in figure 10.9.

**Figure 10.9 Handgun Sales in State A, 1988**

20,000 handguns sold

But what have you done in this case? Considering the vertical dimension of the guns alone, the pictograph is an accurate representation of the data, but pictures have two dimensions. The actual space encompassed by the second gun is *four* times that encompassed by the first, and the visual impact of the two guns reflects this quadrupling of space. While this sort of mistake may seem unlikely, it occurs with surprising frequency and may be easily missed by a casual reader. One simple corrective for such situations is to analyze the raw numbers used to create the graph, and if these numbers are not available, the graph should be ignored.

## *Correlation and Causation*

Perhaps it is worth repeating here that correlation does not necessarily indicate causation, even when the correlation coefficient has a high positive correlation, say $r = +.89$. For example, there is a high positive correlation between the amount of damage done in a fire and the number of fire trucks that respond to the fire alarm: the larger the number of trucks, the greater the damage. There is probably also a high positive correlation between the number of police officers on a scene and the severity of the offense—and between the number of lawyers and the severity or complexity of a crime. However, do any of these correlations represent causation?

One important consideration when examining assertions about the relationship between variables is the definition of the variables themselves. Significant correlations can easily be produced when the two allegedly different variables are "really" two different operationalizations of the "same" or nearly the same thing. Consider the potential correlation between theft rates and the monetary losses due to shoplifting, or between the size of law enforcement agencies' budgets and the number of officers on the payroll. In a sense, monetary losses due to shoplifting may be viewed as an indirect way of measuring the amount of one type of theft. However, a theft rate is also a measurement of the amount of theft. Hence, a correlation between these two variables is "contaminated" by the "fact" that theft rates include shoplifting as a part of the *definition* of theft and, therefore, of theft rates. It would be very surprising, indeed, if two different measurements of the same phenomenon did not produce a high correlation. To avoid misleading or being misled by others in such circumstances requires careful conceptual analysis and definitional precision. One should always be alert to the possibility of using different names for the same phenomenon.

## *Review Questions*

1. Why is it important to distinguish between data and the interpretation of the data?
2. Why is it important to present raw numbers along with graphic displays, percentage and rates?
3. What are the advantages and disadvantages of graphic displays in presenting data?
4. Why is it important to distinguish between correlation and causation?

## *Exercises*

1. Locate articles in magazines or newspapers you own (*not* those in a library) using each of the following:

   a. scientific costumes and/or props
   b. relying on authority
   c. technical vocabulary

   Write an analysis of the article, discussing the reasons the author may have used these techniques and what, if any, relevance they have for the validity of the message being delivered.

2. What else would you want to know about the following statements before you might give them credence?

   a. Two out of three professors believe that students are much more motivated now than they were five years ago.
   b. The crime rate is decreasing.
   c. Fifty percent of those interviewed said they would support a tax increase to raise salaries of judges.
   d. There has been a 100 percent increase in murders in Hitsville.
   e. Brand X has more medicine than Brand Y.

3. What is potentially misleading about the following graphics displays?

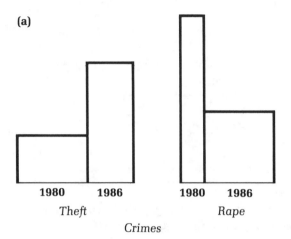

**(a)**

| 1980 | 1986 | | 1980 | 1986 |

*Theft*           *Rape*

Crimes

**(b)**

1970          1985

Cocaine Consumed

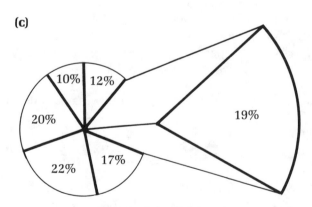

**(c)**

10%   12%

20%

22%   17%

19%

*Federal Allocations*
*for Law Enforcement*

# 11

## Preparing and Reading Research Reports

As noted in chapter 10, most criminal justice practitioners and students are somewhat familiar with the preparation and reading of police investigative reports. To some extent, a research report or article resembles such reports. However, a good research report must contain several elements which may or may not appear in an investigative report. In this chapter these elements are discussed. They include the abstract, the introduction, a review of the literature, the statement of hypotheses, description of methodology, data analysis, conclusions, and bibliography.

There are several accepted ways of organizing research reports and arranging footnote and bibliographic citations; these can be found in recognized style manuals such as *The Chicago Manual of Style*, the Modern Language Association's (MLA) *Handbook for Writers of Research Papers*, or *English Simplified*. It should be remembered, though, that a research report for a professor or a chief administrative officer may require a format and citation style different from the specifications of a professional journal, and that different journals have their own styles. The structure and style of the report should conform to the requirements of the audience or publication for which it is prepared.

## *The Abstract*

An *abstract* is a brief summary (usually 200 words or less) of a research project placed at the beginning of the report. It enables a reader to quickly determine the relevance of the report to his own purposes. Abstracts usually contain a succinct statement of the research topic(s) covered in the report, a brief description of the methodology involved, and a summary of the findings or conclusions.

Although the abstract is found at the beginning of the research report, it cannot be written until the research has been completed, since a brief discussion of the outcome(s) of the research is included. The following is an abstract of a research article* dealing with the validity of self-reported deviant behavior.

> In the study of deviant behavior, current heavy reliance upon data from anonymous questionnaires demands concern for data validity. Responses to anonymous questionnaires involving a wide range of deviant behavioral items, including the Dentler-Monroe and Nye-Short delinquency scale items, were compared to responses made during a follow-up "interview" and polygraph examination. The overall accuracy of the total questionnaire was high although results indicate significant inaccuracy on those items used in delinquency scales. However, a high degree of association was found between the respondent order established by the scales using data from questionnaire and polygraph results. Response inaccuracy was highly related to declared personal norms and reference group norms.

## *The Introduction*

The introduction places the research problem in context. General historical and theoretical frameworks into which the current problem fits are discussed. Major theoretical trends and their principal proponents are mentioned. Finally, the areas in which the subject remains problematic are discussed, leading up to the current research, which addresses one or more of those areas. The introduction may be a distinct section of the research report, or it may be combined with the literature review.

## *The Literature Review*

The literature review is a comprehensive report of existing research and theoretical literature that is related to the problem. Depending on the subject matter and the writer's perspective, the literature review is presented in chronological, thematic, or chronological *and* thematic order.

In most research reports the introduction and literature review sections are separate, while in most criminal justice journals they are combined and left untitled, as the following example from the article on self-reported deviant behavior indicates.

> Because of well-known difficulties, sociologists have tended to avoid direct confrontation with the question of data validity. However, the few attempts that have been made in this respect have furnished every reason

---

*The excerpts in this chapter are reprinted by permission from "Polygraph and Interview Validation of Self-Reported Deviant Behavior," John P. Clark and Larry L. Tifft, *American Sociological Review*, Vol. 31, No.4 (1966), pp.516–524.

to suspect considerable inaccuracy in much of the data we frequently utilize. More specifically, the findings of the few validity studies of interview and questionnaire data "suggest that when people are being interviewed (or are filling out questionnaires) directly concerning behavior about which there is a strong expectation of social approval or disapproval, and in which there is considerable ego-involvement, they tend to err in the direction of idealizing their behavior."[1] Data obtained about deviant behavior via interviews and questionnaires are particularly vulnerable to challenge on the grounds of validity.

In recent years we have become highly sensitized to the great volume and variety of delinquent and criminal behavior which had been largely overlooked in prior analyses based upon official statistics.[2] Findings of studies of undetected crime and delinquency seem to have been so palatable to social scientists that little attention has been given to their accuracy—except to rephrase the question of how much more of such behavior might still lie unmeasured.[3]

The use of self-report techniques has raised the issue of whether some behaviors are under-reported and others over-reported during interviews or on questionnaires, as well as the possibility of differential rates of accuracy under varying circumstances and by offense, irrespective of the direction of possible inaccuracy.

To minimize gross inaccuracy, Nye and Short and others have built trap questions into their techniques to detect the random response-giver, the over-conformer, and the exaggerator.[4] Other attempts have been made to reduce respondents' concern about the identifiability of responses.[5] However, these procedures have not been designed to examine systematically the nature of the errors that are detected.

---

1. Eleanor E. Maccoby and Nathan Maccoby, "The Interview: A Tool of Social Science," in Gardner Lindzey (ed.), *Handbook of Social Psychology*, vol. I, Reading, Massachusetts: Addison-Wesley, p.482.

2. F. Ivan Nye and James F. Short, "Scaling Delinquent Behavior," *American Sociological Review*, 22 (June, 1957), pp. 326–331; Robert A. Dentler and Lawrence J. Monroe, "Early Adolescent Theft," *American Sociological Review*, 26 (October, 1961), pp. 733–743; Fred J. Murphy, Mary M. Shirley, and Helen L. Witner, "The Incidence of Hidden Delinquency," *American Journal of Orthopsychiatry*, 16 (October, 1946), pp. 686–696; John P. Clark and Eugene P. Wenninger, "Socio-Economic Class and Area as Correlates of Illegal Behavior Among Juveniles," *American Sociological Review*, 27 (December, 1962), pp. 826–834; James S. Wallerstein and Clement Wyle, "Our Law-Abiding Lawbreakers," *Probation*, (April, 1947), pp. 107–112; Maynard L. Erikson and Lamar T. Empey, "Court Records: Undetected Delinquency and Decision Making," *Journal of Criminal Law, Criminology and Police Science*, 54 (December, 1963), pp. 458–469; Edward E. Schwarz, "A Community Experiment in the Measurement of Juvenile Delinquency," *Yearbook of the National Probation Association*, 1945; Albert J. Reiss and Albert L. Rhodes, "The Distribution of Juvenile Delinquency in the Social Class Structure," *American Sociological Review*, 26 (October, 1961), pp. 720–732; William

R. Arnold, "Continuities in Research: Scaling Delinquent Behavior," *Social Problems,* 13 (Summer, 1965), pp. 59–65.

3. For an exception to this appraisal see Robert H. Hardt and Sandra J. Peterson, "How Valid are Self-Report Measures of Delinquent Behavior?," Youth Development Center, Syracuse University, paper presented at the annual meeting of the Eastern Sociological Society, Philadelphia, April 16, 1966.

4. Nye and Short, *op. cit.*

5. For a discussion of this see Robert H. Hardt and George E. Bodine, *Development of Self-Report Instruments in Delinquency Research: A Conference Report,* Syracuse, New York: Syracuse University Press, 1965, pp. 22–23; Gene F. Summers and Andre D. Hammonds, "Toward a Paradigm for Respondent Bias in Survey Research," paper presented at the annual meeting of the American Sociological Association, Chicago, 1965, pp. 3–4; and Claire Selltiz, Marie Jahoda, Morton Deutsch, and Stuart W. Cook, *Research Method in Social Relations,* New York: Holt, Rinehart and Winston, 1962, ch.7.

The literature review should include references to classic works in the area as well as professional journals, books, periodicals, newspapers, papers presented at professional meetings, doctoral dissertations, and other sources (see the footnotes included in the example above). The more thorough the review, the less likely that the work will be open to criticism on the grounds that others have conducted the same or similar research in the past, or that important areas which others have pointed out have been overlooked. In addition, the researcher may find much information that will be of assistance in developing measurement techniques, locating relevant samples, deciding what type of an analysis should be conducted, and avoiding pitfalls along the way.

## Initiating the Literature Review

One of the most frequent questions asked by students is, "How do I begin my literature review?" Although there are a variety of possibilities, a first and unfortunately often neglected approach involves asking your criminal justice professor or someone with relevant expertise for any related bibliographic material. This step may well save you considerable time and effort by preventing you from "reinventing the wheel" as far as your project is concerned.

Second, the literature search may begin with a subject search in the card catalogue in the college library. Third, the various indices to criminal justice material contained in the journals and periodicals index in the college library may be of great value (for example, the *Criminal Justice Periodical Index, Psychological Abstracts,* or *Reader's Guide to Literature in the Social Sciences*). These sources generally contain material by subject and author's name and are updated annually. Some of the journals most often used by criminal justice researchers are the following: *Criminology, Journal of Criminal Justice, Police Studies, Crime and Delinquency, Journal of Police Science and Administration,* and *Social Problems.*

Fourth, computer searches by topical area are available through most libraries, which can provide a list of books, periodicals, and audio-visual and other materials available as well as their locations. Although some libraries offer interlibrary loans to allow you to secure materials from other libraries, you should determine how long it will take to procure a particular source, and whether you will need a special library authorization.

Fifth, articles appearing in newspapers and magazines, based upon government reports or recent research may provide leads to further sources of information. By using the government document section of the library or by writing to the authors of the report cited, you may be able to find the source document(s) for the article. Among the magazines commonly used in criminal justice research are *Police Chief, Police,* and *Corrections;* among the most useful government documents are *Crime in the United States* and newsletters of government agencies involved in criminal justice research.

Once the first sources have been identified, the process of locating and reviewing additional literature is under way. By examining the footnotes and bibliographies contained in your sources, you can begin to identify and review the same literature that others interested in your research problem have utilized.

## Completing the Literature Review

Another question frequently asked by students preparing a research report is "How many sources do I need?" The answer to this question depends upon the type of research report being written, but, in general, you will be through with the literature review when you find the same names and the same articles and books appearing repeatedly in your search. After examining these works thoroughly, you will reach a saturation point at which time you will be familiar with the "classics" in your research area and the most recent updates of those classics. At this point further search for literature will only delay the beginning of your report. If, however, new materials become available as you are working on your research project, these also should be reviewed and incorporated into the literature review. The point at which the literature review comes to an end, then, is arbitrary, since you could go on searching for additional literature almost indefinitely.

## Footnoting

Footnotes, an essential aspect of the literature review, are clearly called for under the following conditions:

1. quoting directly from the work of another;
2. paraphrasing closely the work of another;
3. presenting statistics or data that are not common knowledge;
4. referring the reader to a source that will clarify a point which the current report does not elaborate, but which is necessary to a complete understanding of it.

As mentioned above about research reports generally, footnotes may be presented in a variety of styles. Various journals in criminal justice generally employ footnote citations within the text surrounded by parentheses. If, for example, you wished to footnote this book in your journal article, you might do so by reporting the desired material and then referring to the book as follows: (Fitzgerald and Cox, 1987). If we had published more than one book in 1987, you would refer to the first book cited as (Fitzgerald and Cox, 1987a), the second book as (Fitzgerald and Cox, 1987b), and so on. At the end of the article, all books cited are listed alphabetically by author with the year and letter.

Using the more traditional footnoting style, you would number each footnote sequentially, beginning with the number one. Then, at the bottom of each page, following the appropriate number, you would cite the work, with the page numbers following. For example, a citation to this book would be as follows:

1. Jack D. Fitzgerald and Steven M. Cox, *Research Methods in Criminal Justice: An Introduction* (Chicago: Nelson-Hall, 1987).

If you cited this book again as footnote two, you would simply write *Ibid.* and give the page number(s). If you cited the work of another author as footnote three, then cited our book again in footnote four, you would give our last names (Fitzgerald and Cox), the words *op. cit.* (to indicate that you were referring to a work previously cited), and the page number(s). Sometimes, the two types of footnotes are used in the same research report, with the journal style being used to refer to other works and the traditional style being used to make substantive comments which the author feels will provide insight into the subject.

In any case, the specifics of footnoting style should conform to the style manual preferred by your professor or publisher. For further information on acceptable footnoting styles, consult the style manuals mentioned at the beginning of the chapter.

## *Methodology*

The fourth section of a research report, the methodology or research procedures section, describes the procedures employed to collect the data presented later in the report in such detail that any reader wishing to replicate the research project would be able to do so. All the methods used to accumulate information about the research topic are described, including archival research, physical evidence, various types of observation, interviews, and questionnaires. Sampling techniques used to select respondents for an interview or questionnaire survey are described. For example, the number of respondents included in the sample would be indicated, along with the sampling technique by which they were chosen for inclusion, whether a simple random sample, cluster sample, or other type of probability sample, or a systematic or other type of nonprobability sample. The setting in which the research occurred (for example, the size of the community and, perhaps, the mood or attitude of the community associated with research events) is described. Details of the specific research techniques utilized and the rationale for these techniques, such as the development of a questionnaire through any pretest procedures would be discussed. A copy of the questionnaire or interview schedule and cover letter employed are usually provided (often in an appendix).

The methodology section also contains a discussion of the type of data analysis to be conducted. Specifically, it states how the hypotheses will be tested. The researcher should indicate, for instance, what cross-tabulations will be analyzed and what statistical tests, if any, will be applied to the data. Hypothetical tables to indicate the types of findings that would support or refute the hypotheses may be shown. The following methodology section comes from the article on self-reported deviance.

> The study reported here was designed to test experimentally the accuracy of anonymous questionnaire responses by utilizing data obtained via a polygraph examination as external validity criteria.[6] In the first of

---

6. The polygraph is a relatively simple instrument which measures certain physiological reactions of the person being tested. It is a diagnostic tool which indicates whether a person believes what he is saying. There are several conditions in which the polygraph examination can be rendered nearly or completely

two preliminary studies, university students were asked to suggest behaviors which other students might tend to under- or over-report having
done. In the second study, they were asked to estimate the amount of
"normative pressure" on persons of their age and sex to respond in either
direction on these items and items from other research of undetected delinquency. A final questionnaire was then constructed consisting of five
seven-item groups reflecting consensus on their potential under- or over-
reportability (Table 1).

All male students (N = 45) in the discussion sections of an introductory
sociology course at a major Midwestern university were given the final
questionnaire.[7] Respondents were asked to admit the frequency of having committed each behavior *since they had entered high school*—a compromise between having age-specific data but little volume of reported
deviance, and having data covering the student's entire life with the attendant greater ambiguity in recall.

After completion of the questionnaire (in pencil), respondents were
told of a second phase of the study which would require approximately
one hour and for which each participant would receive eight dollars.
While maintaining questionnaire anonymity through a number identification system, students' names and telephone numbers were obtained.
Personal "interviews" were scheduled by telephone during the ensuing
two weeks, but respondents were not aware of the nature of phase two
until they appeared for this "interview."[8]

---

invalid: (1) *physiological abnormalities* such as excessively high or low blood pressure, heart diseases, respiratory disorders, or practically any painful ailment; (2) *extreme nervousness;* (3) *mental abnormalities* such as pronounced neuroses, psycho-
ses, abnormally low intelligence, self-hypnosis, temporary amnesia, or pathological
lying; (4) *unresponsiveness* resulting from extreme fatigue or mental exhaustion,
being under the influence of alcohol or a number of drugs, or even modified yoga,
muscle tension, or exciting imagery; and (5) *bodily movement* such as any physical
or muscular activity that affects blood pressure. See *Use of Polygraph as "Lie Detectors" by the Federal Government,* Part 3: Panel Discussion with Scientists, Hearings
before a Subcommittee of the Committee on Government Operations, House of Representatives, 88th Congress, Second Session, April 29–30, 1964, Washington:
United States Government Printing Office, 1964, pp.12–13. These conditions permit the individual to mislead the examiner. We had no reason to believe that any of
these conditions significantly affected our results.

7. The respondents were all male undergraduates with a mean age of 20; all but
two were white (two were black).   Thirty were single, five engaged or
"pinned," and five were married. One-half were from large cities or their suburbs,
sixteen were from small urban areas, two from rural non-farm areas, and the remaining two from farms. As an index of social class the Duncan Socio-Economic
Index Scores based on occupation of father was used, giving the following distribution: 0–23, 4; 24–27, 10; 48–71, 15; 72–96, 7; and unclassified, 4. See Albert J.
Reiss, Jr., Otis Dudley Duncan, Paul K. Hatt, and Cecil C. North, *Occupation and
Social Status,* New York: The Free Press of Glencoe, 1961, esp. pp. 109–161.
8. As is evident later, these were not interviews in the usual sense in that the respondent was not interviewed directly about his past deviant behavior. However,

During the "interview" the respondent was informed that our primary interest was in the accuracy of his questionnaire. In asking for his utmost cooperation in making his responses accurate, we strongly alluded to the likelihood of inaccurate responses being given on questionnaires administered in group situations. The respondent was then asked to select his questionnaire (using his identification number known only to him) from the entire collection of questionnaires and to make whatever modifications (in private) that were necessary to bring it to 100 per cent accuracy. Before he proceeded, he was advised that in order for us to have maximum confidence in his responses we would like him to take voluntarily a polygraph examination on his final responses, and the nature of such an examination was briefly discussed. (None of the respondents refused to continue participation, N = 40.) He was assured that no probing of any type would occur beyond establishing the frequency of his involvement. The respondent then made the necessary modifications to his questionnaire and was afterwards introduced to the polygraph examiner who completed the examination.[9]

The respondents' initial responses had been surreptitiously recorded,

---

no other term seems more appropriate. The personal engagement was focused upon the establishment of rapport, the giving of information about the remainder of the experiment, and the appeal for continued participation. Forty of the original 45 were scheduled for this interview. Two were not reached by telephone and three stated their academic schedules were too demanding to allow participation. (The experiment was conducted during the final week of scheduled classes.)

9. The polygraph can indicate whether the person is responding emotionally but not why. When an indication of deception occurred with one of our respondents the examiner asked the respondent if he wanted to make a change in his response. Almost all respondents made changes. We, of course, have made the assumption that the difference in both quality and quantity of deviance between that admitted on our initial questionnaire and that detected on the polygraph can be explained by the greater accuracy of the polygraph procedure. The accuracy of the polygraph can be challenged when it is employed under certain conditions. The question of polygraph validity is a judgmental question. It would be better to ask what is the degree of validity and under what circumstances was this validity obtained? For example, some studies show that the more motivated the subject is, the easier it is to detect deception. (See *Use of Polygraph as "Lie Detectors" by the Federal Government, op. cit.,* p. 305) It is also standard procedure, and one which we used, that a belief in the ability of the polygraph to detect deceptions must be established by the examiner. The examiner, like the instruments used, the social characteristics of the respondents, sample of questions, etc., is a crucial variable. The polygraph examiner in our study was a highly qualified licensed polygraph examiner with 18 years of experience who is employed by the State Bureau of Criminal Investigations. Some recent studies show that the polygraph can be used to detect deception (of the type which can be arranged to permit experimentation) by objective criteria in 90 percent or more of the cases. (See Joseph F. Kubis, "Studies in Lie Detection: Computer Feasibility Considerations," *RATC-TR* 62–205, June, 1962; David T. Lykken, "The GSR in the Detection of Guilt," *Journal of Applied Psychology,* 43 (1950), pp. 385–388; Henry V. Baesen, Chia-Mon Chung, and Chen-Ya Yang, "A Lie Detection Experiment,"

and changes made during the polygraph examination were made in ink by the examiner. Therefore, we secured three different sets of responses: (1) initial responses to the classroom-administered questionnaire, (2) responses made after a private "interview" in which subjects were asked to re-consider their initial responses prior to a polygraph examination, and (3) responses made during the polygraph examination.

## *Presentation and Analysis of Data*

In this section of the report, the collected data are described in tables, graphs, and narrative form. The presentation may include percentages and proportions as well as raw numbers. In addition to a description of the data, this section contains an analysis of those data. The results of any statistical tests are given; important points revealed in tables and graphs are noted and discussed. However, statements concerning the reasons for the various results and the conclusions drawn from the data should be reserved for the following section. That is, the presentation and discussion of data should be kept separate from interpretations of the meaning of the data. A look at the discussion of the findings from the article on self-reported deviance will help clarify the distinction between data analysis and conclusions based upon such analysis.

*Findings*

**Table 1  Reporting Error and Percent Admitting Behavior for Self-Report Deviant Behavior Items**

| | | | Reporting Error (Percent)[a] | | |
|---|---|---|---|---|---|
| Items | Deviant Behavior | Accurate | Over-reported | Under-reported | Percent admitting behavior[b] |
| 1. | Run away from home | 100.0 | 0.0 | 0.0 | 12.5 |
| 2. | Attacked someone with the idea of taking his (her) life | 100.0 | 0.0 | 0.0 | 0.0 |
| 3. | Attempted to take my own life | 100.0 | 0.0 | 0.0 | 2.5 |
| 4. | Used force to get money or valuables from another person | 95.0 | 2.5 | 2.5 | 2.5 |
| 5. | Gotten a female other than my wife pregnant | 95.0 | 2.5 | 2.5 | 7.5 |

| | | | | | |
|---|---|---|---|---|---|
| 6. | Bribed or attempted to bribe a police officer or another type of official | 95.0 | 5.0 | 0.0 | 7.5 |
| 7. | Visited a house of prostitution | 95.0 | 2.5 | 2.5 | 17.5 |
| 8. | Carried a razor, switchblade, or gun as weapon | 92.5 | 7.5 | 0.0 | 12.5 |
| 9. | Taken part in gang fights | 92.5 | 5.0 | 2.5 | 10.0 |
| 10. | Used or sold narcotic drugs | 92.5[c] | 0.0[c] | 5.0[c] | 10.0 |
| 11. | Taken things of large value (worth more than $50) that did not belong to me | 92.5 | 5.0 | 2.5 | 5.0 |
| 12. | Broken into and entered a home, store, or building | 92.5 | 2.5 | 5.0 | 20.0 |
| 13. | Struck my girlfriend or wife | 92.5 | 2.5 | 5.0 | 15.0 |
| 14. | Had a steady girlfriend | 90.0 | 2.5 | 7.5 | 90.0 |
| 15. | "Beaten up" on someone who hadn't done anything to me | 90.0 | 5.0 | 5.0 | 10.0 |
| 16. | Defied my parents' authority to their face | 85.0 | 7.5 | 7.5 | 57.5 |
| 17. | Taken a car for a ride without the owner's knowledge | 85.0[c] | 2.5[c] | 7.5[c] | 17.5 |
| 18. | Attempted to force or forced a female to have sexual intercourse with me | 85.0[c] | 2.5[c] | 7.5[c] | 15.0 |
| 19. | Driven a motor vehicle in an unauthorized drag race | 80.0 | 5.0 | 15.0 | 45.0 |
| 20. | Witnessed a crime and neither reported it nor made sure someone else had | 80.0[c] | 7.5[c] | 7.5[c] | 17.5 |
| 21. | Had sex relations with a person of the same sex | 80.0 | 5.0 | 15.0 | 22.5 |
| 22. | Started a fist fight | 80.0 | 17.5 | 2.5 | 22.5 |
| 23. | Purposely damaged or destroyed public or private property that did not belong to me | 77.5 | 10.0 | 12.5 | 55.0 |
| 24. | Driven a car without a driver's license or permit (Do not include driver's training courses) | 77.5[c] | 2.5[c] | 17.5[c] | 62.5 |
| 25. | Falsified information while filling out an application form or report | 75.0 | 0.0 | 25.0 | 57.5 |

Reporting Error (Percent)[a]

| Items | Deviant Behavior | Accurate | Over-reported | Under-reported | Percent admitting behavior[b] |
|---|---|---|---|---|---|
| 26. | Taken things from someone else's desk or locker at school without permission | 72.5 | 2.5 | 25.0 | 47.5 |
| 27. | Gambled for money or something else with persons other than my family members | 67.5 | 7.5 | 25.0 | 80.0 |
| 28. | Had sex relations with a person of the opposite sex (other than my wife) | 67.5 | 15.0 | 17.5 | 55.0 |
| 29. | Masturbated | 65.0 | 5.0 | 30.0 | 95.0 |
| 30. | Bought or drunk beer, wine or liquor illegally | 65.0 | 2.5 | 32.5 | 95.0 |
| 31. | Taken things of medium value (worth between $2 and $50) that didn't belong to me | 65.0 | 2.5 | 32.5 | 45.0 |
| 32. | Driven a motor vehicle at extreme speeds | 52.5[c] | 2.5[c] | 40.0[c] | 85.0 |
| 33. | Had in my possession pictures, books, or other materials which were obviously obscene and prepared to arouse someone sexually | 50.0[c] | 7.5[c] | 12.5[c] | 50.0 |
| 34. | Skipped school without a legitimate excuse | 40.0[c] | 2.5[c] | 55.0[c] | 85.0 |
| 35. | Taken little things (worth less than $2) that didn't belong to me | 32.5 | 5.0 | 62.5 | 87.5 |

Note: The items were presented to the respondents in five seven-item groups (one group per page) in the following order:
Group 1—35, 23, 25,  8, 22, 31,  1
Group 2—34, 24, 16, 26, 17, 33,  9
Group 3—21, 29,  3, 10, 11, 18,  2
Group 4—14, 12, 15, 20, 13,  4,  5
Group 5—30, 28,  6, 32,  7, 19, 27
[a]Reporting error was determined by comparing responses on the initial questionnaire to final responses. A behavior is "over-reported" if the admitted frequency of commission is greater in the initial questionnaire than in the final response. Conversely, a behavior is "under-reported" if the initial admitted frequency is less than in the final response. Accurate responses are those which remained unchanged between the first questionnaire and final polygraph interview. The three percentages add to 100.0.

[b]In general, it appears that accuracy is directly related to seriousness of offense. It is possible that this relationship may be spurious because the lower reported incidence of the more serious offenses provides less opportunity for changes in responses to occur. However, because there is also the possibility to over-admit behavior on an item, items were ordered by the percentage of accurate responses. These percentages are based on the final responses.

[c]Percentages do not add to 100.0 because of inaccuracies arising from respondents misunderstanding the meaning of an item.

*Overall validity.* By the time the polygraph examination was completed, all respondents had made corrections to their questionnaire responses. About 58 per cent of the total number of changes between the initial questionnaire responses and the final responses were made at the time of the personal "interview" and 42 per cent during the polygraph examination.[10]

Three-fourths of all changes increased the frequency of admitted deviance, the remainder were in the opposite direction. In fact, all respondents under-reported the frequency of their misconduct on at least one item but only one-half over-reported on at least one item.

The validity of the initial responses on the questionnaire, based upon the number of items initially answered correctly (as determined by the polygraph) divided by the total number answered was 81.5 per cent. Respondents ranged from 47 to 97 per cent. There was a mean of 6.5 and a median of 6 changes on each questionnaire. (Calculated similarly, the validity of the "interview" responses was 92.3 per cent.) More narrowly, the validity of initial responses based only upon changes out of or into the zero category of frequency was about 92 per cent with the three-to-one ratio remaining between under-reporting and over-reporting.

We *tentatively* conclude that there is substantial empirical evidence that these questionnaire data are externally valid for the population covered and the conditions under which it was given. However, since this collection of items *in toto* has no particular theoretical relevance to the analysis of misconduct, we must examine the validity of the responses to individual items and groups of items which have been used previously as delinquency scales. . . .

### Factors Related to Systematic Error

*Conformity to personal norms.* Assuming that deviant behavior may be in conflict with norms to which individuals generally subscribe, we

---

[10] The changes reported do not reflect changes that were made due to clarification and explanation by the interviewer or polygraph examiner, nor do they include changes where blanks were left in the original questionnaire, nor where the respondent checked the category "over 4" but did not make an estimate of frequency. The reliability of the polygraph was also estimated by asking 10 of the 40 respondents to return again for a retest of the polygraph examination, answering the identical questions. Appointments were set up for these ten persons immediately after the first polygraph examination although they were tested a few days later and again paid eight dollars. Reliability was 99.7 per cent.

would expect persons in threatening situations to make errors in the direction of the norms. Such was the case in this study. Respondents were questioned on their feelings about the acceptability of the behavior described in each of the items. In 53 of 80 instances (66 per cent) in which respondents did not initially admit an act but later did, they stated the act was "never permissible" according to their own feelings.[17] Further, in 20 of the 26 instances (77 per cent) in which respondents initially admitted acts in spite of their not having committed them, respondents reported the behavior was personally "permissible in a few circumstances" or "in many circumstances."[18]

*Conformity to group norms.* Based upon the voluminous literature which suggests that commitment to group norms helps determine public behavior, we first assumed that responding to questionnaires did not represent total escape from the respondent's meaningful group attachments, and then hypothesized that errors would fall in the direction of perceived group norms. Our data tend to support this hypothesis.

In 29 of the 80 instances (36 per cent) in which respondents did not initially admit an act but later did, they stated that the act was "never permissible" according to the perceived standards of their reference group. (Reference group was operationally defined here as "the group of guys you have generally done things with.") The direct relevance of these data to the explanation of under-reporting errors is difficult to assess because every instance of group support coincided with a case of normative personal support. However, in 23 of the 26 instances (89 per cent) in which respondents initially admitted acts in spite of their not having committed them, respondents perceived group support for such acts. There is strong evidence that errors on questionnaires are directly associated with perceived discrepanceies between individual acts and personal and group norms. The errors represent an attempt to make reported behavior compatible with perceived norms. . .

---

[17]The 80 instances involved 34 different respondents.

[18]The 26 instances involved 15 different respondents.

These brief observations should provide a general idea of what is involved in discussing the data presented. If tests for statistical significance are employed, or if means, modes, and medians are used to describe the data, they are also discussed in this section of the report. Notice that the reasons for the results presented, and the conclusions based upon the data presented have not been discussed. These interpretive comments should be reserved for the conclusion section of the report. The analysis contained in this section should allow the reader to examine and comprehend the data presented and to draw his own conclusions, which can then be compared with those presented in the concluding section of the report.

# *The Conclusion*

In the conclusions and recommendations section of the research report, the data presented in the preceding section are interpreted, conclusions are drawn, and attempts are made to relate the data collected in this study to prior research and to the theoretical framework serving as a guide to the current research. Although there is often a strong temptation to draw broader conclusions about the relationships among the variables involved, the conclusions in this section should be limited to the data presented in this research report and not based upon preconceived notions concerning these relationships, as the conclusions section from our article indicates.

The main finding of this study is that self-reporting of delinquency is rather accurate when a wide range of behaviors is considered simultaneously, but that there is differential validity on specific questionnaire items. Those items most frequently used on delinquency scales were found to be rather inaccurate. These findings dictate the need for concern for the validity of indicators and the patterns of response bias to self-report data-gathering techniques. Hopefully, this type of study provides encouragement for further validity studies varying the area of investigation, the identifiability of the respondent, the degree of threat involved in the item content, the research situation, the social characteristics of respondents, and the type of self-report technique used.[19] It has been demonstrated by others that follow up measures which differ from the initial measures probably enhance the validity of self-report data.[20] This study revealed that a particular type of personal interview, following group-administered anonymous self-report questionnaires, was beneficial in improving data validity.

Self-report techniques are well suited for etiological research, and it is time for some causal propositions to be operationalized and tested using these techniques. Validity studies such as ours can point out which qualitative items are accurate enough to use and what methodological procedures elicit the least amount of respondent bias. The latter finding is important in itself, yet has even greater importance for assessing the quality of inferential leaps made from samples to populations and from indicators to concepts in testing theoretical propositions.

This study might also provoke further investigations dealing with the

---

19. Summers and Hammonds, *op. cit.*
20. Winston Ehrmann, *Premarital Dating Behavior*, New York: Bantam Books, 1960; and James Walters, "Relation Between Reliability of Responses in Family Life: Research and Method of Data Collection," *Marriage and Family Living*, 22 (August, 1960), pp. 232–237.

relationships between normative structure and behavior, which has been suggested here as crucial in affecting the direction of reporting error. Inferences such as this may help in reinterpreting, for example, the research findings of a higher degree of delinquency involvement in an institutionalized population compared to a non-institutionalized population, or those in the lower class compared to those in the middle class. Assuming there are differences between the groups with respect to normative acceptance of the behavior items, employing the self-report technique to measure delinquency involvement may magnify behavioral differences, i.e., the institutionalized or lower-class persons may under-report considerably less (or over-report more) than the noninstitutionalized or middle-class respondents.

The extent to which the accumulated data from all our sources supported our hypotheses or failed to support our hypotheses would be discussed, and any known reasons for such support or lack of support would be noted. Any serious problems with the research project and areas requiring further research might also be included. The end product of this section of the report should be a summary of the results of the study, their importance in the development of the theories, and, where appropriate, a critique of the procedures employed.

## The Bibliography

At the end of the research report is a list of the sources and resources employed in compiling the report. It is not necessary or desirable for the researcher to list every book, article, or paper examined in the preparation of the report. Instead, the bibliography should contain a comprehensive list, organized alphabetically by author, of those materials the researcher found to be of sufficient value to use in writing the report, including those from which references, concepts, statistics, or quotations have been taken. This list will enable the reader to examine the same sources used by the researcher and will indicate the extent to which the literature was useful to the researcher. A standard bibliographical style is used, as found in the style manual of choice.

## Appendices

Lengthy documents that bolster or enhance the data presented can be included in appendices. Such documents and their locations are referred to in the main body of the report, and the reader may decide whether it is worth his or her time to read them. For example, the researcher may indicate in the methodology section of the report that a copy of the questionnaire may be found in appendix A.

## A Final Note on Research Reports

Although we have discussed each section of the research report individually, it should be apparent that a thorough consideration of all sections must be accomplished before the report is written or the research carried out. Although the abstract comes at the beginning of the report, it cannot be written until the research is completed. Similarly, the material contained in the introduction and literature review requires consideration of the methods to be employed and the type of analysis to be undertaken. Although the research report can be written a section at a time, it must be conceived in the mind of the researcher as a more or less well-integrated whole.

## Review Questions

1. What purposes do the abstract, footnotes, and bibliography of an article serve?
2. How and why should a researcher review previous research? How should he or she select which previous research to review?
3. Why should a researcher describe the methodology and methods used to collect data?

## Exercises

1. Find an article in a criminal justice research journal that does not have an abstract and write one for the article.
2. Suppose you were preparing a research report on a study you had done examining the relationship between length of sentence and recidivism. Using library resources locate at least three examples of previous research on this topic and write a literature review using the studies you have located.
3. Construct a properly formatted bibliographic listing of the three sources you found in completing 2.
4. Identify three different criminal justice journals in your library and compare the formats of an article in each one, including the outline reflected in the major sections of each article and footnoting and bibliographic styles.

# 12

## Computers in Criminal Justice Research

In 1946, the first digital computer was built at the University of Pennsylvania. It filled a large room (1,500 sq. ft.), weighed 30 tons, and cost more than a half million dollars. Although it relied on 18,500 vacuum tubes and could not run more than seven or eight minutes without a tube failure, it helped revolutionize the world. IBM installed its first computer in 1948 and its first major business model in 1951. With the development of transistors and solid state circuitry in the 1960s, the revolution has continued, and it is now possible to purchase a personal computer for under one hundred dollars and transport it in a briefcase.

In the past decade, the use of computers in all fields of work has increased tremendously, and criminal justice is no exception. It is now possible to access data stored in another computer thousands of miles away using conventional telephone lines to analyze data and generate statistical reports using packaged programs, and to print research reports using a word-processing program. All of these tasks can be accomplished using a computer and accessories that can be purchased for a total of less than $2,000. Computers, then, are economically feasible for most criminal justice agencies and more and more agencies are purchasing, leasing, or sharing time on computers. In addition, virtually all academic and research institutions have sophisticated research-oriented computer systems. The range of possibilities for computer use in criminal justice research is boundless. Those who are not familiar with the basics of computers are going to be at a serious disadvantage in the coming years.

### Components of the Computer

Mainframe computer systems that have a very large storage capacity are capable of supporting many users at one time, while microcomputer systems have a much smaller memory capacity and support only one or a few users. In between are a variety of possibilities in terms of size and complexity. However, all computer systems contain the same basic components: a central processing unit (including memory, input/output circuitry, and support circuitry), data storage device(s), input devices (keyboards and/or card readers), and output devices (CRT screens and/or printers).

The central processing unit controls the operation of the computer and the flow of information within the computer. Complex switching circuits allow it to perform or "execute" a large variety of instructions at a high speed. To perform a particular function, the computer follows a list of instructions called a **program.** Programs may be written in a wide variety of **programming languages** (e.g., Fortran, Pascal, COBOL, or BASIC), but the computer must translate these to its own unique **machine language** before it can follow the instructions. The program is put into the memory of the computer so that the computer can easily find the next instruction to follow. Additional segments of memory are reserved for storage and manipulation of data supplied by the user. There are two basic types of internal memory, read/write **random access memory (RAM)** and **read-only memory (ROM).** Programs may be contained in ROM if they need not be altered, but other programs and all data must utilize the read/write capability of RAM. The support circuitry consists of additional circuits that are required for the central processing unit to function, while the input/output circuitry enables the central processing unit to communicate with other components (peripherals) of the computer system.

Data storage devices permit some or all of the contents of the memory section to be "written" on a magnetic medium and stored for future access. In this way, programs and data can be retained while memory space is cleared for other programs or data. When the stored information is needed later, it can be read back into the computer's memory. The simplest data storage devices use magnetic tape and function like a standard tape recorder. Only entire programs and data sets may be stored and retrieved with these devices. Disk storage devices use a similar magnetic medium on either a hard or "floppy" disk, and may be designed to permit easier access to *portions* of programs or data sets.

Input devices permit the human operator to enter commands or data. The most common input devices are **keyboards,** similar in appearance and function to typewriter keyboards. Large computer systems may also employ **card readers** and **magnetic tape readers** which operate at very high speeds reading cards or tapes prepared by keyboard operators. Also in use are **optical readers** which can read bar codes or pencil marks on special forms such as those used in standardized examinations.

Output devices permit the computer to communicate to the human operator. The **printer** translates the output of the computer into characters typed onto paper, or **hard copy**. Some printers produce hard copy that resembles a typewritten page and are termed "letter quality." Other printers form characters using a dot matrix pattern and are usually capable of very high speeds. When hard copy is not required, data can be displayed on a **CRT**, a **cathode ray tube**, that resembles a television screen.

## Current Computer Applications in Criminal Justice

The wide use of computers in criminal justice has made available a wealth of research information. While there is great variation among agencies and new systems are constantly being introduced, the following computer applications are common.

In law enforcement, local agencies routinely computerize information on criminal complaints and are able to retrieve individual complaint records by incident number, location, type, and name. In addition, reports can be generated from these files showing overall patterns and trends, including those required for state and federal Uniform Crime Reports (UCR). Local systems may also support **computer-aided dispatch (CAD)**, logging calls automatically, verifying addresses, indicating nearest intersection, and even identifying closest available police or ambulance units. These systems often can generate reports on number of calls, types, time and place distributions, response time, and time to clear responding units.

Telephone link-ups to state and federal enforcement agency computers such as the National Crime Information Center or Secretary of State's office permit local agencies to run a variety of checks on information such as vehicle tags, operator's permits, stolen vehicles, stolen/recovered property, and criminal histories. However, these state and federal files/memory banks generally are limited in terms of access for research, and few summary reports are routinely generated. On the other hand, the files maintained by the FBI and many state enforcement agencies on UCR data (including reported crimes, arrests, and manpower/employment information) are designed to support research objectives, and frequent reports are generated and distributed.

In court administration, computer systems maintain court dockets and manage the serving of legal notices. Other systems maintain records for court supervision and probation activities. While none of these systems is primarily designed to support research, an authorized researcher can often pull together information from their files for valuable reports.

In many correctional institutions, computerized files are maintained on all inmates, parolees, or persons under mandatory supervised release. Terminals linked by telephone to other state or federal agencies permit access to criminal histories nationwide and notification of other agencies in the event of escapes or parole or supervised-release violations. Again, although these systems were not designed primarily for researchers, they can yield some reports of great value. A number of criminal justice agencies also maintain computer files on personnel, vehicles, equipment, budgets, expenditures, and so on, that may be useful to an authorized researcher.

The growing use of computers in academic and research institutions also offers a number of new opportunities for the criminal justice researcher. Many major libraries have computerized their card catalogues, permitting "on-line" searches by title, author, or call number and limited searches by subject. The development of national bibliographic data bases also makes it possible to conduct elaborate subject searches (on a time-delayed basis) through most major libraries. In addition, most law libraries now provide access to computerized case-law systems, such as LEXIS or WestLaw, that permit searches by citation or subject.

Further, many data bases are now available to academic and research institutions through the Criminal Justice Archive and Information Network. Data concerning crime, victimization, the criminal justice system, and juvenile delinquency are maintained specifically for use by the criminal justice system researcher.

## *Preparing Data for Computer Analysis*

If you are preparing data for computer analyses, the first step, as we indicated in chapter 5, is *coding* the information on each questionnaire, interview recording sheet, observational log, or whatever other device has been used to gather the data. (To facilitate the coding process, researchers often use the pre-coding technique discussed briefly in chapter 5.) Ordinarily, each questionnaire, individual respondent, or event the researcher is studying is assigned a unique identification number. This number is written on the original questionnaire, event or interview record, etc., so that the researcher is able to return to the original data source to verify the accuracy of the data entered into the computer. For each respondent, event, etc., an array of numbers is created that might be punched on a card or entered onto tape or disc so that the computer can "read" the information. A portion of the array for a particular respondent on the sample questionnaire reprinted in chapter 5 might look like the one below.

The ID number and the data for each variable (e.g., ID number, age, sex) are assigned to a particular location (field) in the array. For every respondent, the ID number is recorded as the first three numbers, age is recorded as the fourth and fifth number, the code for sex as the sixth number in the array, etc.

The process we have just described involves transferring data from the place where it was initially recorded (e.g., on the questionnaires) to another recording device that the computer can read. Accuracy in the transferral process is, of course, vital. Whenever we are transferring information from one place to another and changing its form (e.g., from check marks on the questionnaire to a number code standing for a yes or no answer to the corresponding question), there is a possibility of human error. Errors can be minimized if a competent, well-trained person performs the card punching or other data entry process. Even then, however, it is important to *verify* the accuracy of the transfer process.

There are several ways to accomplish this. Perhaps the simplest one to illustrate (though it is used infrequently now) is the use of what is called a verification punch using a keypunch machine. Essentially, the punched cards are fed through the punching machine again. The machine operator reads the data from its original source again and punches the appropriate keys, as if he or she were punching them for the first time. When a punch entered by the operator does not match the corresponding punch already in the card, the machine buzzes to signal the discrepancy. The operator can then check the original data source to determine which punch is incorrect and make any necessary changes in the "master" card that will be used in the analysis. Essentially the same process may be used for verifying data on more modern data storage media, such as tapes.

There is another strategy for detecting errors in the raw data entry process that can be used with punch cards or other data entry processes. It is more crude than the item by item verification just described, but it is nevertheless useful. The first step in this procedure is to have the computer print out the data arrays for all respondents so that the fields corresponding to each variable for each respondent are listed one under the other. The field for each variable can then be identified, and one can read down the list for each variable field, checking for incorrect or inappropriate code numbers. For example, one could locate the sixth number in the first array on the list (the number corresponding to the codes for the sex variable) and read down that column. The only numbers that should appear in this column are 1 (male), 2 (female), and 9 (no information). If any other number appears in that column, an error has been made and should be corrected. Of course, the computer can be programmed to perform this check as well. These and other procedures for verifying the accuracy of the data entry process are often called "data cleaning." Clean (i.e., accurately entered) data are, of course, essential for accurate data analysis.

Because the relevant codes for each variable are located in the same place (field) in the array for each respondent, the researcher can specify which variable or variables are to be counted, cross-tabulated, or otherwise manipulated by specifying the location of the information in the array. The computer can then count and print out the number of 1's and the number of 2's entered where sex has been coded for all of the respondents, indicating how many males and females have been included. Similarly, the computer can count and print out the number of males (code 1 in the sex field) who answered yes on question 1 (code 1 in the answer to the question 1 field), the number of females who answered yes to question one, the number of males who answered no, etc. and produce a cross tabulation of these two variables. The computer can also calculate descriptive and inferential statistics, among other things. All of these calculations can be done with great accuracy, and in a matter of a few seconds or minutes, depending on the operating speed of the computer and the number of arrays the computer has to read to perform the calculations. Performing these operations by hand would be much less accurate and much more time consuming. The capacity to process great quantities of data accurately in a very short period of time is a principal advantage of computers in research.

A major resource of academic and research institutions is the availability of large capacity computers and sophisticated data analysis programs. There are several prepackaged programs available for use, including SPSS$^x$ (Statistical Package for the Social Sciences) and

SAS (Statistical Analysis System), that are designed for "batch" (time-delayed) processing. Data and commands are entered via punched cards with these systems. SPSS$^x$ is a similar package that allows the user to perform data analysis "on-line," entering data and commands via a terminal. In either case, the data are processed according to the instructions contained in the program, and the results are made available to the researcher in the form of a detailed readout or printout. These programs are particularly attractive because they provide output in the form of tables and graphs that are clearly labeled, as well as a wide variety of statistics. If a prepackaged program is unavailable or inappropriate for the analysis desired, the researcher may use any of a number of programming languages to write his or her own program. However, the variety and sophistication of available programs seldom makes this necessary.

## *Limitations of Computers*

The basic advantage of the computer in research is the speed with which it performs operations that would take the researcher hours or days to perform otherwise. In addition, computers make it possible to communicate and share data with others across the nation and around the world in a very short time. As a result, the rapid growth of computers in criminal justice agencies has created wonderful opportunities for the criminal justice researcher. However, some limitations should be noted.

One major difficulty is that many of the systems discussed are incompatible with one another, and, therefore, information cannot simply be exchanged or transferred from one computer to another. Hardware (the actual machines) and software (the programs) have not been designed to allow such exchanges. A local police agency may automatically generate its UCR statistics, but it is likely that the data will be reentered manually at both the state and federal level. Even programs within the same computer may be unable to communicate with one another (or use each other's data). Systems designed only to store records often do not include the software for analysis that researchers need. Suppose a researcher needs to know whether defendants making bail are more likely to be found not guilty than those without bail. He may have to search an automated docket system for a sample of cases, manually record relevant information, and re-enter the data on another computer system in order to perform the desired statistical analysis.

Just as with numbers and statistics, a basic danger in computer use is that the researcher may come to think of the data as unquestionable. A researcher must constantly be alert to the fact that there is nothing magical about data generated by computers. The value of the data is dependent upon the skills of the researcher as he or she gathers, analyzes and interprets them in terms of a theoretical framework. Whether the output is a simple frequency distribution or complex inferential statistics, the printout should be carefully examined for errors and interpreted cautiously. The researcher must be sure that the computer performed the proper operations on the data and must realize that a great deal of information contained on the printout may not be relevant to the research at hand, especially if "canned" statistical analyses programs that automatically generate a variety of statistical measurements and tests have been used.

Most importantly, the data contained on the printout will be no better than the data entered: "Garbage in, garbage out" is a familiar saying to those who work with computers. If the wrong questions were asked on the questionnaire, if the questions were ambiguous, if the variables were poorly defined, if the sample was improperly selected, if the wrong instructions were given to the computer, or if errors were made in coding or entering the data, the printout will reflect these errors or weaknesses. Only the researcher, then, can interpret properly the meaning of the computer output since the computer cannot think or interpret results. Computers are extremely useful tools, but they are just that—tools. They can only do what they are told to do and cannot compensate for weaknesses in research design or execution.

## Review Questions

1. Why should researchers become familiar with computers?
2. What are the major advantages and the major limitations of computers in criminal justice research? In criminal justice bureaucracies?
3. How is the coding of data related to storage and analyses of data by computer?
4. What is "data cleaning" and why is it important?

## Exercises

1. Using the example of a questionnaire from chapter 5, construct a code book and a corresponding data array for at least ten of the variables included in the questionnaire.
2. Go to the computer center at your college or university, identify the statistical analysis programs that are available and what descriptive and inferential statistics these programs provide.

# 13

## *Conclusions*

In this text, we have characterized science as a process that strives to arrive at *statements of fact*. This formulation clearly indicates the role of symbolic perspectives in science and the results obtained through its methodology and its methods. Hypotheses state what we think to be fact, and hypotheses supported through the application of the scientific perspective and scientific method can be interpreted as statements of fact. A set of logically related statements, at least some of which have been tested and supported empirically, is a theory. If we remind ourselves from time to time that science deals with supposed statements of fact, formulated and tested by researchers, we will be able to keep an appropriately critical attitude toward the processes and products of science.

The entire scientific enterprise is filled with selectivity and choice. At the onset, researchers decide that the scientific perspective, rather than some other perspective, is appropriate to the investigation of some kinds of questions. Researchers further determine, or permit others to decide for them, what topics or issues deserve study. Once these general matters are selected, someone must identify what particular hypotheses will be tested, which research design is appropriate and feasible, which variables are relevant, how to define the concepts and variables operationally, and which research methods and techniques to use. Problems of sampling; choosing a method of observation; preparing a laboratory, questionnaire, interview, or observation schedule; and entering the field must be resolved. A method for organizing and coding the assembled data must be devised, and the type of analysis and form of data presentation must be chosen. Finally, the results of the analysis must be interpreted, and a judgment made about whether the data are consistent with the original hypothesis. Where appropriate, an assessment must be made of whether a causal inference is justified. At each of the stages in the research process, the researcher makes decisions that activate only part of the full range of possibilities. If the scientific method is to be used, these choices cannot be avoided. Each choice carries with it both advantages and disadvantages, and each focuses on some aspects of the problem and ignores others.

If choice is an inevitable component of scientific activity, that choice brings researchers many obligations to themselves, their audiences, and their subjects. First, the investigator should be aware of the many decisions he or she is making, since awareness of making choices contributes to rational research. The researcher should assess the implications of these choices, including both their beneficial and detrimental consequences, and indicate these to the audience in the research report. Reporting the reasoning that led to particular choices helps those evaluating the study, especially when the consumers of the research are not professionals in the researcher's field. Second, the researcher should be cautious in interpreting the results he or she obtains. A researcher who understands the philosophical and practical complexities of scientific study will understand why scientific conclusions are tentative.

Third, researchers should provide as complete a description of the research process as possible to allow other researchers to replicate the study and appraise the research intelligently and critically. Without a detailed description, the usefulness of the study and the presumed validity of its results are minimal.

Fourth, an explanation of the nature, purposes, procedures, and results should be disseminated to the participants being studied. Even if a researcher thought it necessary to give subjects only partial information, or to give them false information, once the research is completed, the subjects should have the opportunity to obtain complete and correct information about the research. In providing this information, however, the researcher has an obligation to protect the individual identities of subjects.

Finally, the ethics of the research process should be carefully considered. Where physical, social, or psychological danger to subjects is a clear possibility, the researcher must take special care to inform the subjects of the risks involved before beginning the research. Most organizations of professional social scientists (such as the American Sociological Association, the American Psychological Association, and the American Political Science Association) and many agencies and organizations that provide funds for research (for example, the National Institutes of Health) publish and enforce a statement of ethical principles for conducting research with human subjects. As in most professions, however, the primary responsibility for abiding by these ethical principles rests with the individual professional conducting the research, and that responsibility should be taken seriously.

The audience, or consumers, of scientific research owe themselves something in this process as well. First, they must invest time and effort to ensure that they understand the process that produced the results presented. Second, the audience should retain a healthy skepticism about research and researchers, and like researchers, regard reported data and conclusions drawn from them as tentative. Third, the consumer should demand that a complete, accurate and understandable account of the research be provided, including alternative explanations for the results obtained, an assessment of the strengths and weaknesses of the study reported, and an evaluation of the extent to which the results correspond to the results of other studies of the same or similar phenomena.

Obviously, all researchers are thoroughly human, possessing the same capacities and subject to the same limitations as other people. Although researchers often construct elaborate instruments to assist them in the observational process, ultimately their own sensory perceptions are limited. Like all humans, researchers learn to speak and write a language that, once mastered, conceptualizes experiences, questions, and explanations. Although language makes communication possible, the symbols used select and organize experiences along particular lines, making some aspects of experiences salient while deemphasizing or obscuring others. By narrowing our focus of attention and interest, however, we can too easily forget that specialization in criminal justice, no less than specialization in other disciplines, can produce a highly selective view of the world.

Like other people, researchers occasionally experience lapses of memory, make errors of observation and reasoning, and fail to recognize the significant or obvious, in spite of precautions taken to avoid such mistakes. Since researchers have invested a great deal of time, money, and effort in their careers, and take pride in what they do, they are inclined to emphasize their successes and hide their failures, to enjoy the prestige that comes with work favorably received by peers, and to respond defensively and sometimes irrationally to criticisms of their work. Researchers also are influenced by personal preferences and prejudices, desires and dislikes, values and vulnerabilities, and their work is at least to some extent a reflection of these personal proclivities, in spite of their efforts to achieve objectivity.

Because most people work for someone else, in order to keep their jobs and earn a living, they must at least occasionally please their employers, and that, in turn, often means sacrificing some personal values and behaving in ways that conflict with their own interests or the principles of science. Those who do hired-hand scientific research are often caught in moral and practical dilemmas regarding research design, analysis, presentation, and interpretation of the data collected. Data can be fabricated, or assembled, presented, or interpreted in ways that deliberately distort their meaning as easily as they can be compiled in ways that are complete, honest, and straightforward. Statistics can be used to illuminate or to mask important aspects of the evidence. Researchers are no more or less honest, no more or less subject to temptations to act in their own self-interest or that of their employers, than anyone else.

Still, science—as a perspective and as an activity—does differ in some important ways from some of the other perspectives by which people try to learn about themselves and the world they live in. Science as a means of justifying knowledge operates according to a set of explicitly stated rules, rules that emphasize the importance of precise statements of problems and hypotheses to be investigated, precise definitions of the concepts or variables to be studied, the careful construction of research design, the strict adherence to the rules of logic, the cautious interpretation of research results, and constant reference to empirical (observable) data as a test of the investigator's hypothesis. The application of these rules is most evident in the researcher's most powerful procedure, the experiment, a deliberate exercise in thorough planning, controlled observation, and careful analysis.

Seldom are ideal conditions available for scientific research, and researchers must, in practice, compromise in varying degrees with the principles of science. Nonetheless, the scientific perspective and method provide—to the extent that they can be employed—a powerful technique for generating knowledge.

We have discussed the basic scientific perspective and some of the basic methodologies and methods of science as applied to the study of human behavior in this text. We have tried to put the reader in a position to appraise intelligently and critically the examples of research he or she may encounter, whether in textbooks, professional journals, or the mass media. We have discussed the pitfalls of scientific research at some length because we believe that this aspect of science is too frequently underemphasized. It is our conviction that students should understand and appreciate the basic strengths of the scientific perspective, as well as its shortcomings.

Consistent with our orientation throughout this book, we should point out that all we have said here is based on a perspective. Like the researcher, we have selected some topics for discussion and excluded others. We have stressed some aspects of the research process and given only brief consideration to others. Each of us has done research, read the research of others, and encountered many of the problems discussed in the foregoing chapters. Each of us teaches research methods. Each of us believes that scientific methodology, properly understood and carefully applied, can make a significant contribution to efforts to understand human behavior.

# Appendix A: Table of Random Numbers

## How to Use the Table of Random Numbers ———

The numbers in Table A have been randomly generated by computer. The researcher can use them to help in drawing a random sample from a population. First, however, each element in the population from which the sample is to be drawn must be assigned a unique number. This is usually done by numbering the elements in the population consecutively. If there were 286 elements in the population, for example, they would be numbered 001, 002, 003, . . . 286. Here is one procedure for using Table A to select a random sample:

1. Determine a starting point in the table by closing your eyes and placing the point of your pencil somewhere in the table.
2. Using the starting point you have selected, begin reading the numbers in the table either across the rows or down the columns. If the population consisted of 99 or fewer elements, you would read the numbers in two-digit units; for 999 or fewer elements in the population, you would read the numbers in three-digit units, and so forth. If a number read from the table does not correspond to a number assigned to one of the elements in the population (for example, 323 for our population of 286), or is the same as a number already read from the table, skip that number and read the next. Continue in this way until you have selected as many unique, valid numbers as there are elements of your desired sample.
3. The population elements that comprise the random sample are those whose numbers correspond to the numbers read from the table.

## Table A    Table of Random Numbers

| | | | | |
|---|---|---|---|---|
| 11805 | 26316 | 36130 | 72714 | 27162 |
| 53798 | 66223 | 30061 | 13563 | 54828 |
| 14027 | 08593 | 86968 | 95905 | 52891 |
| 28607 | 99101 | 22303 | 50520 | 95572 |
| 38547 | 13770 | 52858 | 84369 | 33254 |
| 63317 | 65118 | 03482 | 57702 | 23757 |
| 27398 | 19570 | 61450 | 41899 | 19261 |
| 68622 | 98554 | 07116 | 75341 | 96538 |
| 01648 | 75908 | 53730 | 48420 | 98608 |
| 57619 | 82490 | 74605 | 78133 | 67807 |
| 84213 | 83004 | 00250 | 73800 | 28970 |
| 26441 | 77854 | 25573 | 46711 | 96741 |
| 68696 | 44733 | 05941 | 08194 | 84841 |
| 21762 | 55986 | 67660 | 07426 | 91523 |
| 32494 | 06751 | 02201 | 52567 | 89055 |
| 57490 | 55146 | 73035 | 56771 | 31495 |
| 91697 | 68418 | 12788 | 99723 | 34857 |
| 25747 | 37272 | 14363 | 32062 | 72895 |
| 31560 | 70952 | 74042 | 16372 | 55152 |
| 38200 | 43864 | 46432 | 64863 | 67563 |
| 25236 | 92827 | 61430 | 72439 | 81076 |
| 43783 | 26124 | 70269 | 21758 | 04868 |
| 69379 | 59828 | 76701 | 09757 | 40419 |
| 44336 | 68973 | 01784 | 09980 | 35675 |
| 56793 | 68672 | 51732 | 50831 | 16348 |
| 05572 | 15869 | 65918 | 93576 | 57505 |
| 91221 | 22556 | 20495 | 48881 | 92896 |
| 93289 | 57606 | 44655 | 52074 | 43890 |
| 36826 | 78857 | 42367 | 61222 | 91588 |
| 82311 | 20013 | 79016 | 42047 | 74945 |
| 05418 | 00962 | 01510 | 25556 | 48577 |
| 17093 | 63850 | 42949 | 92775 | 83637 |
| 17228 | 41093 | 14655 | 31509 | 84864 |
| 58404 | 74622 | 02194 | 10688 | 79856 |
| 26755 | 55576 | 28115 | 55501 | 37025 |
| 99277 | 41277 | 65281 | 31048 | 31185 |
| 05372 | 16764 | 25265 | 57526 | 64707 |
| 10275 | 27829 | 78222 | 30479 | 55728 |
| 38277 | 95115 | 98996 | 79178 | 58105 |
| 81728 | 69680 | 06509 | 56831 | 51192 |

Note: Reprinted by permission of The Rand Corporation from The Rand Corporation, *A Million Random Digits with 100,000 Normal Deviates*. Glencoe, Ill.: The Free Press, 1955, p. 59.

| | | | | |
|---|---|---|---|---|
| 50352 | 66593 | 69338 | 07960 | 99411 |
| 92625 | 07337 | 30948 | 09456 | 19121 |
| 58247 | 04001 | 00599 | 33094 | 70302 |
| 42028 | 59691 | 83109 | 51317 | 86211 |
| 90181 | 06951 | 41082 | 01135 | 61973 |
| 95880 | 25087 | 94319 | 10450 | 82572 |
| 93210 | 34949 | 15575 | 34560 | 04589 |
| 52513 | 37099 | 48804 | 61642 | 20111 |
| 12315 | 36592 | 04971 | 00556 | 65335 |
| 01413 | 25163 | 21487 | 47119 | 99682 |
| 17934 | 77862 | 49489 | 73593 | 39933 |
| 17043 | 22264 | 34097 | 14201 | 49308 |
| 35371 | 98701 | 09595 | 47201 | 15108 |
| 31358 | 34890 | 25959 | 03526 | 49036 |
| 26791 | 26979 | 85278 | 40612 | 48973 |
| 82311 | 60301 | 48100 | 14313 | 22570 |
| 35208 | 90923 | 14046 | 40646 | 93067 |
| 81401 | 21608 | 01768 | 56646 | 18168 |
| 64730 | 22009 | 84419 | 32738 | 47953 |
| 03805 | 35936 | 15364 | 19143 | 57613 |
| 38849 | 54269 | 53821 | 47811 | 44106 |
| 73996 | 42503 | 62356 | 12631 | 50452 |
| 30758 | 89897 | 94253 | 71272 | 26652 |
| 08222 | 76753 | 04336 | 75918 | 45037 |
| 38611 | 05163 | 63154 | 18262 | 22888 |
| 22960 | 78799 | 32227 | 29195 | 06750 |
| 93725 | 91389 | 10851 | 91575 | 97765 |
| 18079 | 38119 | 78745 | 88786 | 12134 |
| 56204 | 06838 | 07600 | 34684 | 35518 |
| 36092 | 00478 | 36260 | 16910 | 25925 |
| 04231 | 14492 | 92580 | 31507 | 62353 |
| 22941 | 27077 | 93599 | 85948 | 67835 |
| 23085 | 99884 | 65049 | 02944 | 09276 |
| 75295 | 58425 | 25160 | 94823 | 46768 |
| 23915 | 75472 | 81485 | 10381 | 12465 |
| 95476 | 87922 | 06504 | 40536 | 11267 |
| 94929 | 01637 | 08543 | 77226 | 15286 |
| 17797 | 09714 | 19817 | 52154 | 01887 |
| 26171 | 86969 | 94344 | 41203 | 75834 |
| 22095 | 55143 | 42808 | 85581 | 37355 |

# Appendix B: Areas Under the Normal Curve

## How to Use the Table of Areas under the Normal Curve

The standard normal curve upon which the values in this table are based has a mean 0.0 and a standard deviation of 1.0. The total area under the standard normal curve and the corresponding probability is 1.0000.

The variable in question must be normally distributed. Before using this table, you must convert the raw scores to z-scores. Remember that a normal curve is symmetrical about the mean (that is, 0.5000 of the area lies on either side of the mean), and that z-scores can be positive or negative. Positive z-scores fall above (to the right of) the mean, and negative z-scores fall below (to the left of) the mean. Figure B shows the relationship between the values in the table and the areas (and corresponding probabilities) under the standard normal curve.

**Figure B**

0.5000 of the area under the curve

area between mean and z (col. B)

area beyond z (col. C)

0.00    1.00    2.00

z    scores (col. A)

# Table B   Table of Areas under the Normal Curve

| (A) z | (B) area between mean and z | (C) area beyond z | (A) z | (B) area between mean and z | (C) area beyond z |
|---|---|---|---|---|---|
| 0.00 | .0000 | .5000 | 0.40 | .1554 | .3446 |
| 0.01 | .0040 | .4960 | 0.41 | .1591 | .3409 |
| 0.02 | .0080 | .4920 | 0.42 | .1628 | .3372 |
| 0.03 | .0120 | .4880 | 0.43 | .1664 | .3336 |
| 0.04 | .0160 | .4840 | 0.44 | .1700 | .3300 |
| 0.05 | .0199 | .4801 | 0.45 | .1736 | .3264 |
| 0.06 | .0239 | .4761 | 0.46 | .1772 | .3228 |
| 0.07 | .0279 | .4721 | 0.47 | .1808 | .3192 |
| 0.08 | .0319 | .4681 | 0.48 | .1844 | .3156 |
| 0.09 | .0359 | .4641 | 0.49 | .1879 | .3121 |
| 0.10 | .0398 | .4602 | 0.50 | .1915 | .3085 |
| 0.11 | .0438 | .4562 | 0.51 | .1950 | .3050 |
| 0.12 | .0478 | .4522 | 0.52 | .1985 | .3015 |
| 0.13 | .0517 | .4483 | 0.53 | .2019 | .2981 |
| 0.14 | .0557 | .4443 | 0.54 | .2054 | .2946 |
| 0.15 | .0596 | .4404 | 0.55 | .2088 | .2912 |
| 0.16 | .0636 | .4364 | 0.56 | .2123 | .2877 |
| 0.17 | .0675 | .4325 | 0.57 | .2157 | .2843 |
| 0.18 | .0714 | .4286 | 0.58 | .2190 | .2810 |
| 0.19 | .0753 | .4247 | 0.59 | .2224 | .2776 |
| 0.20 | .0793 | .4207 | 0.60 | .2257 | .2743 |
| 0.21 | .0832 | .4168 | 0.61 | .2291 | .2709 |
| 0.22 | .0871 | .4129 | 0.62 | .2324 | .2676 |
| 0.23 | .0910 | .4090 | 0.63 | .2357 | .2643 |
| 0.24 | .0948 | .4052 | 0.64 | .2389 | .2611 |
| 0.25 | .0987 | .4013 | 0.65 | .2422 | .2578 |
| 0.26 | .1026 | .3974 | 0.66 | .2454 | .2546 |
| 0.27 | .1064 | .3936 | 0.67 | .2486 | .2514 |
| 0.28 | .1103 | .3897 | 0.68 | .2517 | .2483 |
| 0.29 | .1141 | .3859 | 0.69 | .2549 | .2451 |
| 0.30 | .1179 | .3821 | 0.70 | .2580 | .2420 |
| 0.31 | .1217 | .3783 | 0.71 | .2611 | .2389 |
| 0.32 | .1255 | .3745 | 0.72 | .2642 | .2358 |
| 0.33 | .1293 | .3707 | 0.73 | .2673 | .2327 |
| 0.34 | .1331 | .3669 | 0.74 | .2704 | .2296 |
| 0.35 | .1368 | .3632 | 0.75 | .2734 | .2266 |
| 0.36 | .1406 | .3594 | 0.76 | .2764 | .2236 |
| 0.37 | .1443 | .3557 | 0.77 | .2794 | .2206 |
| 0.38 | .1480 | .3520 | 0.78 | .2823 | .2177 |
| 0.39 | .1517 | .3483 | 0.79 | .2852 | .2148 |

| (A) | (B) area between mean and | (C) area beyond | (A) | (B) area between mean and | (C) area beyond |
|---|---|---|---|---|---|
| z | z | z | z | z | z |
| 0.80 | .2881 | .2119 | 1.20 | .3849 | .1151 |
| 0.81 | .2910 | .2090 | 1.21 | .3869 | .1131 |
| 0.82 | .2939 | .2061 | 1.22 | .3888 | .1112 |
| 0.83 | .2967 | .2033 | 1.23 | .3907 | .1093 |
| 0.84 | .2995 | .2005 | 1.24 | .3925 | .1075 |
| 0.85 | .3023 | .1977 | 1.25 | .3944 | .1056 |
| 0.86 | .3051 | .1949 | 1.26 | .3962 | .1038 |
| 0.87 | .3078 | .1922 | 1.27 | .3980 | .1020 |
| 0.88 | .3106 | .1894 | 1.28 | .3997 | .1003 |
| 0.89 | .3133 | .1867 | 1.29 | .4015 | .0985 |
| 0.90 | .3159 | .1841 | 1.30 | .4032 | .0968 |
| 0.91 | .3186 | .1814 | 1.31 | .4049 | .0951 |
| 0.92 | .3212 | .1788 | 1.32 | .4066 | .0934 |
| 0.93 | .3238 | .1762 | 1.33 | .4082 | .0918 |
| 0.94 | .3264 | .1736 | 1.34 | .4099 | .0901 |
| 0.95 | .3289 | .1711 | 1.35 | .4115 | .0885 |
| 0.96 | .3315 | .1685 | 1.36 | .4131 | .0869 |
| 0.97 | .3340 | .1660 | 1.37 | .4147 | .0853 |
| 0.98 | .3365 | .1635 | 1.38 | .4162 | .0838 |
| 0.99 | .3389 | .1611 | 1.39 | .4177 | .0823 |
| 1.00 | .3413 | .1587 | 1.40 | .4192 | .0808 |
| 1.01 | .3438 | .1562 | 1.41 | .4207 | .0793 |
| 1.02 | .3461 | .1539 | 1.42 | .4222 | .0778 |
| 1.03 | .3485 | .1515 | 1.43 | .4236 | .0764 |
| 1.04 | .3508 | .1492 | 1.44 | .4251 | .0749 |
| 1.05 | .3531 | .1469 | 1.45 | .4265 | .0735 |
| 1.06 | .3554 | .1446 | 1.46 | .4279 | .0721 |
| 1.07 | .3577 | .1423 | 1.47 | .4292 | .0708 |
| 1.08 | .3599 | .1401 | 1.48 | .4306 | .0694 |
| 1.09 | .3621 | .1379 | 1.49 | .4319 | .0681 |
| 1.10 | .3643 | .1357 | 1.50 | .4332 | .0668 |
| 1.11 | .3665 | .1335 | 1.51 | .4345 | .0655 |
| 1.12 | .3686 | .1314 | 1.52 | .4357 | .0643 |
| 1.13 | .3708 | .1292 | 1.53 | .4370 | .0630 |
| 1.14 | .3729 | .1271 | 1.54 | .4382 | .0618 |
| 1.15 | .3749 | .1251 | 1.55 | .4394 | .0606 |
| 1.16 | .3770 | .1230 | 1.56 | .4406 | .0594 |
| 1.17 | .3790 | .1210 | 1.57 | .4418 | .0582 |
| 1.18 | .3810 | .1190 | 1.58 | .4429 | .0571 |
| 1.19 | .3830 | .1170 | 1.59 | .4441 | .0559 |

| (A) | (B) area between mean and | (C) area beyond | (A) | (B) area between mean and | (C) area beyond |
|---|---|---|---|---|---|
| z | z | z | z | z | z |
| 1.60 | .4452 | .0548 | 2.00 | .4772 | .0228 |
| 1.61 | .4463 | .0537 | 2.01 | .4778 | .0222 |
| 1.62 | .4474 | .0526 | 2.02 | .4783 | .0217 |
| 1.63 | .4484 | .0516 | 2.03 | .4788 | .0212 |
| 1.64 | .4495 | .0505 | 2.04 | .4793 | .0207 |
| 1.65 | .4505 | .0495 | 2.05 | .4798 | .0202 |
| 1.66 | .4515 | .0485 | 2.06 | .4803 | .0197 |
| 1.67 | .4525 | .0475 | 2.07 | .4808 | .0192 |
| 1.68 | .4535 | .0465 | 2.08 | .4812 | .0188 |
| 1.69 | .4545 | .0455 | 2.09 | .4817 | .0183 |
| 1.70 | .4554 | .0446 | 2.10 | .4821 | .0179 |
| 1.71 | .4564 | .0436 | 2.11 | .4826 | .0174 |
| 1.72 | .4573 | .0427 | 2.12 | .4830 | .0170 |
| 1.73 | .4582 | .0418 | 2.13 | .4834 | .0166 |
| 1.74 | .4591 | .0409 | 2.14 | .4838 | .0162 |
| 1.75 | .4599 | .0401 | 2.15 | .4842 | .0158 |
| 1.76 | .4608 | .0392 | 2.16 | .4846 | .0154 |
| 1.77 | .4616 | .0384 | 2.17 | .4850 | .0150 |
| 1.78 | .4625 | .0375 | 2.18 | .4854 | .0146 |
| 1.79 | .4633 | .0367 | 2.19 | .4857 | .0143 |
| 1.80 | .4641 | .0359 | 2.20 | .4861 | .0139 |
| 1.81 | .4649 | .0351 | 2.21 | .4864 | .0136 |
| 1.82 | .4656 | .0344 | 2.22 | .4868 | .0132 |
| 1.83 | .4664 | .0336 | 2.23 | .4871 | .0129 |
| 1.84 | .4671 | .0329 | 2.24 | .4875 | .0125 |
| 1.85 | .4678 | .0322 | 2.25 | .4878 | .0122 |
| 1.86 | .4686 | .0314 | 2.26 | .4881 | .0119 |
| 1.87 | .4693 | .0307 | 2.27 | .4884 | .0116 |
| 1.88 | .4699 | .0301 | 2.28 | .4887 | .0113 |
| 1.89 | .4706 | .0294 | 2.29 | .4890 | .0110 |
| 1.90 | .4713 | .0287 | 2.30 | .4893 | .0107 |
| 1.91 | .4719 | .0281 | 2.31 | .4896 | .0104 |
| 1.92 | .4726 | .0274 | 2.32 | .4898 | .0102 |
| 1.93 | .4732 | .0268 | 2.33 | .4901 | .0099 |
| 1.94 | .4738 | .0262 | 2.34 | .4904 | .0096 |
| 1.95 | .4744 | .0256 | 2.35 | .4906 | .0094 |
| 1.96 | .4750 | .0250 | 2.36 | .4909 | .0091 |
| 1.97 | .4756 | .0244 | 2.37 | .4911 | .0089 |
| 1.98 | .4761 | .0239 | 2.38 | .4913 | .0087 |
| 1.99 | .4767 | .0233 | 2.39 | .4916 | .0084 |

| (A) | (B) area between mean and | (C) area beyond | (A) | (B) area between mean and | (C) area beyond |
|---|---|---|---|---|---|
| z | z | z | z | z | z |
| 2.40 | .4918 | .0082 | 2.80 | .4974 | .0026 |
| 2.41 | .4920 | .0080 | 2.81 | .4975 | .0025 |
| 2.42 | .4922 | .0078 | 2.82 | .4976 | .0024 |
| 2.43 | .4925 | .0075 | 2.83 | .4977 | .0023 |
| 2.44 | .4927 | .0073 | 2.84 | .4977 | .0023 |
| 2.45 | .4929 | .0071 | 2.85 | .4978 | .0022 |
| 2.46 | .4931 | .0069 | 2.86 | .4979 | .0021 |
| 2.47 | .4932 | .0068 | 2.87 | .4979 | .0021 |
| 2.48 | .4934 | .0066 | 2.88 | .4980 | .0020 |
| 2.49 | .4936 | .0064 | 2.89 | .4981 | .0019 |
| 2.50 | .4938 | .0062 | 2.90 | .4981 | .0019 |
| 2.51 | .4940 | .0060 | 2.91 | .4982 | .0018 |
| 2.52 | .4941 | .0059 | 2.92 | .4982 | .0018 |
| 2.53 | .4943 | .0057 | 2.93 | .4983 | .0017 |
| 2.54 | .4945 | .0055 | 2.94 | .4984 | .0016 |
| 2.55 | .4946 | .0054 | 2.95 | .4984 | .0016 |
| 2.56 | .4948 | .0052 | 2.96 | .4985 | .0015 |
| 2.57 | .4949 | .0051 | 2.97 | .4985 | .0015 |
| 2.58 | .4951 | .0049 | 2.98 | .4986 | .0014 |
| 2.59 | .4952 | .0048 | 2.99 | .4986 | .0014 |
| 2.60 | .4953 | .0047 | 3.00 | .4987 | .0013 |
| 2.61 | .4955 | .0045 | 3.01 | .4987 | .0013 |
| 2.62 | .4956 | .0044 | 3.02 | .4987 | .0013 |
| 2.63 | .4957 | .0043 | 3.03 | .4988 | .0012 |
| 2.64 | .4959 | .0041 | 3.04 | .4988 | .0012 |
| 2.65 | .4960 | .0040 | 3.05 | .4989 | .0011 |
| 2.66 | .4961 | .0039 | 3.06 | .4989 | .0011 |
| 2.67 | .4962 | .0038 | 3.07 | .4989 | .0011 |
| 2.68 | .4963 | .0037 | 3.08 | .4990 | .0010 |
| 2.69 | .4964 | .0036 | 3.09 | .4990 | .0010 |
| 2.70 | .4965 | .0035 | 3.10 | .4990 | .0010 |
| 2.71 | .4966 | .0034 | 3.11 | .4991 | .0009 |
| 2.72 | .4967 | .0033 | 3.12 | .4991 | .0009 |
| 2.73 | .4968 | .0032 | 3.13 | .4991 | .0009 |
| 2.74 | .4969 | .0031 | 3.14 | .4992 | .0008 |
| 2.75 | .4970 | .0030 | 3.15 | .4992 | .0008 |
| 2.76 | .4971 | .0029 | 3.16 | .4992 | .0008 |
| 2.77 | .4972 | .0028 | 3.17 | .4992 | .0008 |
| 2.78 | .4973 | .0027 | 3.18 | .4993 | .0007 |
| 2.79 | .4974 | .0026 | 3.19 | .4993 | .0007 |

| (A) | (B) area between mean and | (C) area beyond | (A) | (B) area between mean and | (C) area beyond |
|-----|-----|-----|-----|-----|-----|
| z | z | z | z | z | z |
| 3.20 | .4993 | .0007 | 3.50 | .4998 | .0002 |
| 3.21 | .4993 | .0007 | 3.60 | .4998 | .0002 |
| 3.22 | .4994 | .0006 | 3.70 | .4999 | .0001 |
| 3.23 | .4994 | .0006 | 3.80 | .4999 | .0001 |
| 3.24 | .4994 | .0006 | 3.90 | .49995 | .00005 |
| 3.25 | .4994 | .0006 | 4.00 | .49997 | .00003 |
| 3.30 | .4995 | .0005 | | | |
| 3.35 | .4996 | .0004 | | | |
| 3.40 | .4997 | .0003 | | | |
| 3.45 | .4997 | .0003 | | | |

Runyon and Haber, *Fundamentals of Behavioral Statistics*, © 1971, Addison-Wesley, Reading, Massachusetts. Pp. 289–91 (Table A). Reprinted with permission.

# Appendix C: Chi Square Table

## How to Use the Chi Square Table ─────────────

To use this table, first compute the value of chi square by using the formula for calculating chi square given in the text. Next, compute the degrees of freedom ($df$) by following the instructions given in the text. Now, to find the probability of obtaining a chi square equal to the one you have computed, locate your table's number of degrees of freedom in the column headed $df$ on the left-hand side of the table. Then read across the row of the table corresponding to this $df$ value until you come to a value in the table equal to or larger than the chi square value you have calculated. If the value in the table is equal to the value you have calculated, the probability is determined by noting the probability indicated above the column in which the value appears. If the chi square value you have calculated falls between the values in adjacent columns in the table, the probability of the calculated chi square value is less than the probability that appears above the left column, and greater than the probability that appears above the right column of the table.

# Table C  Chi Square Table

Probability

| df | .99 | .98 | .95 | .90 | .80 | .70 | .50 | .30 | .20 | .10 | .05 | .02 | .01 | .001 |
|----|-----|-----|-----|-----|-----|-----|-----|-----|-----|-----|-----|-----|-----|------|
| 1 | $.0^3157$ | $.0^3628$ | .00393 | .0158 | .0642 | .148 | .455 | 1.074 | 1.642 | 2.706 | 3.841 | 5.412 | 6.635 | 10.827 |
| 2 | .0201 | .0404 | .103 | .211 | .446 | .713 | 1.386 | 2.408 | 3.219 | 4.605 | 5.991 | 7.824 | 9.210 | 13.815 |
| 3 | .115 | .185 | .352 | .584 | 1.005 | 1.424 | 2.366 | 3.665 | 4.642 | 6.251 | 7.815 | 9.837 | 11.341 | 16.268 |
| 4 | .297 | .429 | .711 | 1.064 | 1.649 | 2.195 | 3.357 | 4.878 | 5.989 | 7.779 | 9.488 | 11.668 | 13.277 | 18.465 |
| 5 | .554 | .752 | 1.145 | 1.610 | 2.343 | 3.000 | 4.351 | 6.064 | 7.289 | 9.236 | 11.070 | 13.388 | 15.086 | 20.517 |
| 6 | .872 | 1.134 | 1.635 | 2.204 | 3.070 | 3.828 | 5.348 | 7.231 | 8.558 | 10.645 | 12.592 | 15.033 | 16.812 | 22.457 |
| 7 | 1.239 | 1.564 | 2.167 | 2.833 | 3.822 | 4.671 | 6.346 | 8.383 | 9.803 | 12.017 | 14.067 | 16.622 | 18.475 | 24.322 |
| 8 | 1.646 | 2.032 | 2.733 | 3.490 | 4.594 | 5.527 | 7.344 | 9.524 | 11.030 | 13.362 | 15.507 | 18.168 | 20.090 | 26.125 |
| 9 | 2.088 | 2.532 | 3.325 | 4.168 | 5.380 | 6.393 | 8.343 | 10.656 | 12.242 | 14.684 | 16.919 | 19.679 | 21.666 | 27.877 |
| 10 | 2.558 | 3.059 | 3.940 | 4.865 | 6.179 | 7.267 | 9.342 | 11.781 | 13.442 | 15.987 | 18.307 | 21.161 | 23.209 | 29.588 |
| 11 | 3.053 | 3.609 | 4.575 | 5.578 | 6.989 | 8.148 | 10.341 | 12.899 | 14.631 | 17.275 | 19.675 | 22.618 | 24.725 | 31.264 |
| 12 | 3.571 | 4.178 | 5.226 | 6.304 | 7.807 | 9.034 | 11.340 | 14.011 | 15.812 | 18.549 | 21.026 | 24.054 | 26.217 | 32.909 |
| 13 | 4.107 | 4.765 | 5.892 | 7.042 | 8.634 | 9.926 | 12.340 | 15.119 | 16.985 | 19.812 | 22.362 | 25.472 | 27.688 | 34.528 |
| 14 | 4.660 | 5.368 | 6.571 | 7.790 | 9.467 | 10.821 | 13.339 | 16.222 | 18.151 | 21.064 | 23.685 | 26.873 | 29.141 | 36.123 |
| 15 | 5.229 | 5.985 | 7.261 | 8.547 | 10.307 | 11.721 | 14.339 | 17.322 | 19.311 | 22.307 | 24.996 | 28.259 | 30.578 | 37.697 |

## Table C  continued

Probability

| df | .99 | .98 | .95 | .90 | .80 | .70 | .50 | .30 | .20 | .10 | .05 | .02 | .01 | .001 |
|----|------|------|------|------|------|------|------|------|------|------|------|------|------|------|
| 16 | 5.812 | 6.614 | 7.962 | 9.312 | 11.152 | 12.624 | 15.338 | 18.418 | 20.465 | 23.542 | 26.296 | 29.633 | 32.000 | 39.252 |
| 17 | 6.408 | 7.255 | 8.672 | 10.085 | 12.002 | 13.531 | 16.338 | 19.511 | 21.615 | 24.769 | 27.587 | 30.995 | 33.409 | 40.790 |
| 18 | 7.015 | 7.906 | 9.390 | 10.865 | 12.857 | 14.440 | 17.338 | 20.601 | 22.760 | 25.989 | 28.869 | 32.346 | 34.805 | 42.312 |
| 19 | 7.633 | 8.567 | 10.117 | 11.651 | 13.716 | 15.352 | 18.338 | 21.689 | 23.900 | 27.204 | 30.144 | 33.687 | 36.191 | 43.820 |
| 20 | 8.260 | 9.237 | 10.851 | 12.443 | 14.578 | 16.266 | 19.337 | 22.775 | 25.038 | 28.412 | 31.410 | 35.020 | 37.566 | 45.315 |
| 21 | 8.897 | 9.915 | 11.591 | 13.240 | 15.445 | 17.182 | 20.337 | 23.858 | 26.171 | 29.615 | 32.671 | 36.343 | 38.932 | 46.797 |
| 22 | 9.542 | 10.600 | 12.338 | 14.041 | 16.314 | 18.101 | 21.337 | 24.939 | 27.301 | 30.813 | 33.924 | 37.659 | 40.289 | 48.268 |
| 23 | 10.196 | 11.293 | 13.091 | 14.848 | 17.187 | 19.021 | 22.337 | 26.018 | 28.429 | 32.007 | 35.172 | 38.968 | 41.638 | 49.728 |
| 24 | 10.856 | 11.992 | 13.848 | 15.659 | 18.062 | 19.943 | 23.337 | 27.096 | 29.553 | 33.196 | 36.415 | 40.270 | 42.980 | 51.179 |
| 25 | 11.524 | 12.697 | 14.611 | 16.473 | 18.940 | 20.867 | 24.337 | 28.172 | 30.675 | 34.382 | 37.652 | 41.566 | 44.314 | 52.620 |
| 26 | 12.198 | 13.409 | 15.379 | 17.292 | 19.820 | 21.792 | 25.336 | 29.246 | 31.795 | 35.563 | 38.885 | 42.856 | 45.642 | 54.052 |
| 27 | 12.879 | 14.125 | 16.151 | 18.114 | 20.703 | 22.719 | 26.336 | 30.319 | 32.912 | 36.741 | 40.113 | 44.140 | 46.963 | 55.476 |
| 28 | 13.565 | 14.847 | 16.928 | 18.939 | 21.588 | 23.647 | 27.336 | 31.391 | 34.027 | 37.916 | 41.337 | 45.419 | 48.278 | 56.893 |
| 29 | 14.256 | 15.574 | 17.708 | 19.768 | 22.475 | 24.577 | 28.336 | 32.461 | 35.139 | 39.087 | 42.557 | 46.693 | 49.588 | 58.302 |
| 30 | 14.953 | 16.306 | 18.493 | 20.599 | 23.364 | 25.508 | 29.336 | 33.530 | 36.250 | 40.256 | 43.773 | 47.962 | 50.892 | 59.703 |

From Fisher and Yates: Statistical Tables for Biological, Agricultural and Medical Research published by Longman Group Ltd., London (previously published by Oliver and Boyd Ltd.) and by permission of the authors and publishers.

286

# Appendix D: A Research Ethics Statement

## Department of Mental Health Guidelines for the Protection of Human Subjects

### I. POLICY STATEMENT

Safeguarding the rights and welfare of human subjects involved in research, development, demonstration, or similar activities is the responsibility of the facility conducting or originating the specific activity.

The facility must assure the Department that no activity involving human subjects will be undertaken unless the activity has been reviewed and approved by an appropriate facility committee, in the manner to be described below.

This review must establish that the activity, as described by the principal investigator or program director, will not interfere with or impair the rights and welfare of the subjects, nor involve risks that outweigh either potential benefits to the subjects, or the expected value of the knowledge sought, nor deny the rights of the subjects to adequate and appropriate informed consent. The committee must establish a basis for continuing review of the activity in keeping with these determinations.

The facility must submit to the Department, for its review, approval, and official acceptance, an assurance of its compliance with this policy.

### II. DEFINITIONS

A. *Subjects*

This term describes any individual who may be at risk as a consequence of participation in any activity, excluding all accepted and established service functions, regardless of the source of funding or of support, conducted in or originating at a department facility.

B. *At Risk*

An individual is considered to be "at risk" if he or she may be exposed to the possibility of harm—physical, psychological, sociological, or other—as a consequence of any activity which goes beyond the application of those established and accepted methods necessary to meet his needs. The determination of when an individual is at risk is a matter of applying common sense and sound professional judgment to the circumstances of the activity in question. Responsibility for this determination resides at all levels of facility and departmental review. The operating agency will make a definitive determination. Appendix I contains a sample of cases obtained from the National Institutes of Health under the title, "Examples of Research Proposals in Sociology, Psychology, and Psychiatry which have put Subject's Rights and Welfare at Risk."

C. *Informed Consent*

Informed consent is the agreement obtained from a subject, or from his/her authorized representative, to the subject's participation in an activity.

The basic elements of informed consent are:

1. A full and fair explanation of the procedures to be followed, including an identification of those which are experimental;
2. A description of the attendant discomforts and risks;
3. A description of the benefits to be expected;
4. A disclosure of appropriate alternative procedures that would be advantageous for the subject;
5. An offer to answer any inquiries concerning the procedures;
6. An instruction that the subject is free to withdraw his consent and to discontinue participation in the project or activity at any time.

In addition, the agreement, written or oral, which the subject enters into, should include no exculpatory language through which the subject is made to waive, or to appear to waive, any of his/her legal rights, or to release the facility or its agents from liability for negligence.

The principles of this policy apply most directly and comprehensively in those instances of social, behavioral and medical science investigations where a procedure may induce in the subject an altered state or condition potentially harmful to his personal welfare. Surgical procedures, the administration of drugs, the requirement of strenuous physical exertion and participation in psychologically or socially harmful activities are examples of experimental arrangements which require thorough scrutiny by facility review groups. Such procedures require a continuing overview and full documentation for the record.

Aside from the above kinds of procedures, there is a large range of social and behavioral research in which no personal risk to the subject is involved. In these circumstances, regardless of whether the investigation is classified as behavioral, social, medical, or other, the issues of concern are the fully voluntary nature of the participation of the subject, the maintenance of confidentiality of information obtained from the subject, and the protection of the subject from misuse of the findings. For example, a major class of procedures in the social and behavioral sciences does no more than observe or elicit information about the subject's status, by means of the administration of tests, inventories, questionnaires, or surveys of personality or background. In such instances, the ethical considerations of voluntary participation, confidentiality, and propriety in use of the findings are the most generally relevant ones. In the foregoing kinds of situations, it may be permissible to adapt informed consent procedures to fit the particular circumstances. In these instances, full and specific documentation is necessary for the record.

Many investigations in the social and behavioral sciences involve procedures designed to alter the status of the individual as, for example, studies of human learning, social perception, or group effectiveness. In such research, even though the effects, if any, on the subject may be transitory or even more or less permanent, they must be judged clearly not to be harmful or not to involve the risk of harm.

Whatever the nature of the investigation, the concern for the subject's protection and for the assurance of voluntary participation becomes most critical when the subject is not of age or competent to make an adequate judgment in his own behalf. Informed consent must be documented. See *Rules of the Department of Mental Health*, Article V, DMH Rule 5.01, "Disclosure of Patient Data and Confidentiality"; Article XII, DMH Rule 12.03, "Consent for Treatment."

D. *Institutional Associates*

Institutional Associates include individuals available to serve as members of a committee to review proposed projects with regard to the protection of human subjects. These individuals should be identified by name, occupation or position, and by other pertinent indications of experience and competence in areas pertinent to the areas of review such as earned degrees, board certifications, licensures, memberships, etc.

E. *Assurance*

The assurance is a formal statement of compliance with department policy executed by an appropriate facility official. (For an example, see Appendix II.)

## III. PROCEDURES

A. *Institutional Assurances*

The Department requires assurances from all of its facilities which sponsor activities involving human subjects. The assurance must provide explicit information on the policy and procedure it employs for review and decision on the propriety of proposed activities involving human subjects.

The document must include a description of the competencies represented in committees of institutional associates utilized for review, the sources of consultants, if used, the administrative mechanisms by which surveillance is provided for projects involving human subjects—particularly to deal with changes in protocol or emergent problems of ongoing activities—and the manner in which the facility assures itself that the advice of a committee of institutional associates will be followed. Copies of documents of the facility's policies on these issues should be attached to the Institutional Assurance.

Nothing in the Institutional Assurance should inhibit any Department staff member, any advisory group, committees or consultants from:

1. Identifying concern for the welfare of human subjects and communicating this concern to the grantee facility.
2. Recommending disapproval of the research proposal or investigation if the gravity of the hazards and risks so indicate.

B. *Project Reviews*

Following the acceptance of the Department's Institutional Assurance, committees of institutional associates for the review of applications for specific activities involving the use of human subjects may be established. Members of a committee must have *no vested interest* in the specific project. The committee should not include the principal investigator or his immediate associates in the proposed research. Committee members may be either or both staff and consultants to the facility. The committee should possess not only specific competence to comprehend the scientific content of the activity under review, but also other competencies pertaining to the decision that needs to be made. The review group must ascertain the adequacy of provisions for protecting the rights and welfare of human subjects in research, the risks and potential benefits of the investigation, and the appropriateness of the methods used to secure informed consent. For example, if the proposed research includes the experimental use of a new drug, the committee must include an individual experienced in the area of experimentation with new drugs. In addition, if any doubt exists as to whether or not the human subject is capable of giving informed consent, the judgment must be made on this matter. In most cases, the facility's clinical supervisor may make this judgment. The committee shall provide the facility with a permanent detailed record of its deliberations. The committee shall summarize its decisions for approved proposals on form DMH-1252 for transmittal to the Research Program Advisor, Chicago General Office, Department of Mental Health.

Note that the human rights review is normally completed after the Institutional Research Committee and the Research Program Advisor approve the proposed Research and Development program through the use of forms DMH-1251 or 1257.

C. *Departmental Actions*

1. *Assurances*

Each Institutional Assurance and its attachments shall be transmitted to the Research Program Advisor for review. Recommendations for action will be made to the Director of the Department of Mental Health. When the Director has reviewed and accepted the Institutional Assurance, the responsible official of the facility will be notified.

Approval for any activity involving human subjects to be authorized by the Research Program Advisor, either state supported (form DMH-1257) or for outside support (form DMH-1251) will require the Department's prior acceptance of an Institutional Assurance.

Each facility shall report to the Department any changes in its policies, procedures, or the competencies represented on its committee of institutional associates. For example, in the event of the addition or termination of individuals to the roster of institutional associates, such changes must be reported.

2. *Project Reviews*

The summary report, form DMH-1252, shall be used to document human rights approval by the Committee of Institutional Associates and acceptance of such approval by the Research Program Advisor for approved proposals.

## IV. CLARIFICATION

All Department facilities are responsible for assuring that activities involving and/or individually identifying human subjects are in accordance with the law and conform to ethical principles which guide innovative or experimental activity. Consequently, all departmental activity must conform to: (1) *Department of Mental Health Guidelines for the Protection of Human Subjects,* (2) Pertinent Department Rules, (3) Pertinent laws contained in Illinois Revised Statutes, and (4) the guidelines of the U.S. Department of Health, Education and Welfare, set forth in *The Institutional Guide to DHEW Policies on Protection of Human Subjects* (DHEW publication No. (NIH) 72-102—Dec. 1, 1971). In general, this latter document is the best reference for the issues and operating mechanisms involved in the protection of human subjects.

Department Rules that are pertinent to the protection of human subjects are as follows:

Article IV.  Personnel.

Rule 4.01–Employee Transactions with Patients.
Rule 4.02–Mistreatment of Patients.
Rule 4.03–Use or Possession of Intoxicants or Narcotics.

Article V.  Records and Reports.

Rule 5.01–Disclosure of Patient Data and Confidentiality.

Article VIII.  Children.

Rule 8.04–Rights of Minors.

Article XII.  Treatment.

Rule 12.01–Autopsies and Inquests.
Rule 12.02–Restraint.
Rule 12.03–Consent for Treatment.
Rule 12.06–Seclusion.

Laws contained in the Illinois Revised Statutes that are relevant to the protection of human subjects are as follows:

Ch 38

| | |
|---|---|
| Methadone | 22-10.1 |

Ch 91-$\frac{1}{2}$

| | |
|---|---|
| Humane Care and Treatment of Patients | |
|     Defined | 12-1 |
|     Mistreatment | 12-9, 15-1 |
|     Negligence | 12-11 |
| Research Funds | 12-12 |
| Responsible Relative, defined | 1-19 |
| Department of Mental Health | |
|     Care and Treatment | 100-7 |
|     Federal Grants | 100-18 |

Ch 111-$\frac{1}{2}$

| | |
|---|---|
| Psychiatric Standards, development and evaluation of | 147-1 |

Ch 127

| | |
|---|---|
| Advisory Committee on Research | 6.04 |
| Psychiatric Advisory Council | 6.04 |

## *Examples of Research Proposals in Sociology, Psychology, and Psychiatry Which Have Put Subjects' Rights and Welfare at Risk*

*Case 1*

This project, supported by a fellowship award to a candidate for the Ph.D. in sociology, concerned the social, political, and economic status of male sexual deviates. The investigator learned the identities of a large number of men involved in impersonal homosexual acts in public places by posing as a participant and volunteering to act as a "lookout" to warn of police intervention. The study plan was approved by both public and institutional advisory committees as being designed so as to protect the anonymity of the subjects, who were never told that they were the subjects of a research project.

Members of the university faculty who were not involved in the study protested that it was ethically undesirable and constituted an invasion of privacy. This controversy forced the resignation of the department chairman, who was also the investigator's chief mentor, and resulted in the matter becoming public and widely discussed in the press. Although the university vigorously defended the scientific merit of the studies, the public outcry damaged its reputation as a protector of human rights and forced it to revamp its system of control of projects involving human subjects, especially as concerns the use of deception and subterfuge in acquiring data.

*Case 2*

This study involved an investigation of the behavioral consequences of chromosome abnormalities in juvenile human subjects. A prevalence study was to be done on the incidence of the XYY anomaly in two populations—one, approximately 5,000 male juvenile delinquents housed in state institutions, the other, a "normal" control group from the outpatient care program of a large urban hospital. Written informed consent was to be obtained for the drawing of a small blood sample from the institutionalized children.

Because there was some inference that the results of these studies might be made available to correctional institution authorities, a parent of one child potentially involved has sought a court injunction to halt the study, contending that inadequate measures are to be taken to provide for confidentiality of findings and that parental consent procedures are inadequate and uninformative.

In this case, the responsible committee of the university noted that the only apparent direct involvement of "human subjects" involved the extraction of a small blood sample, judged that human rights were not at risk, and gave the project full endorsement. Apparently they did not examine the planned use of these samples. As a result the applicant university is re-studying its entire system for administrative "screening" and committee referral and review of projects involving human subjects.

*Case 3*

An investigator with primary interest in the social and psychological problems of the aged planned to study the economic, social, and psychological factors motivating and conditioning occupational retirement and the adjustments thereto. His initial attempt involved interviews with a number of retirees, all of whom were subscribers to the same health insurance plan, and since his questionnaire was designed in a rather innocuous way, his results were inconclusive.

He therefore decided to revamp his protocol, without consulting his institutional committee, and to make the interview procedure much more aggressive and anxiety producing. As a result, a number of his elderly subjects were hospitalized with anxiety-induced syndromes, and a larger number had to consult their physicians with physical complaints which were attributed to anxiety stress.

Since all subjects visited the same group of physicians, inevitably these doctors compared notes about this sudden influx of patients with anxiety neuroses, learned the common source of these complaints, and protested vigorously and publicly to the responsible institution.

The institution was forced to concede that its administrative control of investigators was faulty, so far as impulsive changes in study protocols is concerned, and has taken measures to see to it that these matters will not be implemented without prior committee review and approval.

## Case 4

A psychologist wished to study the adaption to post-graduate life of university students who had been hospitalized during the undergraduate period for treatment of mental or emotional illness. His plan was to locate these people by use of university health center and alumni association records and send them a mail questionnaire inquiring about their marital, occupational, and economic status as well as recurrences of their original illnesses.

At first examination his institutional committee was prepared to disapprove the study. However, on further consideration it was decided that the study had considerable merit, but that careful means had to be taken to assure the confidentiality of the information and protect against invasion of privacy. It was recognized that committing the questionnaire to the mails might result in disclosure to third parties of a previously unknown history of mental illness on the part of the study subjects.

Accordingly, the university committee spent considerable time in conference with the investigator and assisted him in redesigning his questionnaire, his contact procedure, and his methods for protecting the confidentiality of the data acquired. The study was then allowed to proceed.

## Case 5

The aim of this study was to acquire base-rate data on the physiological reactions of juvenile delinquents in natural settings, using a newly developed radio communication telemetry system. Male adolescents with established records of physical aggression and assault would be equipped with a radio sending device to be worn at least 1 hour per day, in normal social situations, and their overt and electro-dermal responses recorded. A matched group of non-delinquents would serve as normal controls.

Although this procedure was approved by the institutional committee, the public advisory panels considered the possibility of invasion of privacy so serious that funding was restricted to that necessary for refinement of the technology, pending further consideration of the required consent procedures and other ethical controls.

*Case 6*

This study was designed to investigate the effects of marijuana on the perceptual and cognitive functioning of humans of various ages and levels of drug experience. Some of the subjects were to be inexperienced juveniles.

The review panels expressed concern about the use of completely naive subjects—particularly minors—as well as about the problems of obtaining fully informed consent. Accordingly, the investigator agreed to limit his study to subjects over the age of 21 who had had some prior contact with the drug.

*Case 7*

The major aim of this study was to examine the role of heightened awareness of breathing in asthmatic children. Patterns of respiration and behavior would be observed, prior to, during, and following experimental induction of a stressful state. Included in these stresses were exposure to a surgical film and exposure to antigens in a pollen chamber.

Although these procedures had been reviewed and approved by the committee at the investigator's institution, the public advisory panels took issue with the ethics of showing a stressful motion picture to pre-adolescent and adolescent children, and with the business of exposing asthmatics to airborne antigens since there existed the possibility of aggravating their condition. The proposal was therefore recommended for disapproval.

*Case 8*

It was proposed to evaluate the effectiveness of a home treatment program of psychiatric care for suicide attempters who refused to come to a hospital or clinic.

Since the subjects would not be volunteers, and typically resisted treatment, the question was raised as to how their consent for treatment would be obtained, by a psychotherapist visiting them at their homes to offer such treatment there.

The scope of the project was reduced to that of a pilot study which did not involve the ethical issue of obtaining consent from unwilling participants.

*Case 9*

This research focused on the effects of contact with blacks upon the racial attitudes of anti-black white subjects. Four stages of inter-racial contact were proposed: preproximity, proximity, actual interaction, and post-interaction. Both laboratory and field studies would be done, and the subjects would not be told in advance of the purposes of the procedures.

Concern was expressed by advisory panels that, although the investigator was sensitive to the ethical issues and planned debriefing procedures for the laboratory phases, these debriefings were indefinite enough to leave the subjects unaware that they had taken part in a study of inter-racial attitudes. Further, the attempt to keep staff-to-mother cooperation at a minimum gave the possibility of breeding suspicion, competitiveness, or inter-racial hostility.

Despite these concerns the study was approved, but with the proviso that these matters be called to the investigator's attention.

*Case 10*

It was proposed to study the cytogenetic effects of repeated dosages of LSD-25 on a population of healthy male prisoner volunteers. The drug was to be administered at monthly intervals over a period of 4 months, and testicular biopsies would be taken to determine the incidence of meiotic chromosome changes.

The review panels felt that the obtaining of truly informed consent from these men would be difficult if not impossible. On the basis of this concern, as well as other serious study design weaknesses, the project was disapproved.

*Case 11*

This project involved two separate investigations of exploitative behavior in which both the cost of exploitation to the exploiter and the level of dependency of the person exploited would be varied. Experimenters posing as customers would negotiate with salesmen for the purchase of cars or shoes and simulate varying levels of dependency by altering personal appearance, apparent discomfort, or degree of need for the product being sold. The general hypothesis of the investigator was that dependency causes exploitation when costs are high.

Despite the fact that arrangements had been made to inform the salesmen of the true nature of these contacts after they had been made, the advisory panels felt that the procedures of deception violated ethical standards to a degree that made support of the project inadvisable.

### Case 12

It was proposed to compare the efficacy of two different types of psychotherapy treatment of married subjects—individual treatment of one of the marriage partners vs. conjoint marriage therapy in which the therapist sees husband and wife together. A questionnaire procedure would be used to assign subjects to one or the other of the two treatment groups. Some of the experimenters were to be inexperienced trainees.

Concern was expressed that, on the basis of an answer to a single questionnaire item, a person seriously ill and needing individual therapy would be assigned to the conjoint therapy unit mainly for research needs. The recommendation was for disapproval.

### Case 13

This was a project to produce a series of films dealing with police activity in a ghetto community. The investigator would accompany police on routine patrol and photograph and record their encounters with private citizens.

Serious questions were raised about methods for insuring that filming of police interrogations would be done only after permission had been obtained from the "suspects." The project was approved, but funding was delayed until specific information was received on how the "consent" matter would be handled, as well as a description of the extent of police cooperation in protecting the subjects' rights. In addition, the program providing the funds will very closely monitor the project as it proceeds.

### Case 14

The purpose of this program was to study the interrelationship between alcoholism and nutritional disease. Most of the research was to be carried out on malnourished and alcoholic persons in a foreign country.

Questions were raised as to whether "consent" elicited by a foreign physician, dealing with citizens of his own country, would be as meaningful and truly "informed" as would be the case in similar research performed in this country.

The supporting program conveyed this concern to officials of the U.S. institution sponsoring the research and elicited their assurance that the "consents" obtained would be such as to conform to U.S. standards.

## Case 15

The main objectives of this study were to determine the effects of "T-group" experiences on a variety of simulated administrative tasks and to compare the behavioral effects of "T-groups" vs. role playing on effectiveness in administrative decision making.

Ethical questions were raised because the student-subjects would be deceived into believing that they were volunteering for a non-credit university course rather than for an experiment. No provision was made for "debriefing" procedures at the study's end.

The recommendation was for disapproval, with the ethical concern to be communicated to the investigator.

## Case 16

This study was designed to test the thesis that the use of deception in laboratory and field social research has ethical and methodological costs. However, the focus of the work concerned the effects of subject deception on the outcome of the research, rather than on its ethical connotations. "Deceived" subjects, considered to be in a high-stress situation, would be compared to "non-deceived" (low-stress) subjects, so far as their attitude changes are concerned.

Although the planned studies were replete with deception procedures, no attempt was planned to control or modify the ethical aspects. It was therefore judged that the ethical issues which the investigators seemed to be concerned about were a significant problem in their own research. The recommendation was for disapproval.

## Case 17

It was planned to compare the effect of systematic desensitization therapy with a placebo therapy which attempted to embody the suggestibility aspects of such treatment. Phobic patients would be given either standard behavior therapy or placebo treatment consisting of attention, suggestion, reassurance, and a placebo drug.

The question was raised whether it is ethically acceptable to have a treating psychiatrist tell a clinically phobic patient over a period of four months that his phobic problem is due to hyperreactivity of the nervous system and that various procedures (bad tasting compounds, false dial readings, pursuit rotor and tachistoscopic tasks) would help him.

It was felt that the risks to the subject's welfare exceeded the possible benefit to him or to research, and the project was recommended for disapproval.

## Case 18

This was a proposal for a detailed examination of the cognitive and attitudinal variables involved in the ingestion of drugs and placebos. The subjects were university students. Performance, affect ratings, and physiologic responses would be measured.

Among the physiologic responses, blood pressure changes were to be measured by use of the arterial puncture method. Objections were raised to this, since no measures were indicated to inform the subjects of the probable dangers and discomforts involved.

The project as a whole was deemed worthy of support, with the proviso that the area of concern be transmitted to the investigator and assurance obtained that subject consent will be properly dealt with.

## Case 19

The general purpose of this proposal was to investigate the relationship between physical aggression and various antecedent conditions, personality factors, reinforcement variables, and physiological indices of arousal such as skin conductance, heart rate, and blood pressure. The race and religion of the subjects were included among the independent variables.

It was felt that including such factors as race and religion might infringe the rights of the subjects, since the test results could lead to their classification as racial or religious extremists. For this reason, and because the study design suffered from other serious weaknesses, the recommendation was for disapproval.

## Case 20

This was a study to explore the possibility of accomplishing the therapeutic effects of electroconvulsive therapy in 1 day by administering successive treatments, monitored by EEG and EKG.

Concern was expressed about the possibility of minimal brain damage from the inducement of six to eight fits, each starting no more than 3 minutes after the end of the preceding one.

The consent issue was a matter of concern. Although all noncommitted patients and their families were to be informed that investigational procedures were to be used, the investigator reported that the Attorney General of his state had ruled that it was not necessary to get signed consent from committed or voluntary patients.

Although most of the consultants who reviewed this proposal were willing to accept the fact that the physical risks of brain damage were not sufficiently serious to bar the study, there was continuing concern about the medicolegal aspects of the informed consent procedures. Since it appeared that the investigator was also not adequately prepared to cope with the problems of determining the therapeutic effectiveness of his experiments, disapproval was recommended.

*Case 21*

This was a pilot study of stimulant drug abuse. Urinalyses would be done on samples from acute psychiatric inpatients and university infirmary inpatients, for detection of the presence of 10 widely used stimulants and appetite depressants. Among other things, it was expected to provide preliminary information about the incidence of stimulant drug abuse among college students and determine if this is related to hospitalization for transient psychiatric symptoms. No provision was made for subjects coming to a student health unit for treatment of physical problems to give consent for urinary drug detection tests for research purposes.

The recommendation was for approval on scientific merit. In the unlikely event that this project was to be considered for funding, program staff was prepared to satisfactorily resolve the ''consent'' issue prior to release of funds.

## *Example of an Acceptable Assurance*

### INSTITUTIONAL ASSURANCE ON
### INVESTIGATIONS INVOLVING HUMAN SUBJECTS
### INCLUDING CLINICAL RESEARCH

The ___(name of institution)___ agrees with the principles of the Department of Mental Health policy (identified as *DMH Guidelines on the Protection of Human Subjects*) with regard to activities involving human subjects. This institution agrees that review independent of the investigator is necessary to safeguard the rights and welfare of human subjects of research investigations and assures the Department of Mental Health that it will establish and maintain advisory groups competent to review plans of each activity involving human subjects to insure adequate safeguards.

Group reviews and decisions will be carried out for each activity to determine that (1) the rights and welfare of the individuals involved are adequately protected, (2) the risks to subjects are outweighed by the potential benefits of the activities, and (3) the methods used to obtain informed consent are adequate and appropriate. No activity with human subjects will be initiated without prior review and approval by both the institutional committee and the central office.

The institution also agrees to exercise surveillance of projects using human subjects for changes in protocol which may alter the activity with regard to the criteria cited above. The institution further assures the Department of Mental Health that it will provide advice and consultation to investigators on activities with human subjects, and also that it will provide whatever professional attention or facilities may be required to safeguard the rights and welfare of human subjects involved in an activity. Records of group review and decision on the use of human subjects and of informed consent will be kept by the institution.

Attached as part of this statement are copies of policy and procedure of this institution with regard to use of human subjects in investigation, as well as a description of the groups utilized to review projects for enforcement of these policies and the manner in which the institution will assure itself that the advice of the committee of associates is followed.

Signature: _____

Title: _____

Date: _____

Attachments.

# Glossary

**abstract**  A brief summary of the issues addressed, hypotheses tested, methodologies and methods employed, and results obtained from a research project.

**accidental sample**  A nonprobability sample composed of individuals who happen to come into contact with the researcher.

**accretion evidence**  Evidence produced by the accumulation of deposit of materials.

**after-only design**  A strategy for attempting to assess the effect of a particular event after the event has occurred, with no prior observation of the dependent variable.

**applied research**  Research addressing specific, concrete questions or pragmatic problems.

**average deviation**  The arithmetic average of the differences between a distribution's mean score and each of the individual scores in the distribution.

**basic research**  Research addressing general and fundamental questions about the nature of phenomena.

**before-after design**  A research strategy in which the researcher observes the dependent variable before the occurrence of the independent variable and then observes the dependent variable again after the occurrence of the independent variable.

**before-after-with-control design**  A research strategy in which the dependent variable is observed in both an experimental and control group prior to the occurrence of the independent variable in the experimental group (but not in the control group). Both groups are observed again after the independent variable's occurrence in the experimental group.

**bibliography**  A listing of the sources and references used in a research report, usually located at the end of the report.

**binomial distribution**  A mathematically derived distribution of probabilities useful as a sampling distribution for determining the probability of outcomes of a series of events, each event having two equally probable outcomes.

**card reader**  A machine that reads data cards prepared by keyboard operators.

**causal chain**  A sequence of three or more variables, each causally related to the one that follows.

**cell**  A location in a table representing the intersection of one value of one variable and one value of the other variable used to construct the table.

**cell frequency**  The number appearing in the cell of a table, representing the number of elements in the sample or population that possess the values of the two variables that intersect in the cell.

**chi-square**  A statistic used to determine the probability of getting the cell frequencies in a cross-tabulation, given the null hypothesis that there is no relationship between the variables.

**coefficient of determination**  A measure of the strength of the relationship between two variables; the amount of the variance in the values of one variable statistically predictable from the values of another variable; varies between $+1$ and $-1$.

**coefficient of multiple determination**  A measure of the strength of the relationship between one variable and two or more other variables taken together; the amount of variance in one variable statistically predictable from the values of two or more other variables taken together; varies between $+1$ and $-1$.

**collapsing categories**  Combining two or more values of a variable, thus creating a smaller number of variable values to facilitate data analysis and presentation.

**computer program**  Instructions that determine which mathematical or other operations will be performed by the computer and in which order they will be performed.

**concomitant variation**  A relationship between two or more variables; one of the three prerequisites of a causal inference.

**conditional proposition**  A proposition that takes the general form "If $a$, then $b$."

**confidence interval**  The range of values between the confidence limits for an estimated population parameter calculated from sample statistics using inferential statistics, with a specified probability that the population parameter falls within the range.

**confidence limits**  The smallest and largest values of the estimate of a population parameter calculated from sample statistics using inferential statistics, with a specified probability that the population parameter falls between these values.

**contradictory values**  The values of a statistic that result in the rejection of a null hypothesis.

**control variable**  In elaboration analysis, a third variable used to construct partial tables (one for each value of the variable).

**correlation**  Synonym for *concomitant variation*.

**correlation coefficient**  A measure of the strength of the relationship between two variables; varies between $+1$ and $-1$.

**critical region**  Synonym for *rejection region*.

**cross-sectional design**  A research strategy in which a larger group is divided into subgroups and each of the subgroups is observed at a given point in time.

**cross-tabulation**  A device for determining whether two variables are related, consisting of cells, cell frequencies, and marginal frequencies.

**curvilinear relationship**  A relationship between variables such that the values change with respect to each other multidirectionally; for example, as the values of one variable go up, the values of the other variable at first go up and then go down.

**data array** A series of codes representing original data gathered on an element of a sample or population and arranged in a predetermined sequence in predetermined locations on a computer-readable storage device (punch cards, magnetic tape, floppy disks, etc.).

**deductive logic** Logic that goes from general to particular observations.

**degrees of freedom** The number of rows in a table minus one multiplied by the number of columns in a table minus one; used with chi-square.

**dependent variable** A variable believed by the researcher to be an effect of an independent variable.

**descriptive research** Research in which the goal of the researcher is to identify and communicate important properties or characteristics of a particular category of objects or events.

**descriptive statistics** Statistics that show relationships between variables or describe and summarize a particular data set.

**determinism** The belief that every event is preceded by one or more events that cause it to occur.

**diagonals** In a cross-tabulation, the cells that lie on or near a line drawn from the upper left to the lower right cells or from the upper right to the lower left cells.

**discrete variables** Variables that can assume only a finite number of values.

**disguised observer** An observer who misrepresents himself to his subjects and observes them while participating as a group member.

**disproportionate sampling** A sampling strategy in which all elements have known, but different, probabilities of being included.

**document analysis** A type of research based on analysis of existing sources of information (documents).

**elaboration analysis** A strategy for analyzing a relationship between two variables by introducing a third, control variable and creating partial tables; helps determine if the apparent (zero-order) relationship is causal or spurious and, if causal, the nature of the relationships among the three variables.

**empiricism** The practice of seeking answers to questions through direct observation.

**erosion evidence** Evidence based on use or wear.

**ethical neutrality** A characteristic of science that requires that moral and ethical beliefs not be allowed to influence data gathering or conclusions.

**exhaustive categories** A set of categories that includes all possible answers to the question posed.

**experiment** A research project bound by the perspective and rules of science, conducted according to a research design, in which the researcher has at least partial control over the environment and some of the variables regarded as independent or causal.

**experimental condition** A condition that involves the researcher measuring the experimental group on the dependent variable.

**experimental design** A research design that allows the researcher to attempt to eliminate possible causes for changes in the dependent variable, other than the proposed independent variable(s).

**experimental group** The group in which the independent variable occurs or is introduced by the researcher.

**experimental treatment**   Synonym for *independent* or *presumed causal variable*.

**explanation**   The result in elaboration analysis when the relationship between the two zero-order table variables disappears in all of the first-order partial tables, the control variable is related to both zero-order variables, and the control variable occurs before the independent variable; the zero-order relationship is spurious.

**explanatory research**   A research strategy in which the researcher attempts to go beyond description to determine why a phenomenon has occurred.

**feedback relationship**   A relationship among variables such that each variable is connected to every other variable; a change in variable *a* will produce a change in some or all other variables, and these changes may, in turn, produce another change in *a*.

**first-order partial tables**   Tables created in elaboration analyses by introducing a third control variable in the analysis of the relationship between two other variables; one partial table is created for each value of the control variable.

**fixed-alternative questions**   Questions that require the respondent to choose an answer from a printed list of choices.

**formal interview**   A structured, standardized interview with a fixed-question content and structure.

**hired-hand research**   Research carried on by an outside organization that is independent of, but paid by, the organization under study.

**histogram**   A line graph.

**hypothesis**   A statement about what effects or results certain causes or actions might produce.

**independent variable**   A variable believed by the researcher to be a cause of a dependent variable.

**inductive logic**   Logic that moves from a number of particular and separate observations to generalizations.

**inferential statistics**   Statistics that enable us to generalize from a sample to the population from which it was drawn with some specifiable degree of confidence that the generalizations are correct.

**informal interviews**   Unstructured interviews.

**Informed consent**   Voluntary agreement to participate in a research project after having been informed of any hazards or dangers that may be present.

**in-house research**   Research conducted by a staff member of the organization being studied.

**interpretation**   The result in elaboration analysis when the relationship between the two zero-order table variables disappears in all of the first-order partial tables, the control variable is related to both zero-order variables, and the control variable is an intervening variable.

**interval estimate**   A range of values around a sample statistic (e.g., the mean value of a particular variable) used to estimate the value of the corresponding population parameter.

**interval variable**   A variable that can be categorized and ordered and for which the quantity of variation between values can be specified.

**intervening variable**   A variable that occurs in time between the independent and dependent variable, creating a causal chain of variables.

**Likert scales**   Measurement scales that allow us to measure the degree to which respondents hold certain attitudes.

**linear relationship**   A relationship between variables such that the values of the two variables tend to change in one direction; that is, as the values of one variable go up, the values of the other go up, as in a positive correlation, or down, as in a negative correlation. When plotted on a graph, the relationship is represented by a straight line that runs diagonally up or down across the graph.

**literature review**   A comprehensive summary of relevant theories and/or research related to the study being described in a research report.

**longitudinal study**   A study in which the same group of subjects is studied over time.

**marginal frequencies**   The sum of a row or a column in a table.

**matching**   A technique for ensuring that subjects in control and experimental groups are as similar as possible on variables believed by the researcher to be relevant in a particular study.

**maturation**   Changes (physical and experiential) that occur in a group of subjects as the result of passage of time.

**mean**   The arithmetic average of the scores that make up a distribution.

**measures of association**   Statistical measures of the degree and direction of a relationship among variables.

**median**   The score in a distribution of scores above which and below which half of the scores are found; the middle score.

**methodology**   The general plan formulated for achieving the ultimate goals of the researcher in a scientific investigation.

**mode**   The most frequently occurring score in a distribution of scores.

**multimodal distribution**   A distribution of scores with more than one mode.

**multiple causation**   Several conditions causally related to a single other condition, with each contributing separately or in combination to the determination of that condition.

**multiple correlation coefficient**   A measure of the strength of the relationship between one variable and two or more other variables taken together; varies between + 1 and – 1.

**multistage sampling**   A probability sampling procedure in which cluster sampling techniques are used in successive stages or combined with random sampling techniques.

**mutually exclusive categories**   Categories established so that there is one and only one response category appropriate for each response.

**nominal level measurement**   A level of measurement in which variables can be placed in mutually exclusive, exhaustive categories, but cannot be ordered further.

**nonparametric inferential statistics**   Inferential statistics that do not assume a normal distribution of variable values in a population; that is, they are distribution-free.

**nonprobability sampling**   A sampling technique in which the probability of any element being included in the sample cannot be determined.

**nonreactive research**   A data collection technique that removes biases introduced by the research process itself by eliminating the subjects' knowledge that they are being studied.

**normal distribution**   A unimodal, symmetrical distribution with specific statistical characteristics.

**null hypothesis**   The hypothesis that there is no relationship between two variables; used to generate sampling distributions for testing hypothesis in inferential statistics.

**objectivity**   A characteristic of science that requires that conclusions be based on careful observation rather than personal prejudices.

**open-ended question**   A question for which no response categories are provided.

**operational definition**   The specification of exactly how the researcher will identify the objects or events that fall into specific categories.

**optical reader**   A machine that reads bar codes or pencil marks on special forms.

**ordinal level measurement**   A level of measurement in which it is possible not only to categorize but to rank elements in a population according to the degree to which a certain attribute is present.

**parameter**   The value of a measure of central tendency or dispersion for the distribution of the values of a variable for a population.

**parametric inferential statistics**   Inferential statistics that assume a normal distribution of variable values in a population.

**parsimony**   A characteristic of science that holds that the numerous alternative explanations of a particular phenomenon should be reduced to the smallest number possible.

**participant observation**   A series of data collection techniques in which the researcher directly observes the people and/or events being studied.

**percentaging in the direction of the independent variable**   Using the marginal frequencies corresponding to the values of the independent variable to convert cell frequencies to percentages in cross-tabulations.

**perspective**   A worldview that selects and organizes our sensory experiences.

**point estimation**   A sample statistic used as a single-value estimate of the corresponding population parameter.

**population**   The entire group of subjects or events from which a particular sample is drawn.

**precision**   Refers to the number of subcategories of a concept (values of a variable) that are available.

**preexperimental designs**   After-only and before-after designs.

**probability**   The likelihood of an event or series of events occurring, usually expressed as a decimal (e.g., .05, .001).

**probability sample** A sample selected in such a way that the probability of each particular element of the population being included in the sample is known before the sample is drawn.

**proportionate sampling** A sampling strategy in which the simple random sample drawn from each stratum of a population is adjusted so that the proportion of elements in the sample is equal to the proportion of the whole population contained in that stratum.

**purposive sample** A nonprobability sampling strategy based on the assumption that the researcher has enough skill to select subjects who ought to be included in the sample; also referred to as typical-case sampling.

**quantiles** The general term used to refer to quartiles, deciles, and percentiles.

**quasi-experimental procedures** Experimental procedures in which the researcher has less than ideal (laboratory) control of the environmental and independent variables (as in experiments conducted in field settings).

**quota sample** A nonprobability sampling procedure in which the researcher attempts to ensure that various elements of the population will be included in the sample.

**random-access memory** Data or program storage areas in a computer whose contents can be altered through the keyboard of the computer and which can be accessed at any specified location.

**random numbers** Numbers generated by a computer programmed so that each number from 0 to 9 is equally likely to be printed next.

**random sample** A sample drawn from a population in such a way that each element in the population has an equal chance of being selected for the sample.

**range** The lowest and the highest scores in a distribution.

**rate** The expression of the frequency of an event in relation to a fixed unit of measurement, usually time.

**ratio level measurement** A level of measurement with the properties of nominal, ordinal, and interval measurement and, in addition, an absolute zero point.

**read-only memory** Data or program storage areas in a computer that can only be read from; that is, its contents cannot be altered through the keyboard of the computer.

**regression line** A straight line that best represents the shape of the area of dots (data) in a scattergram; technically, it is the line that minimizes the distance between it and the dots in the scattergram. If all the dots fall exactly on the line, a true linear relationship exists.

**rejection region** The range(s) of statistical values on the horizontal axis of a sampling distribution curve and the corresponding areas under the curve within which the null hypothesis is rejected.

**relativism** A characteristic of science that requires that scientists not consider their conclusions as universal, absolute truths.

**replication** (*a*) The result in elaboration analysis when the relationship between the two zero-order table variables remains the same in all of the first-order partial tables; (*b*) the repetition of a study previously done.

**research hypothesis**   The hypothesis that two variables are related; it is tested indirectly by testing the null hypothesis using inferential statistics.

**response rate**   The number of completed questionnaires returned divided by the total number of questionnaires distributed.

**sample**   A subset of elements drawn from a population and used to represent the population.

**sample statistics**   The value of a measure of central tendency or dispersion for the distribution of the values of a variable for a sample.

**sampling distribution**   An empirically or mathematically derived distribution of sample statistics, usually assuming random samples drawn from the same population.

**sampling error**   The difference between the values of sample statistics and values of the corresponding population parameters; these differences may arise as a result of many factors (e.g., a researcher's bias, chance); inferential statistics make it possible to estimate sampling error arising only from probability sampling procedures.

**sampling frame**   A list of all the elements in a population.

**scattergram**   A graphic device for determining whether or not two variables are related, consisting of two axes at right angles on which the values of the two variables are arrayed and a dot located at the intersection of values of the two variables for each element in the sample or population.

**science**   A systematic search for the most accurate and complete description and explanation of events, relying on the principles of empiricism, objectivity, relativism, skepticism, ethical neutrality, parsimony, and at least a modified determinism as guides.

**secondary analysis**   A research technique in which the researcher reexamines the method, the data, and the results of earlier research.

**significance level**   The probability set by the researcher that determines whether the researcher will accept or reject a null hypothesis; the probability of making a type I error.

**skepticism**   A characteristic of science requiring that researchers search for disconfirming evidence and continue to question their conclusions and knowledge.

**skewed distributions**   Distributions characterized by a bunching of scores toward one end or the other of the horizontal axis.

**specification**   The result in elaboration analysis when the relationship between the two zero-order variables disappears in some but not all of the first-order partials and the control variable is not related to one of the zero-order table variables.

**spurious relationship**   An apparent but false (not causal) relationship between two variables; the appearance of a relationship is produced by a causal relationship between each of the two variables and a third variable that precedes both of the original two variables in time, as in explanation in elaboration analysis.

**standard deviation**   Expression of the differences of scores from the mean score in units of equal size for a particular distribution.

**standard error**   The standard deviation of a sampling distribution.

**standard normal curve**   A normal curve with a mean of 0 and a standard deviation of 1.0.

**standard score**   A score computed from a given raw score by subtracting the sample mean from the given raw score and dividing by the sample standard deviation.

**statistical explanation**   In correlation analysis, the amount of variance in one variable predictable from the variance in the other variable(s); refers only to correlations, which are not necessarily causal relationships between variables.

**stratified random sample**   A probability sampling technique that assumes that relevant information about the variables that may effect responses is available, enabling the researcher to divide the population into categories (strata) ensuring that each element falls into one and only one of the established categories.

**student's *t***   A statistic used to determine the probability that mean values of the same variable calculated from data for two different randomly selected groups are two samples from the same population.

**systematic sampling**   A probability sampling technique in which the researcher selects every kth element from the population for inclusion in the sample.

**third-party research**   Research conducted by an independent outsider.

**triangulation**   A technique for collecting different types of data from different sources with respect to a single research question; used to increase researchers' confidence in their findings and to bring discrepancies in data to light.

**Type I error**   Rejecting a true null hypothesis.

**Type II error**   Accepting a false null hypothesis.

**unimodal distribution**   A distribution with only one mode.

**validity**   The determination of whether a categorization reflects a characteristic or property of the real, empirical world.

**variable**   A category (concept) that may be divided into two or more subcategories.

**variance**   A statistic computed by squaring the difference or deviation from the mean of each score in a distribution, summing these squared deviations, and dividing the sum by the total number of scores in the distribution.

**verification**   An attempt to demonstrate empirical support for a theory.

**zero-order table**   In elaboration analysis, the table showing the "original" relationship between two variables; this relationship will be analyzed through the introduction of a third control variable and the creation of partial tables.

# Selected Readings

Babbie, Earl R. *The Practice of Social Research*. 3rd ed. Belmont, Calif.: Wadsworth, 1983.

Barr, Anthony J., et al. *A User's Guide to SAS*. Raleigh, N.C.: SAS Institute, 1976.

Becker, Howard S. "Whose Side Are We On?" *Social Problems* 14 (1967) 239–48.

Berger, Peter L. *Invitation to Sociology: A Humanistic Perspective*. Garden City, N.Y.; Doubleday Anchor, 1963.

Bierstedt, Robert. *The Social Order*. New York: McGraw-Hill, 1970.

Binder, Arnold, and Gilbert Geis. *Methods of Research in Criminology and Criminal Justice*. New York: McGraw-Hill, 1983.

Blalock, Hubert M., Jr. *Social Statistics*. 2nd ed. New York: McGraw-Hill, 1972.

Blalock, Hubert M., Jr., and Ann B. Blalock, eds. *Methodology in Social Research*. New York: McGraw-Hill, 1968.

Bogue, Grant. *Basic Sociological Research Design*. Glenview, Ill.: Scott, Foresman, 1981.

Borgatta, Edgar F. and Betty Crowther. *A Workbook for the Study of Social Interaction Processes*. Chicago: Rand McNally, 1965.

Bronowski, J. *Science and Human Values*. New York: Harper Torchbooks, 1956.

Bruyn, Severn T. *The Human Perspective: The Methodology of Participant Observation*. Englewood Cliffs, N.J.: Prentice-Hall, 1966.

Campbell, Donald T., and Julian C. Stanley. *Experimental and Quasi-Experimental Designs for Research*. Chicago: Rand McNally, 1963.

Cohen, Morris R., and Ernest Nagel. *An Introduction to Logic and Scientific Method*. New York: Harcourt, Brace and World, 1934.

Cole, Stephen. *The Sociological Method*. Chicago: Markham, 1972.

Cook, T. D., and D. T. Campbell. *Quasi-Experimentation: Design and Analysis Issues for Field Settings*. Chicago: Rand McNally, 1979.

Cox, Steven M. and Jack D. Fitzgerald, *Police in Community Relations: Critical Issues*. Dubuque, Iowa: W. C. Brown, 1983.

Coyle, William. *Research Papers*. 5th ed. Indianapolis, Ind.: Bobbs-Merrill, 1980.

Denzin, Norman K. *Sociological Methods: A Sourcebook*. Chicago: Aldine, 1970.

_____. *The Research Act: A Theoretical Introduction to Sociological Methods.* 2nd ed. Chicago: Aldine, 1978.

_____. *The Values of Social Science.* Chicago: Aldine, 1970.

Denzin, Norman K., and Kai T. Erikson. "Communications." *Social Problems* 15 (1968) 502–6.

Dornbusch, Sanford M., and Calvin F. Schmid. *A Primer of Social Statistics.* New York: McGraw-Hill, 1955.

Erikson, Kai T. "A Comment on Disguised Observation." *Social Problems* 14 (1967):366–73.

Evans, Christopher. *The Making of the Microcomputer—A History of the Computer.* New York: Van Nostrand Reinhold, 1981.

Farmer, David J. "Thinking About Research: The Contribution of Social Science Research to Contemporary Policing." *Police Studies* 3, no.4 (Winter 1981):22–40.

Filstead, William J. *Qualitative Methodology: Firsthand Involvement with the Social World.* Chicago: Markham, 1970.

Forcese, Dennis P., and Stephen Richer. *Social Research Methods.* Englewood Cliffs, N.J.: Prentice-Hall, 1973.

Galliher, John F. "The Protection of Human Subjects: A Reexamination of the Professional Code of Ethics." *American Sociologist* 8 (1973):93–100.

Glazer, Myron. *The Research Adventure: Promise and Problems of Field Work.* New York: Random House, 1972.

Gold, Raymond L. "Roles in Sociological Field Observations." *Social Forces* 36 (1958):217–28.

Goode, William J., and Paul K. Hatt. *Methods in Social Research.* New York: McGraw-Hill, 1952.

Gouldner, Alvin. "Anti-Minotaur: The Myth of a Value-Free Sociology." *Social Problems* 9 (1962):199–213.

_____. "The Sociologist as Partisan: Sociology and the Welfare State." *American Sociologist* 3 (1968):103–16.

Greer, Scott. *The Logic of Scientific Inquiry.* Chicago: Aldine, 1969.

Hagan, Frank E. *Research Methods in Criminal Justice and Criminology.* New York: Macmillan, 1982.

Harshbarger, Thad R. *Introductory Statistics: A Decision Map.* New York: Macmillan, 1971.

Hay, L. R., R. D. Nelson, and W. M. Hay. "Methodological Problems in the Use of Participant Observers." *Journal of Applied Behavior Analysis,* 13 (1980):501–4.

Homans, George C. *The Nature of Social Science.* New York: Harcourt, Brace and World, 1967.

_____. "The Western Electric Researches." In Schuyler Hoslett, ed., *Human Factors in Management.* New York: Harper, 1951.

Huff, Darrell. *How to Lie with Statistics.* New York: W. W. Norton, 1954.

Hyman, Herbert. *Survey Design and Analysis.* New York: The Free Press, 1955.

James, William. *Psychology: Briefer Course.* New York: Collier, 1962.

Johnson, Edwin S. *Research Methods in Criminology and Criminal Justice.* Englewood Cliffs, N.J.: Prentice-Hall, 1981.

Kaplan, Abraham. *The Conduct of Inquiry: Methodology for Behavioral Science.* San Francisco: Chandler, 1964.

Kidder, Louise H. *Research Methods in Social Relations.* 4th ed. New York: Holt, Rinehart, and Winston, 1981.

Klecka, William R., Norman H. Nie, and C. Hadlai Hull. *SPSS Primer.* New York: McGraw-Hill, 1975.

Lastrucci, Carlo L. *The Scientific Approach: Basic Principles of the Scientific Method.* Cambridge, Mass.: Schenkman, 1963.

Loether, Herman J. and Donald G. McTavish. *Descriptive Statistics for Sociologists.* Boston: Allyn and Bacon, 1974.

————. *Inferential Statistics for Sociologists.* Boston: Allyn and Bacon, 1974.

Lundberg, George A. *Can Science Save Us?* New York: David McKay, 1961.

Madge, John. *The Tools of Social Science: An Analytical Description of Social Science Techniques.* Garden City, N.Y.: Doubleday, 1965.

Mendenhall, William, Lyman Ott, and Richard F. Larson. *Statistics: A Tool for the Social Sciences.* North Scituate, Mass.: Duxbury Press, 1974.

Miller, Delbert C. *Handbook of Research Design and Social Measurement.* New York: David McKay, 1964.

Nie, Norman H., and C. Hadlai Hull. *SPSSH Update Manual.* Chicago: SPSS, Inc., 1977.

Northrop, F. S. C. *The Logic of the Sciences and Humanities.* New York: World, 1959.

Reynolds, P. P. *Ethical Dilemmas and Social Science Research.* San Francisco: Jossey-Bass, 1979.

Ritchie, A. D. *Scientific Method.* Paterson, N.J.: Littlefield, Adams, 1960.

Runyon, Richard P. and Audrey Haber. *Fundamentals of Behavioral Statistics.* 2nd ed. Reading, Mass.: Addison-Wesley, 1971.

Sanders, William B. *The Sociologist as Detective: An Introduction to Research Methods.* New York: Praeger, 1974.

Selltiz, Claire, Marie Jahoda, Morton Deutsch, and Stuart W. Cook. *Research Methods in Social Relations.* New York: Holt, Rinehart, and Winston, 1965.

Simmons, Jerry L. *Deviants.* Berkeley, Calif.: Glendessary, 1969.

Simon, Julian L. *Basic Research Methods in Social Science.* New York: Random House, 1969.

Stouffer, Samuel A., Edward A. Suchman, Leland C. DeVinney, Shirley A. Star, and Robin M. Williams, Jr. *The American Soldier: Adjustment During Army Life.* New York: John Wiley, 1949.

Wallace, Walter L. *The Logic of Science in Sociology.* Chicago: Aldine-Atherton, 1971.

Webb, Eugene J., Donald T. Campbell, Richard D. Schwartz, Lee Sechrest, and J. B. Grove. *Nonreactive Measures in the Social Sciences.* Boston: Houghton Mifflin, 1981.

Whorf, Benjamin Lee. *Language, Thought and Reality: Selected Writings,* ed. John G. Carroll. New York: The Technology Press and Wiley, 1959.

Wiseman, Jacqueline P. and Marcia S. Aron. *Field Projects for Sociology Students.* Cambridge, Mass.: Schenkman, 1970.

Zetterberg, Hans L. *On Theory and Verification in Sociology.* New York: Bedminster Press, 1965.

Zito, George V. *Methodology and Meanings: Varieties of Sociological Inquiry:* New York: Praeger, 1975.

# Index